William E. Donoghue's

COMPLETE MONEY MARKET GUIDE

# William E. Donoghue's

# COMPLETE
# MONEY MARKET
# GUIDE

*The Simple Low-Risk Way You Can Profit
from Inflation and Fluctuating
Interest Rates*

WILLIAM E. DONOGHUE
with THOMAS TILLING

HARPER & ROW, PUBLISHERS, New York
*Cambridge, Hagerstown, Philadelphia, San Francisco,*
*London, Mexico City, São Paulo, Sydney*

1817

*To Norman E. Donoghue, my father*

Charts unless otherwise indicated are © 1980 Donoghue's *Moneyletter* or *Money Fund Report,* Holliston, MA 01764.

*Designer: Sidney Feinberg*

---

Library of Congress Cataloging in Publication Data

Donoghue, William E
    William E. Donoghue's complete money market guide.
    Includes index.
    1. Investments—Handbooks, manuals, etc. 2. Money
market—Handbooks, manuals, etc. I. Tilling, Thomas,
joint author. II. Title. III. Title: Complete money
market guide.
HG4527.D66   1981        332.6'78        80-8200
ISBN 0-690-02008-2

---

81 82 83 84 85 10 9 8 7 6 5 4 3

# Contents

# Illustrations

# Preface

I wrote this book for my mother, Mrs. Norman E. Donoghue, who, like many senior citizens, has saved all her life to prepare for her golden years — only to find that her *savings have been ravaged by inflation*. I wrote this book for my children, Bonnie and Will, who have to count on their parents' ability to *save enough to provide for their education*—a more and more difficult effort. I also wrote this book for other small businessmen, who, like myself, found it difficult before the establishment of money funds to *keep their hard-earned cash working as hard as they do*.

With the advent of the new *money market*—money funds, money market certificates, unit investment trusts specializing in bank certificates, and the old standard Treasury bill — millions of Americans now have a *real* choice to not only keep pace with inflation, but *fight back* and take advantage of it.

However, in writing this book I was struck repeatedly by the fact that even though *the new money market had grown from virtually nothing to over a half-trillion-dollar phenomenon in just two years,* many of the savers and investors who had jumped on the money market bandwagon had invested their money wisely but not well. They were too often opting for low-yielding money market services with the mistaken idea that they were "playing it safe." When, in fact, with the proper guidance, they *could have* used the money market to earn more for their money with even less risk.

It also had become clear to me in my conversations with economists at the Federal Reserve Board that the whole money market movement had not been fully appreciated in Washington. The introduction of the money market's highly interest-rate-sensitive money into the banking system has added an element of instability which is placing the depositor at a risk for which he is not being compensated. Rather than restrict the depositors, it is the banking industry that will have to accommodate this new money market the public demands. Indeed, the new banking laws have created a new agency to oversee the transition period during which Regulation Q and other restrictive banking regulations, which have gotten between banks and their customers in the past, are phased out. The new agency is called the Depository Institutions Deregulation Committee (catchy name, eh?).

As you read through this book you will be introduced to the various instruments of the money market and a host of different strategies tailored specifically to help *you* invest your money profitably in the money market and to make your hard-earned money earn guaranteed high, safe yields despite the ravages of inflation and fluctuating interest rates.

We have always told people that our corporate name is P&S Publications, Inc. The P&S part comes from the expression "When all the world is searching for gold, the thing to be doing is selling picks and shovels." This book constitutes the "picks and shovels" you need to find gold in the money market. Dig in . . . and may the float be with you.

*September 1980*

WILLIAM E. DONOGHUE

# Acknowledgments

I would like to thank some of the people who have helped make this book possible: Dan Butler and David Jones, without whom Donoghue's *Money Fund Report* would never have come into being; Rod Johnson, with whom I conceived the money fund concept; Jim Benham of Capital Preservation Fund, who helped me learn the true genius of the money fund concept; Dr. Paul Nadler, for his insight and humor; my brother Norman Donoghue II, for his support and encouragement; and the members of my staff who have contributed directly to this book: Jennifer Brown, who prepared many of the graphics; Sandra Quinlan and Margaret Smith, who typed the manuscript; and Paul Dreyfus and Lois Estabrook, who kept the business going while I worked on this book. Others on my staff, whose contributions have been more indirect but just as important, are Mary Hogy, Tina Bennett, Vicki Reis, and Kim MacKenzie.

Last of all I would like to thank Nancy Crawford of Harper & Row, who had the vision to see this book in me and the sense to introduce me to Thomas Tilling and his wife, Susan, who taught me how to write a real book, which, I've learned, is an entirely different undertaking from writing newsletters. This book needed to be written and the above people made it happen.

# 1

## The New Retail Money Market — or, Getting Your Interest Wholesale

### "If You Keep Your Money in a Passbook Savings Account, You're a Loser"

This incredible headline on the full-page advertisement placed by Citibank, the nation's largest bank, in the January 9, 1980, *New York Times* tells the whole story. Traditional savings accounts can be hazardous to your wealth. Even the banks are admitting it.

The financial world today is moving too fast for the average saver to keep up simply by depositing money in a traditional savings account. With rates of inflation in the 15-percent-and-more range, letting your cash sit in an ordinary savings account means *losing* 10 percent of the buying power of that money every year. That's like buying tickets on the *Titanic*.

The financial rules of thrift and economy we lived with for almost a century have changed in less than a decade. Yet most people are still playing the old money game, and their piggy banks are being smashed by the sledgehammer of inflation.

*Baseball was always the great American sport,* and savings bonds and savings accounts were the great American nest eggs. Now the baseball players strike at the bargaining table instead of on the field, and people are switching to watching basketball, football, hockey, soccer, golf, tennis, you name it. Savings bonds and savings accounts end up costing you money instead of earning it, and the smart money is turning to the new money market.

The new retail money market — *money funds, Treasury bills, money market and small saver certificates, and unit investment trusts* — opened the door to the formerly exclusive money market. The old money market is still a big numbers game, with $100,000 as the general price of admission.

That is the minimum, and if you have $500,000, Wall Street will begin to treat your cash as if it is almost respectable. The new money market, on the other hand, is for *everyone* and the minimum investment for these "better-than-passbook-savings" yields on your savings is only a few hundred dollars.

The amazing thing about this market is that, to all intents and purposes, it did not exist in early 1978. In slightly more than two years, it has attracted over half a trillion dollars (that's $500,000 million) of savers' money. The new money market now accounts for nearly *half* (46 percent) of all the savings in this country.

### The New Money Market—A Victory for Savers' Libbers

Although, like any major movement, the growth and popularity of the money market evolved over time and started in many places, I like to refer to June 1, 1978, as Savers' Liberation Day. That's the day banks were first authorized by the Federal Reserve Board to begin offering the six-month money market certificates. Prior to this time, you had to lock in your money for eight years to qualify for even an 8 percent interest rate.

With the advent of the money market certificate, suddenly you could earn as much as 10–15 percent interest from the bank. The rate was tied to the Treasury bill rate and fluctuated with general market conditions. No longer were savers tied down to the inflation-trampled rate of 5 percent. All they needed to earn the new interest was $10,000 and the willingness to leave their money in the bank for six months. That was certainly better than eight years.

At last the consumer had access to the rising money market interest rates. And the small investor's financial future was to improve even more with the advent of money funds and the many other high-yield savings plans.

Suddenly an incredibly complicated array of interest rates was being quoted each day by banks, money market mutual funds, savings and loan associations, stockbrokers, and others—all bidding for your savings dollar. Well, there's a method to this madness, and deciphering it is the purpose of this book. You see, while interest rates change daily in the money market, they do move in concert. I'm going to show you how to read the sheet music for this concert. Then I'll show you how to plan your investments to play a happy and profitable tune—without a sour note.

The method is called the SLY system, and by the time you've read this book, not only will you be able to find your way through the money market maze, but you'll be equipped to get the best return on your money — whether interest rates go up or down. *Fluctuating interest rates* is the name of the game, and you play it for profit.

### The SLY System

The SLY system is a conservative, low-risk, commission-free approach to investing in the money market and related investments. It's a sophisticated approach — sophisticated doesn't mean complicated; it does mean smart — which takes into account the saver's and investor's need to consider fully the *S*afety, *L*iquidity, and *Y*ield of each investment, in that order. Now you know what SLY stands for.

### Safety First

Truly the first thing you must keep in mind in investing your nest egg during these perilous times is the safety of your investment. There are three ways to build this safety factor into your investments, each of which has its use:

1. FDIC or similar government insurance.
2. A diversified, professionally managed portfolio — the don't-put-all-your-eggs-in-one-basket and don't-try-to-manage-the-eggs-yourself philosophy — in a highly regulated and reputable industry.
3. The guarantee of a major financial institution.

Nearly all the investments we will be considering fit one or another of these profiles.

### Liquidity—The Ability to Change Your Mind and Get Your Money Back

Liquidity does not refer to a hot tub, nor does it refer to a drink. It's being able to convert your investment into cash without a penalty whenever you want to.

With the notable exception of some of the bank-offered money market accounts, long-term deposits of six months or more, each of the investments we will be discussing allows you to get at your money, free of any restrictions, right away. Often it's as easy as writing a check or making a telephone call.

### Yield—How to Get the Best, and How to Know What It Will Be Next Month

In most investment situations, if you want more yield you have to assume more risk. In the money market, however, that's often not the case. As I will show you, a safer investment may yield more than a riskier one. The secret is knowing when that's true.

### Getting at the Really High Yields—While Letting the IRS Wait

Using the SLY system, you will learn how to earn high money market yields—and how to defer 100 percent of the taxes, if you want to, until you draw on your profits. And that's without tying up your principal. If you are in a high income tax bracket, you can even avoid taxes entirely, although the interest rates you earn will be lower.

### Souping Up Your Investments

The SLY system will also teach you how to soup up your money market investments so your nest egg can begin to keep ahead of inflation, rather than merely staying even with it.

### A Totally New, Yet Proven Way to Accurately Predict Future Interest Rates

More amazingly, *the SLY system will actually show you how to predict which way interest rates are headed*—months before yields make their move. And up or down, whichever way the fluctuating interest rates move, you'll profit all the way.

### Money Funds—Your Cash's Key to Growth

Central to your inflation-fighting strategy will be money funds. What is a money fund? It's a mutual fund that invests in the money market—another great idea that rose from the ashes of inflation-burned investments after Savers' Liberation Day.

"Whoa! Hold it right there," you say. "I've been ripped off by mutual funds before, and I'm not about to have that done to me again." Right you are. But money funds are mutual funds only in the sense of being pooled funds with a specific investment goal.

*There's no commission to pay with a money fund.* Hence the term *no load*— you're not playing with loaded dice. That much money funds owe to the unfortunate history of the older mutual funds. By the time money funds were conceived, fund managers had realized that the average investor was sick and tired of being ripped off by salesmen. Mutual funds with 6 and even 8 percent sales fees, or loads, had been common in the sixties and early seventies. You took a 6–8 percent loss on your investment the day it was made. So just about the only one profiting from the deal in those days was the swiftie who sold it to you.

Most of the fund salesmen took their high-pressure tactics and high commissions into the gold, diamond, and other commodity markets or into the tax shelter schemes when Mr. and Mrs. America and all investors at sea saw the light and simply said No to their demands. Mutual funds didn't expire, however. They changed. To accommodate the sensible sentiments of the more sophisticated small investor, they, too, became no-load funds. That was the only way to sell, they learned. Bye-bye, commissions. Hello, more equitable equity investment. For without the sales commissions, funds really were a fair deal. And don't worry about any poor starving fund managers, either. They still got their share.

But investors didn't return to the mutual funds in droves. The stock market held little allure for them once the sagging seventies had replaced the sizzling sixties.

Money, on the other hand—now, that really interested the investors, particularly when they began reading that loans were being offered at 10, 12, or even 14 percent, and that big companies were getting still higher yields on their cash investments. If only everyone could take advantage of these higher yields, not just the big guys. Enter the money mutual fund.

Now, a mutual fund is by definition a pooling of people's money to take advantage of professional management and investment opportunities not readily available to the individual investor. A mutual fund, then, can be designed to purchase anything—stocks, or bonds, or both, or stamps, or trees, or what have you. When interest rates soared, the time was ripe for a whole new breed of funds to take advantage of and profit specifically from the high-yielding money market. Money funds were born to buy money, money in all the forms available on the money market.

Of course, to buy money you need money. But you don't need a lot of it to buy into a money fund. And even if your ready savings don't meet the minimum required, you're apt to find, somewhere among your belongings and investments, a fund of cash you hadn't thought of to make up the difference.

Nearly every American has money stashed away in one or more of the four most untapped stores of idle wealth there are. These stores aren't working as hard as you are, and they should be. One such treasure chest may provide you with enough money to start investing more aggressively for your future.

So what are these treasure chests? Well, one of them is the cash value of your *life insurance*. Did you know that many insurance companies are obligated to lend you money at 5 percent or less in many circumstances? Another underutilized source of funds is the *equity in your home*. Do you know when to get a second mortgage? Savings accounts are a definite source, if you're what Citibank means by a loser, and many of us are. I was. Another is those old stocks and mutual fund shares your dad bought for you or someone talked you into buying. Now they can be put to work in a real system.

## Now, What's This Money Market All About?

The money market has been much in the news in recent years. We've heard about money market certificates, T-bills, the prime rate, the discount rate, the Fed funds rate, and similar topics almost every day on the national news. The money funds are part and parcel of this market. But where is this money market, exactly? What is it? And more important, what does it mean to you?

The money market has no single location, although it is concentrated in New York and a few money-center cities, like San Francisco, Chicago, Dallas, and Atlanta. And what is it? It's simply an informal telephone network of borrowers and lenders of money ensconced in small offices in banks, brokerage houses, and private firms. The forms of money being traded are simply different types of loans, or, to use the legal term, debt instruments. Hence the term money market instruments, which simply describes what the money market investor trades.

Long a hidden part of our country's financial system, the money mar-

**THE MONEY MARKET RATES**

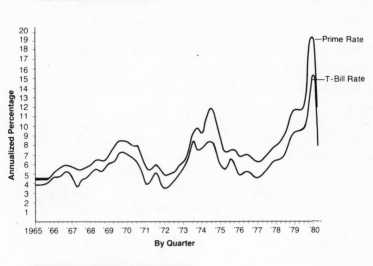

PRIME RATE VS. T-BILL DISCOUNT RATE
(3-MONTH, 13-WEEK T-BILL)

### The Money Market Roller-Coaster Ride

Over the last 15 years we have seen three interest rate cycles, whose peaks have been increasingly higher and whose roller-coaster ride has become increasingly steeper. This chart, with 3-month Treasury bills on the bottom and the prime rate at the top, shows the traditional boundaries of money market rates, during a period when passbook savings accounts never exceeded 5.25%.

ket has suddenly gone public. While the U.S. capital market has always been divided into three parts — the bond market, the stock market, and the money market — formerly only corporations, banks, and supersophisticated investors were in a position to profit from the money market, the key segment of the capital market during times of inflation. At last, after Savers' Liberation Day, there was a crack in the door for the small investor.

But it wasn't to remain a crack for long. During the years 1978 and 1979, the door opened wide. As investors became aware of its potential, a new money market developed, offering a complete smorgasbord of cash-compounding alternatives, new and old, for Everyman. It was a veritable supermarket of savings alternatives. And the image is more than appropriate, for, as at a supermarket, the careful shopper in the money market is the one who comes out ahead, way ahead.

*The size of the U.S. money market is staggering.* Hundreds of billions of dollars are traded — every day. Consider, for a moment, just one billion dollars on the time scale of man. Counting dollar bills for sixteen hours a

Where America Stores Its Money
(In billions of dollars)

| | 1/77 | 1/78 | 1/79 | 1/80 | 6/80 |
|---|---|---|---|---|---|
| **Traditional Banking** | | | | | |
| Checking accounts | $ 226.4 | $ 242.8 | $ 251.9 | $ 263.5 | $ 259.9 |
| NOW accounts | 2.8 | 4.2 | 9.9 | 17.3 | 19.6 |
| Time deposits less MMCs, SSCs (under $100,00) | 401.8 | 457.4 | 438.7 | 368.0 | 308.4 |
| Savings accounts | 453.7 | 489.1 | 468.1 | 411.7 | 381.4 |
| SUBTOTAL | $1084.7 | $1193.5 | $1168.6 | $1060.6 | $ 969.3 |
| **The New Money Market** | | | | | |
| Money Market Certificates (MMCs) (6 mos.) | --- | --- | $ 107.6 | $ 290.6 | $ 361.7 |
| Small Saver Certificates (SSCs) (30 mos.) | --- | --- | --- | 3.2 | 50.2 |
| Money market funds | 3.6 | 4.2 | 12.1 | 49.1 | 74.2 |
| Unit Investment (CID) Trusts | --- | --- | 1.2 | 4.7 | 3.7 |
| Treasury (T-) bills, non-competitive bids (3 & 6 mos.) | 7.7 | 8.9 | 11.2 | 20.0 | 22.4 |
| Savings bonds | 72.2 | 77.0 | 80.6 | 79.2 | 73.3 |
| SUBTOTAL | $ 83.5 | $ 90.1 | $ 212.7 | $ 446.8 | $ 585.5 |
| **The Old Money Market** | | | | | |
| T-bills, competitive bids (3 & 6 mos.) | $ 73.0 | $ 82.1 | $ 89.5 | $ 107.6 | $ 128.8 |
| Repurchase agreements (overnight) | 12.4 | 17.0 | 21.2 | 22.6 | 19.6 |
| Certificates of deposit (CD) (over $100,000) | 117.6 | 148.8 | 197.4 | 222.5 | 230.7 |
| Bankers' acceptances | 9.9 | 13.0 | 22.4 | 28.4 | 30.2 |
| Commercial paper | 52.1 | 64.3 | 81.0 | 99.0 | 96.3 |
| Eurodollar CDs | 10.3 | 14.1 | 24.5 | 34.1 | 36.9 |
| SUBTOTAL | $ 275.3 | $ 339.3 | $ 436.0 | $ 514.2 | $ 542.5 |
| GRAND TOTAL | $1443.5 | $1622.9 | $1817.3 | $2021.6 | $2097.3 |

day—let's allow eight for sleeping and eating—and averaging 150 bills a minute between flying fingers, you'd be in the counting house for twenty years inventorying a billion dollars. And that's just one billion.

### Inside the Money Market

Visiting a money market trading room is a nerve-racking experience. There is a steady underlying tension that makes the SALT talks look like a church picnic. The brokers sit by enough telephones and buttons to control the Pentagon's War Room. There is no ringing, however. The noise would be overwhelming. So the telephones just blink—with the speed of a hyperactive pinball machine.

As if to make up for the stilled bells, telephones and buttons are always banged down with sledgehammer force. Then there's the din of prices, rumors, information, and gossip all being exchanged under controlled shouting conditions. Or sometimes not so controlled.

It's when your senses settle down after you first enter a trading room, however, that real shock overcomes you. There's that kid in his twenties. He just traded $90 million worth of CDs in the time it took you to catch your breath after hearing the amount. The guy next to him, for heaven's sake, brokered $200 million in overnight bank funds between the time it took him to strike a match and light his cigarette.

Lest you dream of becoming a money broker and making million-dollar commissions, however, please note that the rate is $1 per $1 million in overnight funds. Even a billion dollars in trades earns the broker only $1,000. Maybe that's why no one seems awed at the figures bouncing around the trading room. But that's the old money market, where a million dollars is just so much change.

In the new money market, on the other hand, as little as $1,000 can put you in the catbird seat of finances. Let's explore that new money market and see what your cash is going to be getting into so profitably.

# 2

## The Money Market Instruments—What They Are, What They'll Do for You

On a small scale, you've been in the money market ever since you earned your first dollar cutting the neighbor's lawn or baby-sitting. You already trade in what are technically money market instruments, even if these instruments are limited to the consumer money market, because that dollar bill in your wallet is a Federal Reserve note.

No longer legal species redeemable for something of value such as gold or silver, the pieces of paper money we carry about are merely notes, "legal tender for all debts, public and private," but notes nonetheless. In other words, IOUs. In the case of your dollar bill, the IOU is from the Federal Reserve. Being from the government, it's the most widely circulated and common IOU available.

You've probably also borrowed money from your bank, perhaps when you bought your car or your home. That piece of paper, the loan agreement you signed, is another IOU, or note, or money market instrument. In this case you actually helped to create the instrument. The bank holds it. And while most people aren't aware of it, the bank can sell it. It's transferable, tradable, exchangeable, just like money. It represents money owed, and it's an example of a money market instrument.

*The money market deals in different types of very high quality IOUs with various types of repayment guarantees.* Money market instruments such as bank certificates of deposit (the $100,000-plus variety), commercial paper (corporate IOUs), and U.S. Treasury bills are some of the safest investments you can buy—if you have enough money. Deals in these instruments are often in million-dollar quantities, and for very short periods, even overnight.

**THE NEW MONEY MARKET**
**TOTAL OUTSTANDING ($ BILLIONS)**

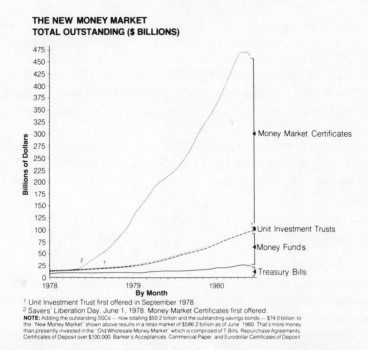

By Month

1 Unit Investment Trust first offered in September 1978.
2 Savers' Liberation Day, June 1, 1978. Money Market Certificates first offered.
**NOTE:** Adding the outstanding SSCs — now totalling $50.2 billion and the outstanding savings bonds — $74.0 billion, to the "New Money Market" shown above results in a retail market of $586.2 billion as of June, 1980. That's more money than presently invested in the "Old Wholesale Money Market" which is comprised of T-Bills, Repurchase Agreements, Certificates of Deposit over $100,000, Banker's Acceptances, Commercial Paper, and Eurodollar Certificates of Deposit.

The new money market, to which you might also add the over $50 billion of small saver (30-month) certificates outstanding, now rivals the old money market in size. For savers, it symbolizes the response the financial markets can expect to find from offering a fair return on your money. To the banking and thrift industry, it symbolizes a ticking time bomb of increasingly interest-rate-sensitive deposits. To the author, it symbolized a crying need for saver/investor education, since the instruments of greatest value to the saver—money funds and unit investment trusts—were being outsold by the restrictive and lower-yielding money market certificates.

## Wheeling and Dealing with the Federal Reserve

For an idea of the kind of money and the kind of turnover involved in large-scale money market trading, consider Federal Reserve funds, or Fed funds, as they are known in the financial community.

The Federal Reserve system requires member banks keep a certain percentage of their money on deposit at the local Federal Reserve bank. Your local bank is probably a Federal Reserve member. Most banks are.

Each day, some banks have too much money in their reserve accounts. Since the reserve accounts don't earn interest, these banks will lend their deposits to a bank that is short of funds that day. This is called lending Fed funds, and literally billions of dollars are lent every day.

To understand why the Fed funds market exists, it helps to know that the interest on a million dollars at 10 percent is $400 for just one business day. (If you're trying to test my calculation, I figured on 250 business days to a year, to take account of holidays.) The interest on ten million dollars is $4,000 a day. A billion dollars is worth $400,000 a day. I'd surely like to have just one day of interest earnings like that. With figures like this before you, you can see the importance of the Fed funds market to a bank which must squeeze every cent of interest it can out of the money it manages in order for you to have a free checking account. Let me tell you, this money moves fast, and in quantities much larger than John Q. Public can deal with.

### Money Market Instruments You Should Invest In

If you can't beat 'em, and you can't join 'em, the thing to do is to join forces, form a co-op, get an army together. Then you can storm the bastions of high finance. The name of the army is money funds, and it's waiting for you to sign up.

1. *Money funds are perhaps the ultimate in money market investing convenience.* They're going to be the backbone of your high-profit savings plan using the SLY system.

Money funds invest in a broad spectrum of money market instruments, which will be described later in this chapter. For now, consider them an investment opportunity with nearly all the convenience of a checking account. It takes *as little as $500* to open a money fund account. You can both open your account and add to your investment by mail if you wish. Every mailbox is, in effect, a money fund office. And you can withdraw your money by either a telephone call or simply writing a check (usually in $250–$500 minimums, please) on your account. You can deposit a money fund check in your checking account, or you can use it to pay someone else — your bank, for example, to cover a mortgage payment.

Money fund yields vary daily, following the general direction of the money market. In the spring of 1980, several funds were earning at an annual rate as high as 23 percent. That's not bad for a checking account.

2. *Treasury securities constitute a massive chunk of the money market* and represent borrowings by Uncle Sam. He's the all-time great when it comes to borrowing, one might add.

Series EE and HH savings bonds are what the government sells to consumers. In today's inflationary age, they are absolute rip-offs. One wonders

Money Market Accounts Classified by Type End of December 1979

| Type of Account | Value of Accounts (in millions of $) | Percent Distri- bution | No. of Accounts | Percent Distri- bution | Average Account Size ($) |
|---|---|---|---|---|---|
| Individual | $24,435 | 53.7 | 1,743,974 | 73.0 | $14,011 |
| Institutional | | | | | |
| Fiduciary accounts | 11,875 | 26.1 | 322,516 | 13.5 | 36,820 |
| Total employee benefit plans (include pension & profit-sharing plans, Keogh & IRA accounts) | 2,866 | 6.3 | 160,064 | 6.7 | 17,905 |
| Business corporations and other nonfinancial businesses | 4,686 | 10.3 | 105,116 | 4.4 | 44,579 |
| Financial institutions (other than bank trusts) | 546 | 1.2 | 31,057 | 1.3 | 17,581 |
| Nonprofit institutions (charitable organizations, hospitals, churches, etc.) | 728 | 1.6 | 14,334 | 0.6 | 50,788 |
| All other institutional accounts | 364 | 0.8 | 11,945 | 0.5 | 30,473 |
| Total Institutional Accounts | 21,065 | 46.3 | 645,032 | 27.0 | 32,657 |
| Grand Total (Total Net Assets) | $45,500 | 100.0 | 2,388,006 | 100.0 | $19.046 |

Source: Investment Company Institute, Statement Before Subcommittee on Financial Institutions of Senate Banking, Housing and Urban Affairs Committee, January 24, 1980.

As you can see by the above chart, institutional investors account for nearly half of the money invested in money funds. Bank trust departments, corporations, pension and profit-sharing plans, and nonprofit organizations use money funds as the most efficient and cost-effective way to manage short-term portions of their investment portfolios. By the end of June 1980, money funds had grown to over 74.2 billion in assets and counted 3,633,563 accounts.

how government officials can sleep at night, taking widows' and orphans' money and paying 6.5 percent while inflation is running 10 percent and even the banks are offering 10–15 percent, albeit on a limited basis through their certificates of deposit. Yet sell the bonds they do.

On the more sophisticated level, there are Treasury bills, T-bills for short. These are issued due in less than one year. Treasury notes, with a maturity of from one to seven years, and Treasury bonds, with a maturity of five years or more, also keep the government's debt afloat. All these instruments pay high market interest. That is, as overall interest rates rise, the yield of new Treasury bills, notes, and bonds rises as well. The opposite occurs, of course, if interest rates decline. All these government instruments have been more or less unavailable to the consumer until recently.

You could have bought T-bills before, if you'd happened to have heard of them. And the minimum investment was then, as it is now, only $10,000. But where and how? That's what nobody told you. Your local friendly banker didn't make a substantial profit on T-bill transactions, and they didn't add to the bank's assets. That's why he forgot to mention them to you.

I'll be telling you about T-bills. And I'll show you how to ride the yield curve so *your T-bills can earn more interest than the government is actually paying.*

3. *Money market certificates opened the doors of the private money market club to Everyman* when they were first authorized by the Federal Reserve Board on that momentous day, June 1, 1978. That's the good news they delivered. Now the bad news. They aren't all that great an investment most of the time, even though the banks and thrift institutions that sell them will try to convince you otherwise. Under very specific interest rate conditions, however, MMCs, as the money market certificates are abbreviated, have their definite purpose, as you'll see when I go over with you the strategies for a fluctuating-interest-rate market.

The minimum MMC investment is a fairly hefty $10,000, the same amount as for a Treasury bill. The interest of both instruments is also the same, since money market certificate yields are tied to those of the T-bills. The exception to note is that when general interest rates are 9 percent or above, T-bills will yield a slightly higher return than money market certificates will.

The real drawback of money market certificates is their severe penalty for early withdrawal. Before investing in these instruments, you had better be certain that any money you tie up in them is definitely not going to be needed for the full six months of the certificates' life. You can profit from this type of investment. It simply takes a little sophisticated, though not difficult, planning.

4. *Small saver certificates* were first offered late in 1979 with four-year maturities. In consideration of the speed with which interest rates fluctuated during 1980, the maturities were reduced to a more popular two-and-a-half-year, or thirty-month, time span. Small saver certificates offer an opportunity to lock in yields as high as the 12 percent upper limit imposed on them by law. Since they can be used as collateral for low-cost loans, they also offer you a chance to borrow the money back to invest at still higher rates when such rates are available.

5. *Unit investment trusts are the brokerage firms' answer to the changing money market.* In 1978, Merrill Lynch, recognizing that many of its clients were buying the six-month money market certificates, began offering a new type of mutual fund. The funds, technically trusts invested primarily in bank CDs, were set up on a specific date, sold out in a few days, and expired on a specific date six months later. The funds sold in $1,000 units (unlike the $10,000 minimums of the banks), paid a higher rate than money market certificates were paying, and had no early withdrawal penalties. In fact, if interest rates fell, you would be paid a premium for selling your unit back to Merrill Lynch.

That wasn't a bad deal at all. But only a few thousand people found out about it in time to take advantage of it. You see, trusts like this tend to be creatures of high-interest-rate periods like the one in the spring of 1980. They are usually not available after interest rates decline below about 12 percent.

But they'll be back. And when they are, using the SLY system, you'll be able to profit from unit investment trusts to the fullest.

### What Money Funds Invest In

No matter how liberated the money market is, there are yet highly profitable debt instruments, or IOUs, which the individual cannot purchase without being extremely wealthy. However, you and I can still participate in this extra-high-yield sector of the market through money funds. The fund managers will make the actual investment decisions. But knowing what their options are will help you to choose among the various funds.

1. *Bankers acceptances provide a way for banks to bet on the future* and spread their risk at the same time. Let's say the bank agrees to lend a

company short-term money. And let's say the loan is to cover an import deal involving coffee that an importer hasn't the money to pay for until three months later, when he in turn has been paid for the coffee. To insure an incoming flow of money, the bank often sells to other parties part of its acceptance of this loan. Hence the term bankers acceptance.

**WHERE THE TWENTY LARGEST MONEY FUNDS INVEST**
**JUNE 1980**

|  | Percent |
|---|---|
| 1. U.S. Treasury Obligations | 4.87 |
| 2. U.S. Government Agency Issues | 9.48 |
| 3. Repurchase Agreements (Repos) | 3.59 |
| 4. Certificates of Deposit (CDs) | 24.73 |
| 5. Bankers Acceptances (BAs) | 11.82 |
| 6. Commercial Paper | 35.01 |
| 7. Eurodollar CDs | 9.66 |
| 8. Other | .84 |
|  | 100.00 |

The loan itself is secured by the importer and the coffee as well as by the accepting bank. Since there are, in effect, three sources of funds to cover a bad debt, a bankers acceptance is considered very safe and offers a slightly lower yield than something like commercial paper.

2. *Commercial paper is a short-term promissory note,* that is, an IOU, issued by a corporation. Usually sold for a period of thirty or sixty days, such a loan provides a way for the company to compensate for seasonal earnings distortions, inventory irregularities, and the like. Commercial paper from, say, IBM or AT&T would be considered safer than commercial paper issued by Western Worm Farms. The size and financial position of the corporation are crucial in determining the yield of commercial paper. The spread between a top-rated corporation and the lower-tier companies is very large, often as much as 5 or 6 percent.

3. *Certificates of deposit in the big-money world* are a way to get around the infamous Regulation Q, the government's pronouncement that, among other things, keeps your savings account in the 5 percent interest range. Regulation Q is why banks advertise "the highest interest rate allowed by law." It's true they can't pay more, at least not on savings accounts.

One of the anomalies of Regulation Q when it was formulated was that on deposits of $100,000 or more left intact for a specified time, the banks could pay as much interest as the market demanded. Corporations loved it — except for the fact that their money was tied up. CDs were an illiquid investment for them, just as the smaller CDs now available to you through the banks are.

If you bought a $10,000 CD six years ago, you've been stuck with the preinflation interest rates of the past ever since. Legally, a bank can refuse to cash in your CD prematurely. And recently, as the banks' funds have been withdrawn at alarming rates, some of them have indeed done just that — even when someone needed the money for something as unexpected and desperate as hospital bills.

Small investors rush in where the big ones fear to tread. CDs would never have become a multibillion-dollar market for corporations had it not been for the fact that they found a way around the lack-of-liquidity problem.

One reason why the money market works so well is that every time the government tries to wrap it up in red tape, it simply changes. It evolves to avoid government strangulation. In this case, large CDs developed an aftermarket. A corporation in need of cash and sitting on a $10 million CD not due for three months simply sold the CD to someone who had $10 million he didn't need right away. He in turn might wait the three months and collect lots of interest, or he might resell the CD a week later if the need arose.

4. *Eurodollar CDs have a similarly large liquid market.* In this case, the dollars are deposited by a U.S. bank in an overseas branch. They are actual dollar deposits, even though they are held overseas. Much of the Eurodollar CD market's dealings involve extremely short-term money, as short as overnight — something made possible only by modern communications and electronics, which put a CD dealer in Brussels in an office right next door to one in New York.

The whole Eurodollar market is, in fact, held together by communications cables. Hundreds of banks worldwide participate in the Euromarket. For a specific branch in need of Eurodollars to contact all the possible lending banks in search of the best rate would probably take longer than the loan was needed for. That's the reason the brokerage market in this money instrument came about. And brokerage is, in turn, what makes Eurodollar CDs so liquid.

With all these dealers trading like lightning in money market instruments, one might validly wonder if some of them don't occasionally get stuck with more securities than they want. As dealers, they must, of course, buy and sell for their own account. That's their inventory. If they believe interest rates are going to fall, they will increase their inventory.

Why? Because if interest rates go down, the value of the securities goes up. Say an instrument sells at $100 to yield 10 percent. If interest rates fall to 5 percent, new instruments issued at $100 will yield 5 percent. Old instruments will in theory increase in value to $200 so that they, too, yield 5 percent. After all, why should anyone sell something at a price that yields 10 percent when the market is yielding only 5 percent?

5. *This is where repos, or repurchase agreements, come in.* Now, while money market dealers aren't exactly what you'd call poor, there are limits, even for them. So they often have to borrow money to carry their inventory. As arcane as this may sound, essentially they are borrowing money to put money into their inventory. It's just a different form of money in either case. Dealers do this by entering into repurchase agreements. They sell an investor, say, $25 million worth of securities for a little less than $25 million. At the same time, they agree to buy the securities back for exactly $25 million the next day.

Most repos are very short term, overnight to a few weeks. They are generally backed by government or other top-quality paper as collateral. And they are highly liquid. Paying high market rates usually just below Fed fund rates, they can be an investor's dream — as long as he can afford to dream in the $10 million range.

At least that's the way it used to be. Now, through money market funds, you can participate in the repo market for as little as $500. It's all part of the SLY system.

### Onward and Upward

The Savers' Liberation Movement has opened a wide variety of money market investment options to you. Before we begin to describe how and when to use all these alternative investments and the SLY strategy to build up your financial base, I'd like to relate a story about getting started.

Waiting for a flight in the San Francisco airport, in United Airlines' Red Carpet Club, I struck up an interesting conversation with a fellow passenger.

The lady was, she told me, sixty-five years old and just retiring as president of her own travel agency. The conversation turned to the subject of money funds, as so many of my conversations tend to do.

"Money funds remind me of porcupine hunting," the lady said, much to my surprise.

"How so?" I reacted quickly. I wanted to hear this one.

"Well," she began, "have you ever hunted porcupines? What you do is get one of those galvanized washtubs and head for the woods. When you find a porcupine, you sneak up on it real quiet-like and throw the washtub over it."

She paused. "Then you've got time to think about what your *next* move is."

Well, getting started in investing entails some of the same anxiety and risk. The first step, before you do anything else, is to put your money into a money fund. Once it's under cover, then you can "think about what your next move is."

Let's begin.

# 3

# Finding Safe Harbors in Perilous Times

Seeking out the highest yield without checking the investment's safety is pretty much like buying the fastest car without looking at the brakes. You could be in for a real thriller of a ride.

For these are perilous times — particularly for savers. Everyone is trying to get your money, including the government. This isn't meant to sound paranoid. But while people have been after other people's money ever since it was invented, today they're after it with a vengeance.

*So if you are asking: "When will the money fund bubble burst?"* you have a good reason for wondering. After all, over the past few years, many people have been stung by the stock market, the commodity markets, the stock funds, and real estate investment trusts, or REITs. Back in the mid-seventies, many REITs went bankrupt — just a few years after being the hottest investment vehicles around. Why shouldn't the same thing happen to money funds?

## The REITs Guessed Wrong

Here's why. It's because you are talking about apples and oranges. Or maybe I should say jackasses and turtles.

REITs were highly leveraged investments. In other words, they were bought primarily with borrowed money. They were shaky pyramids that could come tumbling down if interest rates rose. And interest rates did just that, to a much greater degree than expected.

## Money Funds Don't Guess

Money funds, on the other hand, are not leveraged. They are not speculative. They simply put your money into other forms of money, forms of money that yield higher interest than you, as a less-than-multimillion-dollar investor, could obtain by yourself. They provide a savings base for money, and they provide limited—but very useful—services. *The money funds are slated to become the more efficient savings banks of the inflationary eighties.* And they are *just as safe,* even though their insurance policies are based on prudent diversification rather than on government guarantees.

There's no bubble to burst. What will happen to money funds is that when interest rates fall, the funds' yields will decline as well. But so will those of the banks. Banking overhead being what it is, in fact, money funds will in all probability always yield more, over the long run. And *one of the most profitable of all times to invest in money funds is a period of overall declining interest rates,* as you will discover later in this book. Meanwhile, there is one key to safety, and it's not government regulation, which somehow always appears after the disaster has already occurred.

### If Someone Offers You the World on a Silver Platter, Take the Platter

*No amount of legislation will protect your investment.* Safety, that paramount value, is up to you. Any investment that looks too good to be true probably is. So investigate any money market investment before you buy, evaluating not only the investment's safety, but its safety relative to your goals.

Buying only supersafe T-bills, for instance, would be a mistake for most people. Balance your portfolio, remembering that risk and yield go up together. With enough cash, it might even be worthwhile to take a really speculative flyer—checking with particular thoroughness, of course, to be sure that it is indeed a flyer, and not a fly-by-night scheme headed for a crash.

### What to Watch Out for

*There are four distinctly different risks in any financial transaction—market risk, rate risk, credit risk, and liquidity risk.* Though interrelated, they can work independently because of the effects of time and market rates on an investment. So when you check out an investment's risks, think about all four and how they might affect your particular financial situation.

### INVESTMENTS RATED ACCORDING TO RISK

| | Risk Profile | | |
| --- | --- | --- | --- |
| | Credit Risk | Liquidity | Rate Risk* |
| T-Bills | Full faith and credit | †Market risk | Fixed yield |
| 6-Month Money Market Certificate | FDIC insurance to $100,000 | †Substantial penalty | Fixed |
| Money Fund | Diversified and professional management | †None, except in short run | Varies daily |
| Unit Investment Trusts | Same as MMF (Money Fund) | †Market risk | Fixed yield |

\* If held to maturity.
† Principal risk—you could lose principal if you had to redeem prior to maturity.

## Market Risk—Winning One Day, Losing the Next

Weigh the market risk carefully. If you buy an instrument yielding 10 percent, and the following week the interest on the same type of investment rises to 11 percent, well, then you've taken a paper loss. You've taken both a 1 percent loss on yield and a small bite out of your capital, because your lower-interest instrument is worth less in the marketplace.

If what you've purchased is a short-term instrument — say, a six-month certificate of deposit — why, then at the end of six months, when it matures, you will receive all your capital back. In that case, your only sustained loss is the 1 percent in interest you would have been able to earn had you invested a week later.

But if your 10 percent instrument is a long-term bond and interest rates remain at 11 percent or go even higher, then you would take a small loss on your capital if you sold after the same six months. The marketplace would value your 10 percent bond at less than you paid for it, and would continue to do so until and unless interest rates fell. This is the market risk you take when dealing in money.

## Rate Risk—Will It Keep Its Promise?

What about the rate that is quoted for an investment? Can you be sure you're really going to get it?

Treasury bills, money market certificates, and unit investment trusts guarantee you that if you hold them to maturity, you will receive the rate stipulated at the outset. That's why these instruments are called fixed-income investments. Of course, if interest rates rise, a fixed-income instrument isn't going to budge.

Money funds do not guarantee a fixed return. They promise only the best they can do in the market. And they pay dividends daily, distributing what they have earned after expenses. If interest rates rise, money fund rates will rise too. If interest rates fall, on the other hand, in some cases money fund rates will actually rise at first, and in all cases, they will fall more slowly than the general rates.

### Credit Risk—Is There a Money-Back Guarantee?

Credit risk involves the question: "Am I going to get all my money back when the instrument I'm considering matures?" In the case of federally insured bank deposits, the answer is: "Of course I am, in any situation except, perhaps, the total collapse of the banking system."

Treasury bills are even safer from a credit-risk standpoint. Even if the banking system collapsed, the Fed would print enough money to keep turning T-bills over. What exactly that money would be worth under those circumstances may be open to question. But you would get it.

Lower on the scale of credit risk is commercial paper. It is unsecured, backed only by the issuing corporation, a company you may really know nothing about except perhaps its general reputation. Even the best of money managers, in fact, know little about the true financial workings of the companies behind the commercial paper they buy. With seven or eight hundred companies constantly issuing large quantities of paper, and numerous other companies offering a few million dollars' worth of paper here and there, no one person could even begin to keep up with the information necessary to truly know and assess a given company.

*Enter the rating services, Standard & Poor's, Moody's, and Fitch.* These are the statisticians keeping track of the number of runs, hits, and errors the players of your potential money team make. Moody's strength lies in its coverage of municipal bonds, and its rating there carries more weight than does Standard & Poor's which, in turn, is considered a more reliable judge of corporate securities. Fitch generally is in third place by most accounts.

Standard & Poor's top rating is A1, Moody's P1, and Fitch's F1. In these times of turmoil, when there is need to preserve capital as well as to maximize interest, most investors should limit their funds to these top categories, excepting only any speculative part of their portfolio.

The rating services, incidentally, are not perfect. For instance, Standard & Poor's, as well as Moody's, rated Penn Central tops the day before the railroad failed. But it's the only major mistake they've made and that was back in 1970. All in all, their record is good. As an investor you should always check a company's rating before you consider letting it hold your money even overnight. You can check a company's standing easily by looking it up in the books published by the rating services. These are usually available in your local library.

### Liquidity—Can You Stay Afloat?

Liquidity risk is a matter of when you can get your money back without incurring an extra penalty. In the case of a six-month money market certificate, for instance, you will lose at least ninety days of interest for early withdrawal, regardless of how long you've held it. The liquidity of this instrument, then, is poor.

Its credit risk, on the other hand, is excellent. So you want to balance out its worth in your given situation. Other conditions being equal, if you have cash that you absolutely and positively will not need for the next half year, a six-month certificate may be the right investment for you. But if there's a chance you might need that capital in a few months, then, even considering the very low credit risk, it's not the right choice at the moment.

Liquidity risk is a particularly important aspect of investing during an economic downturn. People who find themselves in adverse financial circumstances brought about by illiquid investments plus a shortage of cash often are forced to dispose of assets below their true value. Not having money when they need it, they end up selling things at a loss to gain survival cash. If you're liquid, on the other hand, their predicament is your profit.

### Money Talks—Nobody Walks

During a recession or a high-interest period, money really talks. And just about everyone listens. That's when the person who can't keep up the payments on the extra car will give it to you for $100 plus the responsibility of taking over the monthly installments. It's when the $150,000 house sells for $100,000 because there simply aren't enough bidders around who can cover the down payment.

If you are offered the chance to buy a car for $1,500 less than it's worth, the $1,500, in effect, can be considered additional interest you earned simply because you were liquid—assuming, of course, that you need the car. Never, never put the total of your investment in an illiquid instrument, no matter how high the yield. There's real safety in balance. This same balanced-portfolio safety factor is one of the underlying principles of the money funds, and it's built into them for very sound investment reasons.

The balanced-portfolio principle involves not simply diversity of the investments themselves, but diversity *over time* as well. The staging of the maturities of money fund holdings not only gives you a smoother and basically higher-yielding return on your investments, but since the spread spans several quite distinct markets—certificates of deposits, commercial paper, bankers acceptances, and so on—even problems in an entire market segment cannot affect you very much.

Other safety-promoting features of the money funds include research and street savvy. Money fund managers have research sources far more extensive than those available to the individual investor. The fund manager's studies are also much more timely. You may receive some of the same information they receive; but you'll do so days, if not weeks, later, after the news has already been discounted.

## "The Street" Knows Long Before You Do

Street savvy is much harder to quantify. But it's never to be underrated. When the Franklin National Bank hovered on the edge of collapse in 1974, a lot of people panicked and sold their Franklin certificates of deposit at a considerable loss. No one could really blame them—things were looking bleaker with each day's news. No money fund would even consider investing in Franklin. Yet money fund advisers would have counseled investors to stay with the bank and even to buy up the discounted certificates of deposits. Why? Because they knew the bank was in so much trouble that the FDIC would have to protect the depositors (as opposed to the shareholders) or risk starting a full-fledged panic, which could only lead to the complete collapse of the banking system. They knew that in this case one could count on getting the full dollar value of one's investment back at maturity.

With a lot of banks lining up at the brink, the story could be quite different. Discriminating between the two situations is the kind of street savvy that makes the difference between uninformed panicking and profiting from trouble—other people's, that is.

## Where Was the Equity in Equity Funding?

*There is, of course, fraud.* Many investors remember the Equity Funding scandal. Millions of dollars' worth of nonexistent insurance policies ended up on the books, generating equally nonexistent profits, which, in turn, drove Equity Funding's stock price skyward—until, that is, the fraud was exposed and the stock collapsed.

Couldn't a scandal like Equity Funding's occur in the money fund world as well?

## Fraud-Proofing the Money Funds

That's certainly a fair question, and one you should always ask when approaching a new investment vehicle. But the answer is, it would be an almost impossible occurrence in a money fund. Nothing is completely impossible, of course, not even forged Treasury notes, a favorite criminal pastime in the seventies. The Equity Funding fleecing, however, was an internal corporate heist executed through complex computer machinations. The outside checks and balances required of a money fund were absent.

In order to embezzle, the perpetrator—crook is the obvious word, but you won't find it bandied about in banking circles or on Wall Street—needs to have a source of forged bank certificates of deposits, government securities, or other suitable instruments. Printing these is extremely difficult. But with determination, it can be done. A money fund's custodial bank, however, would probably notice the forgeries right away. It has the responsibility of dealing with millions of dollars' worth of certificates every day. A document that might appear perfectly legitimate to you or me would stand out like milkweed in a rose garden to the bank.

Then there's the time factor again. Money funds, at the time of this writing, have an average maturity of thirty-nine days. On the whole, their maturities are usually less than six months. This means that the potential embezzler would have to keep the printing presses busy almost every month turning out replacement collateral. In addition, he'd have to keep the blinders on the bank with strict regularity, somehow getting the fake certificates in and out of the trustee's vault.

Cajoling even a genuine document out of the custodian's hands is a major undertaking. Bruce Bent of the Reserve Fund, the inventor of money funds, told me how once, out of sheer curiosity, he decided he'd like to see the physical certificate of deposit behind one of his fund's investments. So he called up the custodian bank and asked to have the CD sent over. It arrived promptly — with an armed guard. The guard never left his side as Bent read the certificate from top to bottom on both sides. Handing it back to the guard, he commented, "You know, I've bought and sold billions of dollars' worth of these things, and I'd never seen one." The guard nodded coolly, locked the CD in his case — which was handcuffed to his wrist — and marched off to his armored truck.

Imagine, given a routine like that, trying a monthly smuggling act with false certificates!

On top of such security measures, a custodian bank must balance out its accounts daily with the transfer agent of the fund, often another bank. Most of the funds' transactions are in fact processed by banks. This is why I'm always tickled when someone says, "The real problem with money funds is that they're such young organizations. They're not as seasoned as the banks."

### Cross-checks on the Checkers

Now, you have a money fund watching two banks and two banks watching the money fund. Considering how much faith the public has in banks, what could be safer than two of them watching over a third entity while it earns you a larger yield?

Frankly, money fund embezzlement is simply not worth the risk. There are many more attractive long-range multimillion-dollar deals to fleece the unwary investor. Why bother with the difficult buck when there are easy ones to be picked?

### Human-Error Insurance

As to honest errors and omissions, yes, they do occur. But then again, there's such a thing as error-and-omissions insurance to cover those contingencies. Basically, then, while a money fund is not government insured like a bank, it is protected by its own safety checks and by portfolio diversification. If you were to rank the two on a safety scale of 0 to 100, the banks might rate 99 and the money funds 98.

The bank's major safety problem is the nature of the FDIC, or Federal

Deposit Insurance Corporation, and the FSLIC, or Federal Savings and Loan Insurance Corporation, insurance pools. It's true, as the television ads put it, "No one ever took a bath at a savings bank." What the ads fail to state is that with 5 percent interest your money bleeds to death slowly through inflation. At their current rate of return, bank savings accounts simply aren't a viable alternative for the eighties while the average annual inflation rate hovers at 10 percent or more.

Some years it will be more, some less. But overall it will remain above what was at the time considered the "horrible" inflation of the seventies, the one that brought down the greatest number of banks since the Depression—and with a swiftness the public could not even anticipate.

### Franklin's Kite Flew High—for a While

Consider the speed of events in the Franklin National Bank case. On May 11, 1974, the bank denied rumors that it was in trouble. (Don't they always?) One day later, on May 12, Franklin's chairman, Harold V. Gleason, completed an all-day Sunday marathon commute from New York to Washington and back by announcing that the bank had lost $14 million plus some possible currency trading losses—of $25 million.

The Federal Reserve pledged loans to help overcome liquidity problems. After all, the Comptroller of the Currency had assured the Fed that Franklin was solvent.

On May 14, the stock in Franklin was suspended from trading for a month. The Italian financier Sindona set about raising $50 million to keep his ship afloat. Depositors scurried off with their money.

By June 14, the bank had lost $1 billion in deposits. The big money had pulled out. The smaller savers hung around to get their monthly interest.

On June 20, Franklin reported its first five months' earnings for the year—a stunning $63.5 million loss. The bank denied it was involved in merger talks, which, of course, meant it was about to merge, and which it eventually did. The point is, only a few weeks intervened between Franklin's status as a respectable pillar of the community and its insolvency.

The FDIC pulled off a rescue that time. But those who keep all their money at the bank may be doing more than simply penalizing their financial growth. In all fairness to the FDIC, should a series of major bank failures occur, the insurance pool would be sorely pressed to meet all its obligations to the savers.

By all means include banks in your investment strategy. But don't have blind faith in them. And remember, there's more overall safety in diversity than in insurance, even government insurance.

## Money Fund Miscalculations

The only real horror story for money fund investors was First Multi Fund for Daily Income. It was a real horror story, that is, until you examined the facts.

First Multi was part of a small mutual fund complex that also included a mutual fund which invested in other mutual funds. This was a very popular vehicle among a then small group of switchers. The investors would simply switch between the equity fund and the money fund to take advantage of whatever interest rate fluctuations they thought were in the offing.

The so-called money fund, however, was not really a money fund. It looked like a money fund. It behaved like a money fund. But it wasn't one. Why? Because it didn't follow one of the basic money fund rules, which is to keep your maturities short. The portfolio manager reasoned that if he had a portfolio with a long maturity, it would always outyield the other money funds. So he went out almost two years in his average maturity while other money funds were keeping their maturities to under ninety days. Consequently, he was profitable right during 1975, 1976, and 1977.

However, when rising interest rates caught up with him in late 1978, First Multi found itself in a real bind. Its current yield was too low to keep investors interested. Yet, if it sold its portfolio to lower redemptions, the fund would take a real loss — a loss of 7 percent on the portfolio value. The day after Christmas, the fund manager notified shareholders that the portfolio had been devalued from $1 to 94¢ a share. (Later the auditors would mark it down to 93¢.) First Multi merged into another money fund six months later, and charges were filed against the managers.

The investors in First Multi enjoyed the highest yields in the industry for the three good years, and it was essentially the same investors who ate the resulting loss in 1979.

So in a sense their profits and losses balanced. The First Multi portfolio devaluation was an unfortunate incident, but one not likely to be repeated, as newer regulations have forced all the money funds into much shorter average maturities than those of First Multi. In addition, the incident alerted SEC auditors to the necessity of being more vigilant.

Holding Trust, the second black sheep of the money fund family, was a complex similar to First Multi Fund. It included three funds: FundPack, the fund of funds, Holding Trust, and a fund with the reassuring name HUGSI, or Holdings of U.S. Government Securities, Inc.

Though Holding Trust was a problem fund, in this case no investor lost money, to the best of our knowledge. The fund was essentially forced into liquidation by the SEC, which assigned an administrator to handle the fund after charges against its managers were settled — with no one admitting guilt. The improprieties cited by the SEC involved the fund's promotion of the switching strategies used by the investor.

Neither First Multi nor Holding Trust accounted for more than 0.1 percent of the then current money fund industry, and although a little consumer money was lost in the First Multi situation, it is only fair to note that by most definitions it was not actually a money fund, even though it masqueraded as one.

### Safety and Security, or Sominex

*By now you're probably wondering whether it's possible to have savings and sleep at night too.* Of course it is. T-bills, for example, are as secure as the United States government itself. If that goes under, you'll probably have a few weeks' notice. But what would you do about it?

In the end, no matter what you invest in, you have to accept some risk. You have to balance the risk and return — and they always go up and down together — of each investment against your own total financial picture. For *not* investing is the riskiest course of all when money is losing its worth week after week as it is today.

Investing safely means diversifying your investments. You simply shouldn't lock all your money into one money market instrument, such as T-bills, any more than you should lock it all in a bank. Don't concentrate on safety to the exclusion of yield, or inflation will bleed you.

On the other hand, while Will Rogers' advice "Invest in inflation — it's the only thing that's going up" is sounder than ever, you can't simply look at yield, either. A 90-percent-return investment that ends up not returning is no investment at all.

And that's why money funds are the perfect place for your cash today. You get the top interest rates of the money market plus the safety of diversification and quality — as well as a real chance to keep up with inflation and the tax man.

# 4

## Your Hidden Treasure Chest:
## Finding More Money

*So now there's a whole wide world of financial instruments out there* that can earn you up to two to three times the minimal 5 percent yields of savings accounts — even more if inflation keeps up its dizzy ascent. What have you got to put into this high-yield haven? Probably a lot more than you think.

Most of us feel poorer these days, if not downright broke. That's one of the psychological consequences of inflation. You can't help noticing, with a nickel pack of gum costing a quarter. It's up 400 percent. Bananas used to be on sale for 19¢ a pound only a few years ago. Now 39¢ a pound is a good buy. Percentagewise, this is horrendous. Prices seem to explode in front of our eyes day by day.

Now, I'll be the last one to deny the ravages of inflation, or the fact that it will probably get a lot worse. Oh, there will be a few months' respite now and then; there may even be a whole year when inflation stabilizes at around 10 percent. There will be times of rapidly declining inflation as well, perhaps a month or two after major elections. But you can safely discount these inflation fluctuations, for the overall trend is up, up, up and away.

What is devastating, however, is not so much inflation itself — at least not yet, in this case — but rather the attitude it engenders. A nation that has not faced runaway inflation in recent memory is a vulnerable nation. Its people don't know how mentally to cope with the phenomenon. With bad news everywhere, despair, outright or subconscious, shapes everyone's spending and investment. Buy now! Go into debt and pay off the debt later, with cheaper inflated dollars! Spend, spend, spend! Until finally the inflation everyone worried about becomes a self-fulfilled superinflation.

I'm not a Pollyanna, and I wouldn't expect you to be. The point is, if you are aware of the negative atmosphere permeating our everyday lives and if you can break free from it, there *are* opportunities. *There's always a winner, even when most people are losers.*

### Hunting for Cash

The fact of the matter is, however strapped and up-against-the-wall broke you may feel, you *do* have money to invest. Everyone runs low on cash occasionally — including the billionaire Hunt brothers. In their case, when it came to covering some margin calls on silver one day, they were short a couple of hundred million dollars. A week later they were out buying Gulf Resources & Chemical Corp. stock for $2.5 million. Where did they get it from?

We all have more money around than we're aware of. It may not amount to $2.5 million. But it's there.

Someone once described money as being like quicksilver, slithering through your fingers. The standard tactic, then, when money gets tight, is to stop up the cracks. Cut back on spending.

Fine. But in times like these, stopping up the cracks isn't enough. We need to actually reach down into the cracks and retrieve the silver there.

### Melting Down the Silver Lining

An example par excellence of reaching for unnoticed silver was businessman James Ling, one of the original conglomerate builders of Wall Street in the sizzling sixties. Eventually he reached too far into the labyrinths of high finance and lost a multimillion-dollar fortune. But he still kept one large enough to shelter himself in a mansion.

Ling came up with the concept, or at least the term, "redeployment of assets." There were other businessmen who used the concept too, but not to anywhere near the extent Ling did.

*Redeployment of assets essentially means finding hidden value* and doing something profitable with it. When, for instance, in the middle sixties, James Ling bought controlling interest in the Wilson Company, with its $100 million-plus sales, he did it because he felt the company was worth much more than the stock market said it was — worth more, that is, after the judicious application of a scalpel to redeploy the company's assets.

Wilson had three main thrusts to its business — an old meat-packing line, a pharmaceutical division, and sporting goods products. This may sound like rather an odd combination. But consider the old management's rather ingenious game plan.

Meat packing is a thin-profit-margin business. Profits depend primarily upon volume and using every possible slaughterhouse by-product. That's how meat packers developed a reputation for selling everything but the squeal.

Pharmaceutical companies use slaughterhouse by-products in numerous ways. Owning your own pharmaceutical firm makes more sense than selling these by-products to someone else.

As far as sporting goods go, such terms as pigskin for footballs and gut in tennis rackets have their roots in the original materials used. Meat packing and sporting goods fit well, like a baseball mitt.

## Making the Whole Greater Than the Sum of the Parts

The concept of combining seemingly unrelated but integrated companies is called synergism. That's when $1+1=3$. It was all the rage on Wall Street for the decade of the sixties.

Ling looked at Wilson and decided that while this was all well and good, he knew how to sell even the squeal. He took the Wilson Company and redeployed its assets by splitting the company into three separate companies — a meat packer, a sporting goods company, and a pharmaceutical company, nicknamed meatball, golfball, and goofball by stock traders. Each had its own stock listed on the exchange.

There's no need to go into the complicated methods Ling used. Suffice it to say that the combined value of the three companies' stock far outweighed the value of the original Wilson Company in the marketplace.

Nothing had really changed. But Ling & Co. had lots more money. With an intelligent redeployment of your assets and available cash, you will too.

## Finding Your Hidden Assets—Equity in Your Home

Actually, many people have redeployed one of their most obvious assets without even thinking about it in those terms—they've gotten a second mortgage. House values have risen tremendously in the last decade. And when interest rates were low, it paid handsomely to borrow against the accumulated and inflated value of your house. All the interest paid out is tax deductible. So getting 2–4 percent more on Treasury bills than you were paying for the second mortgage meant a true gain of up to 8 percent on found money, depending on your tax bracket. At the moment, with the cost of borrowing so high, this is no longer a valid game plan. But temporary dips in mortgage rates may afford such opportunities once more.

### Long-Term Mortgage Rates Can Often Be Lower Than Short-Term Money Market Rates

Overall, mortgage rates will probably not return to their cozy 5–8 percent range within this century. Still, there will be peaks and valleys. And second-mortgage capital building is something to keep in mind for the next interest valley. So when interest rates are as low as you think they'll go for quite some time, take out a second mortgage and invest the cash in the meantime.

Let's do a cash survey of your other assets. Start small, remembering that even ten- and hundred-dollar found assets will add up to thousands of dollars of found money in the long run.

### Fluff in the Finances

*Do you suffer from an overstuffed checking account,* one with more money in it than you need on a weekly basis? Are there periods between your bill paying when there are fifty to a hundred or even several hundred dollars just idling in the account? Lazy money that just lies around loses its value to inflation.

Adjust your cash flow so that all your bills are paid on one day each month—at the last minute possible without impairing your credit rating. Deposit your paycheck and other earnings directly to a money fund. Then write your checking account a check from the money fund at the same time you pay your bills. For the average individual, this means a float of around $1,000 for a period of twenty or more days a month. Multiply by twelve, and you have about 250 days a year of float. The better part of a year's interest can be earned on that $1,000. The figures may be nothing compared to the Hunt brothers' fortune. Still, for the average investor, they represent over $100 a year in found money.

### Don't Lose Interest on Your Certificates

While you're running through your bank holdings, consider whether it might be worth redeeming any outstanding long-term certificates of deposit you may have. Such redemption makes sense and money in many instances. However, cashing in CDs might not be worth it for a 15 percent current return if the penalty, a loss of six months' interest, is too high. Each CD position must be carefully weighed in the given circumstances and should be reviewed with your banker. However, for now, simply consider liberating your old under-interested CDs as a real possibility in redeploying your assets.

### What's in the Cookie Jar?

Still on the subject of the bank, what about those old savings accounts? Had you forgotten all about the one with $50 in it from when you were saving for that vacation? Or that $200 you keep in a separate account just for emergencies? A money fund account is fully as good for emergencies. It will keep your money bringing top yields while it waits.

### Giving Up the Ghost

Then there's the ten shares of Horror Movies, Inc., or maybe it was Consolidated Electrobionics, you bought five years ago because it was supposed to double in price soon. It still hasn't. So why keep hoping? Liquidate any old and losing stock holding you might have. Liberate the cash.

### How Your Insurance Policy Can Chip In Some Cash Before You Cash In Your Chips

*Probably the biggest hidden silver vein minable by most people is life insurance.* Without our becoming mired in discussion of the pros and cons of whole, or ordinary, life insurance versus term insurance, the fact is that a lot of people have paid-up cash value just lying dormant with their insurer.

For example, a policy written before January 1, 1978, carries a maximum loan rate of 5 percent. That is to say, you can borrow up to the full paid-in value of your insurance at a cost of no more than 5 percent. Policies written after January 1, 1978, may carry loan interests as high as 8 percent. They're still a bargain compared with what anyone but your relatives might charge you.

The arbitrage — the spread or difference — in value between a 5 percent loan and a 15 percent money market rate would be 10 percent. Let's say you have a $20,000 life insurance policy taken out ten years ago, with a current paid-in loan value of $3,000, placed in a money fund yielding 15 percent. You would earn $450, and end up with $300 found money, after the $150 interest cost.

The most common argument against life insurance loans is that if you borrow, as in this example, $3,000 of a $20,000 policy, you then have only $17,000 of insurance. True indeed. But so what? Add the $3,000 in the money fund and you still have $20,000 in coverage. Actually you're ahead, because your coverage will be $20,300 come year's end.

One negative aspect of this type of loan, which the insurance companies don't mention, perhaps because they don't want to frighten you, is that the cash value of an insurance policy is usually sheltered from the clutches of all creditors, except the IRS in a case of tax evasion. So if you're expecting to file for bankruptcy soon, don't borrow against your life insurance. Under all other circumstances, borrowing against your life insurance is almost mandatory at today's interest rates.

Of course, you will have to pay taxes on the interest you earn from the money fund, as the insurance company will hasten to point out. Yes, but you will also get to deduct the cost of the interest you pay, something insurance companies again fail to mention.

Minimizing one's taxes is fine. I'm all for paying no more in taxes than is necessary by law. Still, to refuse an extra $300 in earnings because you might have to give Uncle Sam $50 as his share seems rather self-defeating.

Apparently a lot of people agree. In 1979, customers cashed in over 8 percent of the insurance industry's total $34.2 billion in assets. That's just below the cash-in rate of 1974, when interest rates last skyrocketed. And it's the second-highest incidence of life insurance borrowing since the Depression year of 1935. Do you have inflation-ravaged paid-in cash value wasting away in your insurance plan?

### "Excellent Deduction, Sherlock"

Homeowner's insurance is another silver vein to be mined. First of all, what's your deductible? With inflation, a $100-deductible policy doesn't make the sense it did back when a good sofa could be bought for $200 and your salary was half what it is now. Switching your homeowner's coverage to a $500- or even a $1,000-deductible policy should reduce your premiums considerably. And $500 is an amount you can readily self-insure out of the liberated cash and the interest it earns.

### You "Auto" Look Here Too

*The same principle holds true for automobile insurance.* Do double-check the deductible. Chances are it's $100 or $200 too low for today's stratospheric automobile prices. You can easily absorb an additional $100 loss in case of an accident. Meanwhile, over the years, the premium savings could be substantial, particularly if you also cancel the collision coverage on any car over four years old. At that age, the insurance value of the vehicle is probably so low as to make collision insurance (not, of course, liability insurance) an empty hole in which to throw your money.

### Taxes and Insurance—Pay Direct

Apart from adjusting the deductible to the inflation index, there's a further ploy to be used on homeowner's insurance, namely, *separating it from your mortgage payments.* Separate out the tax payments as well. Together these two items can equal up to one third of your total monthly payment. If you currently deposit to the bank a monthly lump sum to cover the actual mortgage plus insurance and real estate tax, the bank is taking a very lucrative ride on your money. Both insurance and real estate taxes are paid quarterly, semiannually, or even on a yearly basis. Until they come due, the bank is earning good interest on your money—the interest you could be earning if you paid the insurance and taxes directly rather than through the bank.

Don't let the mortgage department of your bank tell you it's obligated to pay the taxes and insurance for you. It's not. I do the job myself. Any bank should let you do the same if you have made your payments reliably in the past. Just remember to pay the insurance and real estate tax on time, or you could be in big trouble. The bank may, in fact, be entitled to foreclose, although it's unlikely to do so except in extreme cases.

Since we've touched on taxes, let's tackle another question right here. *Are you giving the IRS an interest-free loan?* It doesn't really make sense to do so. Yet one of your tax collector's biggest sources of interest-free loans is *overwithholding*. Usually this is no one's fault but the taxpayer's. Many people file for half the exemptions they are allowed—some even with zero exemptions—just so that at the end of the tax year there's a substantial refund in store for them rather than the chance of making out a check to Uncle Sam. Somehow it makes them feel better not to owe the taxman a cent. It's all part of the fear that the IRS has spent so much time and money instilling in us.

How good does, say, a $200 refund look when you realize that you're getting back only $160 after inflation? Worse yet to contemplate, had that withheld $200 been in a money fund instead during the 1979 tax year, for instance, you would have had $230 rather than your inflation-fractured $160 refund. So what, you say, $70 is no fortune today. True, but it still buys a lot of hamburgers for a family of four. Better to feed your family than Uncle Sam. And in a higher tax bracket, we're speaking of amounts like $1,000 or more tied up in overwithholding. That's at least $350 directly out of your pocket.

*Financial finesse applied to withholding tax means end-loading your payments.* End-loading is simply a fancy term for taking the maximum number of deductions you are allowed beginning on January 1. Then, in the middle of the year, switch to the minimum number of deductions or whatever is necessary to bring your total withheld income tax in line with what you will owe for the year.

End-loading your payments this way means you *underwithhold* on your income in the beginning of the year, when that inevitable economic whirlpool, the social security tax, is being taken out of your pay, and *overwithhold* later, to catch up on the income tax due the IRS. The result is that your paycheck stays on a more even keel all year round. And the money saved in the beginning earns interest all year.

## Taking Credit for Being Special

Carried to its full potential, underwithholding can be so remunerative that the IRS even has a name for it—"the W-4 problem." The problem is the IRS's, however, not the taxpayer's, since underwithholding is not illegal. At least not yet.

The W-4 form is what a company files with the IRS for each employee, and it indicates how much is being withheld for the employee's taxes. But it's the employee who determines the exact figure filled in on the form, by listing his or her exemptions or allowances for anticipated tax credits.

Anticipated tax credits include such items as energy credits, child-care expenses, and alimony, items that would not show up directly on salary computations. These credits are simply enumerated for the employer. They don't have to be itemized. And a student, for instance, with no expected tax liability, can file for tax-exempt status and eliminate withholding altogether.

In a recent *Wall Street Journal* example, a $45,000-a-year married executive claiming four allowances would have $205.34 withheld weekly. Increasing his allowances arbitrarily to fifteen would reduce the government's advance take to $127.05. The difference would represent a yearly net gain for his redeployed assets of $4,071.60. As the *Wall Street Journal* points out, although "he might have to pay it back on April 15—plus possible penalties—he would have its use during the year."

You should be aware that there is a penalty if taxes withheld are insufficient by 20 percent or more. That is, if the government gets in advance or in quarterly payments less than 80 percent of the tax money you owe them at the end of the year, they will penalize you. Currently, underwithholding leads to a 12 percent penalty on the excess. The exact amount you decide to redeploy, then, will depend on your individual finances as well as the applicable money market rate the found cash can earn. The gentleman claiming fifteen allowances would probably be stretching matters. Twenty percent underwithholding, on the other hand, is certainly a safe source of funds since it will incur no penalty.

### Borrow a Little Now So You Can Borrow a Lot Later

That American dream, *the automobile,* can also be used to generate unexpected investment funds. A surprisingly large percentage of car buyers will pay cash for their vehicles. Part of the old conservative saver's ethic, it was once a most laudable notion. But it's no longer a very profitable one in these inflationary times.

Now, I'm not one to recommend that you profit from inflation by getting yourself in debt up over your ears and then slowly paying off the debt with devalued dollars. In theory, it might work. In practice, too often it doesn't. Instead, the debt pyramid comes tumbling down when the unexpected occurs. Personal bankruptcies are going to increase tremendously in the coming decade because personal debt has got out of hand.

This does not mean, however, that a *certain amount of debt* isn't profitable, indeed necessary, in inflationary times. After all, any debt paid in the future is paid with dollars that will be worth less than they are today and at a time when you will, you hope, be earning more than you are now. High on the list of desirable liabilities are completely covered debts such as what I'd like to call the "you acceptances" of car buying.

*"You acceptances" are much like bankers acceptances on a personal level.* You borrow money to buy a car—even though you have enough money saved for it. The loan is backed by both the security of the car itself and the actual cash you have on hand.

Looking at it in round figures, let's say the car costs $10,000, a not outrageous figure given a year or two more of inflation and a vehicle with all the options. If you pay for the car in cash, that's the end of the cash. You have the car. The dealer has the money.

In opposition, let's look at the "you acceptance" approach. Currently, an automobile loan goes for 14 percent. Because money is tight, it's a hard loan to get, but not an impossible one if you have an established-customer relationship with your bank.

So instead of paying cash for the car, you put down $5,000 and take out an automobile loan for $5,000. Now you have the car plus $5,000 cash—plus, of course, monthly payments.

But the loan is costing you 14 percent. If a money fund is paying 16 percent on your $5,000, that's an extra 2 percent, or $100 found money a year. Meanwhile, the bank loves you. Since banks are in the business of giving loans, taking out a loan—especially if you already have a track record of having borrowed and repaid on time—makes you a good customer. Additionally, the 14 percent interest you pay on the loan is tax deductible, which raises your found money to $150, $200, or even more, depending on your tax bracket.

So where's the catch? Of course there is one: the free lunch really doesn't exist. The catch is that if interest rates fall, you'll end up getting less from the money fund, or the other money market investments, than you're paying for the loan. So in order not to get caught with your interest down, you need a loan with no loan prepayment penalties. Some banks offer them. Some banks don't. Penalties may vary too. Also, some banks may let you renegotiate a loan at a better interest if market conditions justify a switch. Shop around. You should be able to find a bank in your region offering no-prepayment-penalty loans, or loans with penalties low enough to make the gambit work. Shop for a bank just the way you do for groceries or a car. Get what you want, but do so from the place that offers you the best deal.

*Whatever you do, don't prepay too early.* If money fund yields drop from 16 percent to, say, 14 percent, the level at which your loan was negotiated, you will still be ahead because of the loan interest deduction on your income tax. For someone in a high tax bracket, the money fund rate could conceivably drop to 3 or 4 percent below the loan rate before the spread is no longer profitable. It's all a matter of timing your take.

### Time and Money—The Dynamic Duo

*Timing is crucial to your financial health.* Whether it be in the planning of tax payments or in simply never paying your bills early, much less buying for cash, timing is an essential part of money management. In today's roller-coaster interest rate environment, this is truer than it ever was in the past. Watch the clock and the calendar and you'll discover they're money machines that can unearth cash you were never even aware of.

The velocity of money is why this financial timing is so important. Money, like everything else, moves—out of your pocket into someone else's. It moves the other way around as well, of course. But the fundamental speed at which money moves has changed drastically without most people noticing it. It's like the expanding rate of technological progress that has turned a transatlantic voyage from a month-long journey into a few hours' ride on the magic carpet of a supersonic plane, and a transcontinental letter from a six-week pony express communiqué to a six-second telecopied message. So, too, money runs a lot faster these days.

Not so long ago, most working Americans were paid their salaries quarterly. Then the pay period became monthly, then weekly. Banks paid interest annually, bonds semiannually. Then banks went quarterly. Not so many years ago, the banks began compounding interest daily, a few even hourly. Zip, zip, faster and faster went the money.

*As inflation becomes a more important factor in our economy, the velocity of money speeds up even further.* And with this acceleration, the velocity of money becomes the power turning your cash management wheels, because the faster money travels through the economic system, the more important cash, and the interest it generates, becomes. This is particularly true for a society used to dealing in credit.

Consider the 1974–1975 recession. A friend of mine shopping for a house at the time attended a lecture by Pierre Renfret, a consulting economist. Never having purchased that ultimate of high-ticket items, he was amazed to hear Renfret suggest that when money was in short supply, buying a house wasn't a matter of bidding a few thousand dollars below the asking price. For an expensive house, at that time anything over $100,000, it was possible to bid 20 or 30 or even 40 percent below the seller's expectations and close the deal. So, knowing he had enough cash to make a mortgage tempting to the bank even during the tight money times, he offered $90,000 for a $135,000 house. And got it.

He was liquid and the world wasn't. Money is something saved as well as earned—if you have cash in the first place. That's the second reason to reorganize your finances to maximize your cash position. It pays not only to channel your money into the high-interest yields now available to the small investor, but also to be liquid enough to take advantage of the bargains that become available during the economic dislocations of recessionary inflations.

After having told you to pay your bills at the last possible moment, and after telling you to borrow to build up capital, this might seem to be a contradiction. But really it's just another example of that old maxim "The exception proves the rule." In your day-to-day operations you should never pay cash. But if by paying cash you can get a huge savings on something you need, why, then you're in a position to deal.

The key word is *need*. Most of us have far more things than we need, than we are even aware of having, for that matter.

What exactly do you have in your safe-deposit box, for instance? Marriage certificate, birth certificates, passports, insurance policies, sure, but what else? A couple of old U.S. savings bonds that someone gave you or your children years ago? They're still earning interest; so you never cashed them in? Don't be embarrassed. I found three in my own safe-deposit box. I'd forgotten all about them.

Go through your safe-deposit box and other caches with the goal of finding hidden, not to mention forgotten, value that you can liquidate. Get the lazy assets into cash to take advantage of today's high interest rates.

Then do the same thing with your home. Garage sales are for someone else. Right? Wrong. Some friends I never thought I'd see having a garage sale, and certainly never thought of as needing more money, spent a Saturday peddling all sorts of hidden "junk" to passersby. The spring cleaning removed a lot of clutter and brought in $500. A lot of miscellaneous dusty objects were redeployed into interest-earning cash.

Some of these find-the-hidden-money games may sound petty and penny-pinching. And taken by itself, something like borrowing on your life insurance may well be only penny wise. Certainly these ideas for pulling together more money are not going to make you rich by themselves. They're not even going to make you close to rich. But taken together, *they could increase your annual cash flow by $1,000 to $10,000 or even more*, depending on your overall income.

The question then is simply, considering that you don't even have to work for it, couldn't you use this much found money? If your answer is yes, read on, and we'll see if we can't raise your income even more.

### Hidden Money Mines for You to Explore

- Capitalizing on your house equity in your home with a second mortgage
- Low-interest life insurance loans
- Stripping extra cash from checking and savings accounts
- Cashing in low-earning CDs, bonds, and stocks
- Borrowing to invest
- Increasing homeowners and auto insurance deductibles
- Adjusting withholding taxes to keep the cash for a year
- Increasing your manageable debt load to liberate cash
- Emptying the safe-deposit box of forgotten treasures

# 5

## Money Funds: Your Parking Lot
## Paved with Gold

*How do you start managing your money to survive inflation?* The answer, in two words, is money funds. In today's high-velocity-money and inflation-incapacitated economy, *every cent you have that's not immediately spoken for should go directly into a money fund.*

Whether interest rates are rising or falling doesn't matter . . . and yes, as you saw in the snappy seesaw of the rates during 1980, interest rates can fall—if only temporarily—even during inflation. Your available cash should go into a money fund. Why? Because it's a parking lot paved with gold.

Remember, though, it *is* a parking lot, not a graveyard. You don't put your cash into a money fund and forget it. No investment is permanent and totally carefree. You wouldn't expect a potted flower to grow on your windowsill without being watered and cared for. You can't expect your cash to grow without tending, either.

While flexibility has always been important, in these rapidly changing times it is an absolutely essential key to personal financial growth. Your money has to be able to go with the flow, as the mellow millionaires in California put it. And the flow is through these new mutual funds called money funds.

### How It All Began

*It was early in the sagging seventies that I devised what I thought was the first money fund,* mulling over the possibilities of the money market with my finance professor at Temple University in Philadelphia. At the time, early in 1974, I was finishing up my MBA in finance—and financing my degree in the subject with my consulting work on the subject.

**$10,000 INVESTMENT IN PASSBOOK SAVINGS VS.
MONEY FUNDS VS. STOCK MARKET'**

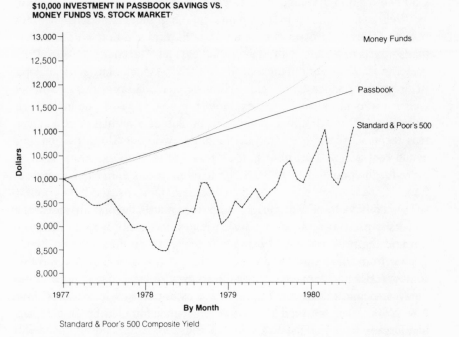

Standard & Poor's 500 Composite Yield

The consulting I was doing focused on small businesses, part of my work being under a contract with the Small Business Administration. In the course of my work, I encountered several independent clients who had considerable excess cash on hand—for part of the year. They were in a situation most small businesses would envy, but not a truly unusual one in seasonal operations. The question was, however, what could they do with that part-time cash besides sit on it?

At the time, the prime rate was already heading for the then unbelievable peak of 12 percent it was to hit in July of that year. And yet even our biggest clients, small businesses with less than $100,000 in cash, had to settle for leaving their money earning nothing in their checking accounts or investing in T-bills. Corporate savings accounts were not to be authorized for another fifteen months. Remember, $95,000 wasn't enough to play the money market. You had to have $100,000 to buy a bank certificate of deposit (CD).

With a 7 percent spread developing between T-bills and CDs, a client's lack of $5,000 could cost him $7,000 annually, just because he was short a few thousand dollars in cash for that $100,000 investment. And with more than one client in the same low-interest boat, a lot of money was being lost.

Well, as a certified public accountant, I'd had some experience with the pooling of assets through mutual funds, both from auditing various mutual funds and as an auditor with one of the "big eight" accounting firms, Price Waterhouse & Co. My finance professor, Dr. Rodney Johnson (later deputy director of finance for the city of Philadelphia), had previous experience with investment clubs. So we explored the possibility of pooling our clients' money through either an investment club or a mutual fund. For various technical reasons, the mutual fund idea won out. But a mutual fund would cost $50,000 up front in legal fees and start-up expenses. Also, in order for the pool to be liquid enough to allow clients immediate in-and-out transactions as necessitated by their business demands, the initial pool itself would have to be $20 million. Both were a little beyond the reach of a university professor and his student. Besides, in his enthusiasm, Dr. Johnson told the press we would manage the investments *free*.

Far from that being the end of the matter, however, I discovered that someone else had arrived at the same concept. Like so many ideas whose time has come, the money fund notion was not conceived in isolation. In New York, a money fund called Reserve Fund, founded by Bruce Bent, had already been in existence since 1972.

That fall I began to plan a series of corporate cash management semi-

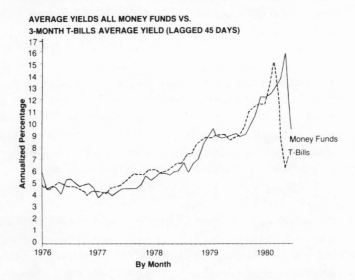

**AVERAGE YIELDS ALL MONEY FUNDS VS.
3-MONTH T-BILLS AVERAGE YIELD (LAGGED 45 DAYS)**

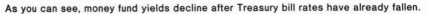

As you can see, money fund yields decline after Treasury bill rates have already fallen.

nars for my clients, including Temple University. Central to my presentation was the money fund concept and its applications.

Corporate cash management professionals, including the head of cash management at Chase Manhattan Bank, thought I was a little crazy talking about mutual funds. You see, the small investors weren't the only ones who had been stung by those investment vehicles. Large-scale investors, too, had lost a bundle of equity, or stock, funds. Besides, they said, mutual funds were for investors who couldn't get enough money together to invest directly, and surely corporate cash managers could do it better themselves.

Bit by bit they saw the light. Even though many corporate cash managers had enough money to invest directly in CDs and other large-scale deposits, they really didn't have the time and staff to do the actual managing. Leaving that to the full-time management company controlling the investments of a money fund seemed not such a bad idea. For the lone investor adrift on the ocean of finance, having the benefit of the contacts and the day-to-day, even hour-to-hour, information of professional managers makes, if possible, even more sense. Remember, money funds charge no commissions. Money fund managers know that even with the higher interest rates they offer, they're competing with no-sales-charge banks, so they don't try to market anything but no-load money funds.

To every rule, of course, there are exceptions. Currently among the money funds there are three loaded ones: MIF/Nationwide Money Market Account; the Lutheran Brotherhood Money Market Fund, with $100 one-time sales charges; and the CG Money Fund. If you really insist on paying salesmen's commissions (or loads, as they are called), these are the funds for you.

But the vast majority of money funds cost nothing to use. Also, unlike stock funds, money funds are interested in only one thing—the highest possible yield consistent with safety. There's no attempt to outwit the stock market, no temptation to invest in go-go stocks that may double in a month—or become almost worthless in less time.

### Money Funds Buy Money for You

*Money is what money funds essentially invest in.* This gives them stability, much more stability than stock funds have. Money is, after all, the one universal in the world of business, the bedrock on which commerce is based. Of course, investing in money gives the money funds less long-term growth than stock funds should have if and when the stock market ever goes once more into a sustained rally. But over the past three years, money funds have outperformed the widely followed Standard & Poor's 500 stock average.

Think of the money fund as a special-purpose savings bank with an investment company charter and probably the best yield opportunities for the future. Like the bank, the money fund is free. There's normally no sales fee.

There is, however, a management fee. A tightly regulated part of the funds, this management fee can't exceed 0.5 percent. Many money funds charge less. And fund managers earn their fee. With their entrée to the markets, they can maneuver higher yields than you and I could ever do.

At the same time, the managers have a very real incentive to keep costs down. Management fees are based on assets, not on yields. In order to increase assets, and hence the management fee, then, the managers must, of necessity, obtain the highest yields safely possible. For you, it's the *reverse* of the old vicious circle. The managers need to convince you to invest more by paying you the highest yield they possibly can in order to increase their own take.

Let's look a little more closely at how, and why, this works. Perhaps the best way to do this is to trace the organization of a money fund from its beginnings and see how it develops its checks and balances.

### How Money Funds Work

*The management company starts it all.* A group of financiers gets together with the intent of establishing a money fund. The parent organization they form is the management company, and it, in turn, selects a board of directors. The two groups, managers and directors, are separate entities functioning to protect the investors, a relationship much like the checks and balances of the U.S. government.

*The board of directors is directly responsible to you, the investor.* They have a legal fiduciary commitment to watch over your money. They're also liable to be sued if they don't do it right, so you know they're on their toes. And while a certain amount of overlap is permitted, at least two thirds of the directors must be disinterested parties unaffiliated with the management company. They can't even be consultants or advisers to the management company, much less its employees.

Once this yin and yang of the money fund is established, the real fun can begin. For the company now commences to deal with the SEC, the Se-

## MONEY FUND ORGANIZATION CHART

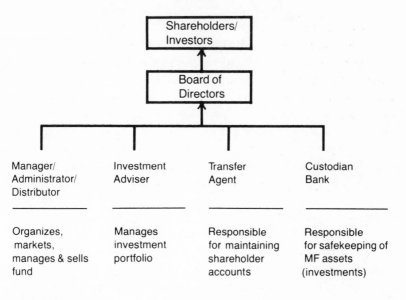

curities and Exchange Commission, guardian of the nation's fiscal finaglings. Even something as basic as the fund's name comes under the scrutiny of the SEC.

Bruce Bent of Reserve Fund tells how, when he originally tried to register the money fund as "The Savings Fund," an SEC official said, "See that pile of work? Your application can be on top of it—or at the bottom." The word "savings" has a complex and rather guarded meaning to this country's financial watchdogs. It simply sounds too bank-like to be used by any other type of institution.

Reconsidering quickly, Bent agreed to the name Reserve Fund. But then he said he'd like to call the fund's management company "The Guaranteed Profit Management Company"—a marketeer's dream of a name. To which the SEC official replied, "See that pile—"

"All right, all right," said Bent. "Reserve Management."

Bent's experience with the SEC is not an isolated case. Money Market Management, for another instance, originally applied for the name "Federated Cash Management," only to be told by the SEC, "You can't *manage* cash." And Capital Preservation Fund tried to capitalize on its T-bills-only portfolio by applying for the names "The First Real Bank" and "The First State Fund." Needless to say, it didn't get very far, either.

### The Prospectus—Essential Gobbledygook

If the SEC is reserved about names, it is more so about prospectuses. A prospectus is a statement by the fund giving information concerning its methods of operation, its investment policies, and the individuals involved in it—their birthdays, their experience, their favorite foods, the color of their eyes, etc., etc., etc. It is written by lawyers, for lawyers, who need lawyers to aid in its interpretation. About the only people who really read it word for word are members of the SEC. Designed to protect the investor, the prospectus, like most documents grinding through the mills of the government, shreds English into a mush the average individual simply can't deal with. The name for this gobbledygook is MEGO, which stands for "Mine Eyes Glaze Over."

Just to test its prospectus readership in May and June of 1980, the Northwestern National Bank of Minneapolis offered a hundred of its customers ten dollars if they would merely send a self-addressed postcard to the bank. The details of the offer were buried in a 4,500-word federally mandated disclosure notice, similar to a prospectus, describing the customers' and the bank's rights and obligations under the Electronic Fund Transfer Act. The gambit was a safe bet on the bank's part. It didn't have to pay out a single ten-dollar bill. Customers simply didn't read their rights.

After all that, let me hasten to add that you should not be put off by all the legalese in a prospectus. Compare the funds you're interested in with all the others in *Donoghue's Money Fund Directory*. Here, the basic information about the funds is displayed in a simple, stripped-down version. Then simply double-check your recent prospectus for each of the funds you're seriously contemplating to see that nothing about them has changed in the last few months. With the *Money Fund Directory* to help you, reading prospectuses becomes feasible.

Should you have any questions, you can always call a fund on its toll-free 800 number. If there's no toll-free number listed, call collect. The fund is trying to get your business, so your collect call will always be accepted. Save your cash to put into the fund itself.

### The Rest of the Money Fund Crowd

While the board of directors is registering the fund and drawing up an SEC-approvable prospectus, it also hires two more entities. It engages a custodian bank, to be charged with safekeeping the fund's assets, and a transfer agent, to control the actual physical processing of your funds and the issuing of shares.

*The transfer agent runs the "who owns how much" department.* Who bought shares. Who sold. Who's holding. Payment of dividends is also the transfer agent's bailiwick. If there's ever a foul-up in your payments, this is the office to deal with. Go to the top for quick action. And send copies of all correspondence to the fund's management company as well.

*The custodian is the one with all the money,* and subsequently all the purchased money market instruments. This, given the nature of things monetary, means a bank or a trust company. It is only, as the name implies, a safekeeper. The fund's assets are segregated from those of the bank. The bank cannot use the custodial funds as part of its assets—nor does federal bank insurance cover these funds.

When all the arrangements have been made and overseen by the government, the money fund is in business.

What you have when you join them is common stock shares of a pool of short-term money market instruments. Your money is part of daily multimillion-dollar deals, high-profit trades. Without the money fund, there would have been no way for you to join this exclusive club unless you had a few hundred thousand dollars of your own lying around or you pooled with a lot of wealthy friends.

Millions of dollars start flowing into the money fund's pool once it opens its doors. And they go right out again. A money fund can't sit on cash. Cash that doesn't move doesn't earn interest. The faster it's moved into investments, the better. Exactly where it is channeled depends on the fund's philosophy. But looking at the total invested fund assets as of the beginning of 1980 gives us an interesting picture of safety through diversity.

U.S. Treasury bills, your most conservative money market investment, accounted for 3.8 percent of all moneys placed. Additionally, 6.9 percent of the funds' assets were in U.S. government agency issues. At first glance, this would seem to indicate that slightly more than 10 percent of all the funds' money was invested in government instruments. Actually, however, these investments were placed primarily by specialty funds focusing on government instruments only.

The breakdown of how the remaining money fund assets were allocated is as follows: major bank CDs, 28.2 percent; repurchase agreements, 5.6 percent; bankers acceptances, 10.2 percent; commercial paper, 32.7 percent; Eurodollar CDs, 11.1 percent; and other, 1.5 percent.

To put all this in perspective, as well as to show the increasing importance of money funds today, one may note that their share of all outstanding CDs in this country was 13.1 percent; of commercial paper, 13.5 percent; and of bankers acceptances, 10.7 percent. The Eurodollar holdings of money funds as a percentage of total Eurodollar CDs outstanding is truly amazing. While it is difficult to get up-to-date figures from the Bank of England—after all, it is the Bank of England—projections from older figures indicate that the American money funds own over 31 percent of all Eurodollar CDs in London branches of U.S. banks.

The picture that emerges is one of money funds actually supporting the banks. Nearly 40 percent of fund money makes its way back into the banking system. Granted, the money funds do skim the safest cream off the top by putting their money in only the largest and safest banks. But that's to your and your pool's benefit. The fact that they channel money back to the banks at all is what the bankers will have to settle for.

So how and when do you split the goodies with all the silent partners in your pool? Again the current high velocity of money comes into play.

Had money funds evolved fifty years ago, chances are the pool would have divvied up its loot quarterly, or maybe monthly. Today it's daily. In "The Oedipus Transaction," a science fiction story by Robert Abel published a few years ago, J. D. "Steady" Stedmund managed his money with a high-speed computer, pyramiding loans and gambling on the fact that "the normal amount of cash in the system was about $15,036 a minute." Money funds, of course, never gamble, nor do they pyramid loans. But within the decade, they may well end up calculating their distributable assets on an hourly basis. And at that rate, an annualized 10 percent of, say, $20 million could buy a couple of cars at least. Now, why should someone who liquidates his shares in the morning get as much as someone who liquidates in the afternoon? For the moment, however, the funds evaluate their position and pay dividends daily.

### How to Evaluate a Money Fund Portfolio

*There are several ways of valuing a money fund's portfolio.* Knowing which method of valuation a fund uses gives you an idea of its day-to-day operations. However, in the long run, the means of valuation rarely makes a major difference.

Stock and bond mutual funds price their portfolios to market every day. That is, they add up the current price of all the securities they own, add the day's earnings, and simply divide the total for their portfolio by the number of shares they have outstanding on the same day. That's the net asset value per share, or price per share, listed in your newspaper. Typically it varies every day.

A money fund portfolio is different. It is unique, in fact, in that for most funds, the per share price always stays the same. Usually it's a dollar a share. Buy $1,000 worth of a money fund and you get $1,000 shares of a money fund. Buy $1,012 worth and you get 1,012 shares.

The next day you may find you have 1,015 shares. The previous day's dividends have been added to your portfolio in the form of 2 or 3 more shares. Then $1,012 + 3 = 1,015$. All you really have to know, however, is dollars. Because each share represents a dollar, for transaction and bookkeeping purposes the two can be considered one and the same. The simplest way to visualize your money fund holdings is to forget about shares entirely. Just think dollars.

For the fund, the accounting is not quite that simple. The fund is dealing with two distinct values—the interest its investments earn and the fluctuating market value of those investments.

Consider the simplified case of $1 million in discounted Treasury bills bought by the fund for $970,000 and due to mature in 300 days. The interest is easy enough to figure: it comes to $100 a day ($100 x 300 = $30,000). But what if interest rates drop in that intervening period? Why, then the value of the bills themselves would increase. If interest rates dropped 1 percent overnight, the T-bills valued at $970,000 would probably be revalued to $975,000 the next day. How do you reflect that $5,000?

On the one hand, the portfolio is worth $5,000 more, plus, of course, the $100 for a day's interest. On the other hand, it's not, for on the day the bills mature, the fund still gets only $1 million. On the third hand, maybe the fund should sell the bills for $975,000 and reinvest the cash. That, of course, is a management decision. The way it's reported to you is not.

There are four approved valuation methods for reporting: constant net asset value, mark to market; variable net asset value, mark to market; penny rounding; and amortized cost. Which is all I'm going to say here. (Turn to Appendix B for a more detailed explanation of these terms.)

What all these methods boil down to is simply the inescapable fact that interest on a money fund fluctuates daily. You are, in fact, buying a form of savings account which has a variable rate of return floating along with the general interest rate trend in the money market. Overall, it parallels the rate of a three-month T-bill.

The funds traditionally list their yields as "annualized average yields."

A recent Oppenheimer Monetary Bridge advertisement, for instance, claimed 13.36 percent as its current yield—in large bold letters followed by an asterisk. At the bottom of the ad, the asterisk was followed by this explanation: "13.36% was the annualized average yield for the seven-day period ending January 15, 1980. During this period the average dollar-weighted portfolio maturity was 22 days. The yield will fluctuate daily as money market rates and expenses vary, so don't consider this rate to be a representation of future rates. The yield of any investment is generally a function of portfolio quality and maturity, the type of investments made and operating expenses. For more complete information including all charges and expenses send for a free prospectus. Read it carefully before you invest or send money."

In other words, if everything stayed the same in the world for a year, and interest rates did not fluctuate, you would get a 13.36% yield for the whole year. But since the real world isn't like that, what the fund does is to promise you the best rate it can obtain.

Being used to banks, whose passbook rates have hardly varied from decade to decade, many people find the concept of a fluctuating interest rate uncomfortable at first. However, once you learn, as you will later in this book, that with good money management fluctuating interest rates can lead to even higher yields for you, you will learn to love them.

### Page Skippers, Pick Up Your Wealth-Increasing Reading Here

*How safe are money funds?* This is a question that's no doubt nagging at the back of your mind by now. Banks, after all, are insured to $100,000 per account by Federal Deposit Insurance Corporation, or FDIC, protection. Money funds are not. On the other hand, when you give your money to a bank, it can do anything it wants to with that money. It can even lend money to people like you and me. No wonder it must be insured! In the case of a money fund, on the other hand, you know exactly what will be done with your money. It's all in the prospectus.

Insurance is only as good as the pool of money behind it. The fact is, should two or three large banks go under, there really wouldn't be enough cash in the till to cover the losses. Another fact is, contrary to what you may have been led to believe, the FDIC has never paid off the depositors of a big bank. Sure, when the Sugar Creek Manufacturers Savings and Loan and the First National Small Town Trust Company folded, the FDIC was there overnight, reassuring everyone and paying out what was needed.

But according to a front-page story in the *Wall Street Journal* on April 28, 1980, when a big bank is threatened with failure, "the agency usually arranges a 'shotgun wedding' of the ailing bank into a healthy one, which takes over its deposits and most of its assets, mainly loans, sticking the FDIC only with the worst loans. . . ."

Finding a willing takeover partner, however, is becoming harder and harder these days. And as banks weaken, so does the FDIC.

Consider the FDIC's history. Formed during the Depression to keep the banks that hadn't caved in yet from collapsing under the weight of panic withdrawals, the FDIC covered accounts up to $5,000. There was $1.61 in the pool for each $100 of insured deposits. In other words, if all the banks went under at once, for each $100 you had on deposit the insurance would give you $1.61. On the other hand, the chances of all the banks going under was extremely slim. If only a few failed, there would be enough cash in the insurance pool to pay you a full $100 for each $100 on deposit.

By the beginning of 1980, the FDIC coverage had increased to $40,000 per account, and there was something like $10 billion in the cash drawer to cover contingencies. But deposits had exploded to $805 billion. So there was only $1.22 for each $100 of insured deposits.

Then, early in 1980, things really crumbled. Congress raised the insurance ceiling to $100,000. That was a nice thing to do and the people back home really liked it. It made them feel their representatives in Washington knew what they were doing, making the banks safer and all that.

Unfortunately, Congress hadn't bothered to confer with the FDIC beforehand. So when President Carter signed the new banking bill into law on March 31, 1980, the FDIC's risk exposure immediately jumped another $75 billion. The ratio of coverage plummeted to $1.11 for each $100 of deposits, the lowest ratio on record.

Now, there are two outside sources of funds for the FDIC. The agency can borrow up to $3 billion from the U.S. Treasury. And there's always the Federal Reserve Board, normally the lender of last resort for solvent banks needing short-term funds.

Under the new banking law, the Fed is allowed to lend money to any depository institution with checking-type accounts—money funds excepted, of course. Its umbrella is thereby extended to the previously unsheltered savings and loan associations.

With some two hundred banks on the problem-bank list, the chance of a couple of biggies needing rescuing is not out of the question. Far from it. At this writing, First Pennsylvania Corporation, parent company of First

Pennsylvania Bank, the twenty-third largest bank in the United States, has barely averted insolvency, according to articles in *The New York Times*.

A $1.5 billion rescue operation was mounted in an attempt to keep the bank's doors open. According to the plan, the company's shareholders had their ownership reduced from 100 percent to 43.9 percent. That meant for every $100 of stock they owned, they had only $43.90 after the rescue. The remaining equity was owned by the FDIC and a syndicate of thirty rescue banks.

According to First Penn's president, George A. Butler, if the shareholders hadn't accepted this better-than-50-percent overnight loss in equity, the result could have been failure of the bank and the holding company.

Now, the bank's depositors, as opposed to stockholders, did not lose a cent. The FDIC honored its obligations. But how many more troubled banks are on the verge of closing their doors? And how many banks are there left that have the funds to play rescuer before the Federal Reserve is called upon to play lender of last resort?

Unfortunately for the banks, not to mention depositors, using the Fed as a lender of last resort in the case of an impending bank failure presents a problem. It's called jail. The Fed is not allowed to lend money to banks that would be insolvent without the Fed's help. Members of the Federal Reserve Board could go to jail for doing so. I'm sure there are a lot of self-sacrificing and upright members of the Federal Reserve Board, but could you really expect them to go to jail for your money?

After all this, I'm not suggesting that you hurry out and withdraw all your money from the bank. Just remember, the old saying about the only certain things being death and taxes doesn't include the FDIC. So diversify. Keep some money in the bank, some money in hard assets, like gold, and your flexible short-term cash in money funds and other money market instruments such as T-bills. Diversification is your means of protection.

*Diversification is the insurance behind money funds* too. By law, money funds can't place more than 5 percent of their assets in any of the obligations of any single issuer other than the government. Now, there's real diversification.

A second safety valve for money funds is the *quality of these diversified investments.* Consider the much-in-the-news troubled Chrysler Corporation.

When the first doubts crept into the financial community about Chrysler's ability to manage its debt, there were some $1.3 billion of this automobile company's commercial paper outstanding. While it was not yet suitable for wallpaper, both Standard & Poor's and Moody's, the major rating companies for commercial paper, had reduced Chrysler's paper to A2 and P2 respectively. In plain English, that means second rate.

To be on top of the ever-changing money fund market, I decided to survey the funds to see what their exposure to this potential problem was. As I expected, not a single fund held Chrysler paper. It simply wasn't up to their standards. Considering the fact that at the time the funds together held considerably more that 10 percent of all the commercial paper outstanding, that's quite a record of prudence—and safety.

I'm sure that at the same time a number of banks held considerable amounts of Chrysler paper. Individuals alone, even wealthy individuals, certainly hadn't put $1.3 billion into this investment.

The reason I say I'm sure the banks were holding Chrysler paper, without being able to document what I say, is that there's no way for the public to know what bankers are doing with their moneys. Banks don't have the same constraints as money funds, and depositors have no way of knowing what their investment policies are. You can find out that a bank invests in commercial paper. But what kind of commercial paper is it? What quality guidelines, if any, does the bank use? Money funds are much more open about their investments. You can always check the prospectus to find out what they are getting into. In the case of a bank, just keep your fingers crossed. It's none of your business, because you're insured.

Now, as far as I know, the people holding that $1.3 billion worth of Chrysler paper haven't lost a cent. Yet. Of course, if they tried to sell it before the due date, if they needed money tomorrow, there could be a heavy discount penalty.

And, not to pick on banks too much, when the Franklin National Bank went under because of questionable practices on the management's part, the holding company's commercial paper holders were indeed left holding the bag. Again, we found no money funds among those holders.

The Franklin depositors, after this country's largest bank failure, did get all their money back, though they could have been required to wait sixty days, as the depositors of the much smaller St. Joseph's credit union in Atlanta, Georgia, insured by the FCUSI or Federal Credit Union Share Insurance, are being asked to do. According to an article in the *Atlanta Constitution,* St. Joseph's went under just as I was writing this chapter. In the estimation of the *Wall Street Journal,* another 10 percent of all existing credit unions may well fold in 1980. This brings us back to the question: How often will rescue operations work?

Consider the front-page story in that staid chronicler of the banking industry, the *American Banker,* on April 15, 1979. It began: "Some Fed insiders are becoming reconciled to the likely occurrence of a few key bankruptcies among financial institutions this year and next." Reconciled, indeed. If the Fed is reconciled, the FDIC must be near panic.

The FDIC will probably be able to handle a number of massive bank failures. But not too many, please.

By comparison, the money funds, as we have seen, are insured by the sheer diversity of their investments. They are also insured by the almost paranoid, supercareful caution of their managers. And some money funds are, in a sense, insured by the government, since they limit their investments solely to government obligations, a policy clearly stated in their prospectuses. In general, you'll get ½ to 1 percent lower yield in return for this extra margin of safety. But the interest is still well above what the banks pay in inflationary times.

## How to Find a Money Fund

*But, you say, there's no money fund located in my area.* Well, that's true and not true. It's true the funds don't have branch offices spread around the country. Remember, the money market is a telephone market. A single office is all a money fund needs, which means low overhead and a higher return for you.

The fancy offices of banks and their branches are paid for out of your money. Were money funds to open a chain of offices dotting the countryside like McDonald's stands, it would really do nothing but increase their overhead and reduce the yield they could offer.

Think of money funds as bank-by-mail or telephone operations. More and more energy-conscious people are saving gas by mailing deposits and withdrawal requests to their local banks. The convenience of banking by mail is the way these venerable institutions advertise this service. Very progressive banks are even beginning to offer telephone service. And it really makes sense. Recently I calculated the depreciation and gas cost of driving to my bank. Seven dollars and fifty cents a trip it costs me. (That's for a thirty-mile round trip at 25c a mile.) We live a little farther from the bank than the average individual, but not that much farther. Then there's the time wasted.

Still, on occasions when you drive by the bank, in the back of your head is the comforting thought: There's my bank. A certain calming atmosphere is fostered by the banking community. Their superthick vault doors don't have to be open for all the customers to see. Psychologically they instill a mood of safety by just being there. This aura is also largely why banks have traditionally been designed as heavy, imposing granite structures just oozing integrity and solidity from every pore.

Modern architecture is rapidly changing all that. Glass, steel, and open spaciousness are replacing the old solidity. People are even banking at trailers converted to bank branches. Now, I'm not suggesting that just because banks don't look as solid as they once did, they are less dependable institutions. But if you can get used to entrusting your money to a computer in a glass cage, adjusting to banking by mail is a snap.

Old habits do die hard, nevertheless. If you really need a physical office to handle your money, stockbroker-sponsored money funds such as E. F. Hutton's Cash Reserve Management, Oppenheimer Money Market, and Shearson Daily Dividend are your answer. Just look up the nearest one in your telephone book.

### A Money Fund Office on Every Corner

If you can adapt to banking by mail, why, then your nearest money fund is as close as your mailbox or telephone. That means, in fact, there are literally thousands of money fund offices scattered all around the country. So even if you're vacationing far from home, if you suddenly find yourself low on cash, you have fast direct access to your funds by check or in the case of Merrill Lynch's CMA Money Trust, by VISA cash advance.

With your "local" money fund situated in New York, or California, or somewhere in between, like Cincinnati, how do you go about finding it? As is so true of much that one searches for in this information-saturated world of ours, all you need and could possibly want to know about the money funds is readily available once you know the right place to look.

And now, time out for a commercial. But don't flick the dial. For commercials, in spite of their often boring repetitiveness, do offer a service. That is to say, at least the first time you hear them, they offer you information about something which may prove useful. In this case it's Donoghue's *Money Fund Report*, for the professional or $100,000-plus investor, and Donoghue's *Moneyletter*, for Mr. and Mrs. Average Dollar, as well as Donoghue's *Money Fund Directory*.

Actually, our full name is a bit longer, and I'll explain why. In starting a newsletter, the largest outlay is for advertising. Believe me, the bills for that alone are enough to make you cry. Interviews and other editorial write-ups, on the other hand, are free publicity, so I'm always more than happy to oblige the besieging press. And because I don't like the idea of people having to buy a pig in a poke, I always tell reporters that if their readers would like a free sample copy of my report, they can just drop me a line.

Dutifully the reporters used to mention to their readers that they could get a free copy of Donoghue's *Money Fund Report* by writing for it. But they never used to say where to write. So we changed our name officially to *Donoghue's Money Fund Report of Holliston, Massachusetts 01746.* Everyone was happy—except perhaps the mailman, who began to develop a bit of back trouble what with delivering 60,000 letters last year. Anyway, now you know how—and where—to get your free sample copies of the newsletters.

*Donoghue's* Money Fund Directory *lists all the basic information on every money fund available.* You'll find a recent issue in Appendix A of this book. It is updated twice a year to include the newest funds as well as any changes in the established ones. Besides giving the funds' average yields and assets, it covers information on checking privileges, investment limitations, fees, wire redemption where available, and other factors to guide your investment decisions, including a complete breakdown of the funds' various approved investments. All this will be covered in detail in the next chapter.

Additionally, each week in the *Money Fund Report,* and monthly in the *Moneyletter,* we list for each money fund the annualized seven-day yield, the thirty-day yield, and the average twelve-month yield updated to our press time. As you will recall, the yields of money funds run parallel to the overall money market yields, How individual funds express their yields is up to management. Therefore, the yield of fund X and the yield of fund Y as advertised by the funds themselves may not be directly comparable. Also, these yields are usually expressed as annualized seven-day yields, which are not necessarily indications of longer-term performance. Still, they will help you evaluate the funds by indicating which are currently the highest yielders and which have the best long-term record.

The only sources of directly comparable yields for all the funds are Donoghue's *Money Fund Report* and *Moneyletter.* Utilizing the funds' own information, which we gather weekly by telephone directly from over a hundred money funds, we report, using *our* standardized formula, the yields of each fund. Just let your fingers do the walking down the yield column and you can determine which among the funds that interest you has had the highest yield.

But don't base your judgment of a fund solely on its seven- or thirty-day yield unless you're thinking of a very short-term holding pattern for your money. For your basic parking lot account, the funds' long-term performance, such as their last two years' record, detailed only in the *Money Fund Directory*, is a key determinant.

Besides the Donoghue publications, other sources of information on money funds—once you've found one that interests you, the thing to do, of course, is to contact the fund directly—include major newspapers such as *The New York Times*, (New York) *Daily News Tonight*, *Chicago Tribune*, *San Francisco Examiner*, *Washington Post*, *Washington Star*, *Los Angeles Times*, *Miami News*, *Miami Herald*, *Detroit News*, *Boston Globe*. Even the *Tallahassee Democrat* covers the funds. Besides the advertisements of the funds themselves, these papers carry, every Friday, a "Top Fifty" list of money funds. That's the top fifty in assets, not necessarily in performance. The information source for the Top Fifty list is—what else?—Donoghue's *Money Fund Report*.

You are also likely to see in most newspapers a money market mutual fund table prepared and distributed to the press by NASD, the National Association of Security Dealers, which is the investment dealers' self-regulatory organization. I must caution you about this table. For reasons that are very technical, some of the yields presented in this table are unobtainable for the average investor. Also, because NASD uses different time periods to report on the yields of different funds, their statistics, though accurate, cannot be used to compare one fund's yield with another.

For example, one fund reported to NASD a yield of 12.7 percent for the first week in June 1980, with the note that this figure did not reflect capital gains and losses. To my firm, the fund reported that considering the capital losses incurred that week, when interest rates rose, it paid investors a yield of only 8.7 percent annualized. It paid 8.7 percent, yet the press was told it paid 12.7 percent. Do you see why my firm has set the standards for the industry?

We report what the investors actually receive, in a way that is easy to understand and that makes it simple to compare the yields of different funds. It's not an abstract figure. What you see is what you get.

Another problem with the NASD figures is that because many of the funds price at 4 P.M. and NASD collects the data on Fridays at 3:30 P.M., about a quarter of the funds cannot report Saturday-to-Friday yields. Instead, they report seven-day yields ending on Thursday.

So, investors, for the most accurate tables, stick to mine. The reason I've always offered to give a free sample copy of my newsletter to anyone who sends me a postcard is that I want to make sure people have the right information. Investing is a big decision.

## MONEY FUND NEWSPAPER TABLES
### Donoghue's Money Fund Table

# MONEY MARKET FUNDS

Funds with assets of $100 million or more ($50 million or more for clone funds) available to individual investors. For period ended September 17, 1980

| Fund | Assets ($ million) | Average maturity (days) | 7-day average yield (%) | 30-day average yield (%) |
|---|---|---|---|---|
| Alliance Capital Reserves | 655.0 | 26 | 9.3 | 8.8 |
| American Liquid Trust | 212.5 | 23 | 9.0 | 8.8 |
| Capital Preservation | 755.4 | 17 | 8.1 | 8.2 |
| Cash Equivalent | 1,410.9 | 43 | 9.7 | 9.2 |
| Cash Mgmt Trust | 315.4 | 74 | 7.0 | 7.4 |
| Cash Reserve Mgmt | 3,099.0 | 39 | 8.9 | 8.4 |
| Columbia Daily Income | 340.4 | 26 | 8.8 | 8.5 |
| Current Interest | 595.7 | 35 | 9.2 | 8.8 |
| Daily Cash Accum. | 2,266.0 | 26 | 9.8 | 9.6 |
| Daily Income | 610.7 | 39 | 10.0 | 9.6 |
| Delaware Cash Reserves | 639.4 | 48 | 9.1 | 9.0 |
| Dreyfus Liquid Assets | 4,053.0 | 43 | 9.3 | 8.9 |
| Eaton & Howard | 114.2 | 23 | 9.5 | 9.1 |
| FedFund | 581.0 | 37 | 8.5 | 8.3 |
| Fidelity Cash Reserves | 1,072.3 | 50 | 8.7 | 8.7 |
| Fidelity Daily Income | 3,484.0 | 51 | 9.0 | 9.0 |
| Fidelity MMT Domestic | 300.3 | 52 | 8.6 | 8.2 |
| First Investors Cash Mgmt | 195.3 | 23 | 9.4 | 9.1 |
| First Variable Rate | 460.1 | 25/a | 9.0 | 8.9 |
| Franklin Money Fund | 256.0 | 31 | 9.3 | 9.0 |
| Fund/Govt Investors | 424.2 | 55 | 9.6 | 9.2 |
| Government Investors Trust | 107.8 | 9/a | 9.7 | 9.4 |
| Gradison Cash Reserves | 316.6 | 27 | 9.0 | 8.6 |
| IDS Cash Mgmt | 391.8 | 54 | 9.7 | 9.6 |
| INA Cash Fund Inc. | 268.2 | 31 | 9.3 | 9.0 |
| InterCapital Liquid Asset | 4,545.3 | 47 | 9.3 | 9.1 |
| Kemper Money Market | 974.7 | 42 | 9.6 | 9.2 |
| Legg Mason Cash Rsrv Trust | 126.1 | 42 | 8.6 | 8.5 |
| Liquid Capital Income | 914.3 | 19 | 9.6 | 9.2 |
| Lord Abbett Cash Reserve | 175.4 | 20 | 9.5 | 9.0 |
| Mass Cash Mgmt Trust | 310.8 | 45 | 8.9 | 8.6 |
| Merrill Lynch | | | | |
|   Government | 160.0 | 34 | 9.0 | 8.7 |
|   Ready Assets | 12,069.6 | 54 | 7.5 | 7.3 |
|   Institutional | 803.8 | 38 | 9.3 | 9.1 |
| Midwest Income | 114.8 | 27 | 8.0 | 7.4 |
| Money Market Mgmt | 302.3 | 56 | 8.9 | 8.7 |
| MoneyMart Assets | 1,810.0 | 31 | 9.3 | 9.1 |
| Mutual of Omaha | 122.1 | 44 | 9.2 | 9.0 |
| National Liquid Reserves | 1,850.8 | 37 | 8.8 | 8.6 |
| NEL Cash Mgmt Acct | 291.2 | 61 | 9.0 | 8.7 |
| Oppenheimer Money Mrkt | 652.5 | 20 | 9.7 | 9.2 |
| Paine Webber Cashfund | 2,519.1 | 43 | 9.1 | 8.7 |
| Putnam Daily Div.Trust | 165.5 | 50 | 8.1 | 7.9 |
| Reserve | 2,007.0 | 15 | 9.6 | 9.2 |
| Rowe Price Prime Res | 1,189.3 | 25 | 9.5 | 9.1 |
| Scudder Cash Inv Trust | 203.4 | 35 | 9.6 | 9.0 |
| Scudder Mged Reserves | 469.8 | 97 | 4.3/b | 6.7/b |
| Shearson Dly Div. Inc | 2,252.9 | 19 | 9.6 | 9.2 |
| SteinRoe Cash Reserves | 379.7 | 39 | 9.3 | 8.9 |
| TempFund | 2,511.6 | 43 | 9.2 | 8.9 |
| Union Cash Mgt Inc. | 322.7 | 22 | 9.9 | 9.4 |
| United Cash Mgmt | 136.9 | 35 | 9.5 | 9.1 |
| Vanguard Money Mkt Trust I | 344.3 | 55 | 9.5 | 9.2 |
| Webster Cash Reserve | 629.7 | 36 | 9.5 | 9.1 |
| Donoghue's Money Fund Average (All funds) | | 43 | 9.0 | 8.8 |

Yield represents annualized return in 7- and 30-day periods.

Past returns not necessarily indicative of future yields.

(a) Average term to next rate adjustment date.

(b) Seven- or 30-day average not representative of current yield due to effect of varying net asset value.

Reprinted with permission from Donoghue's Money Fund Report, Holliston, 01746

SOURCE: Donoghue's *Money Fund Report*

NASD's Money Fund Table

# Money Market Funds

Friday, September 5, 1980.

| Money Market: | Days | Yield | Chg. | Money Market: | Days | Yield | Chg. |
|---|---|---|---|---|---|---|---|
| AlliaCpRs f | 27 | 8.83+ | .36 | LexMMkt | 25 | 8.58+ | .44 |
| AlliGvRs af | 18 | 8.35+ | .46 | LqdCapit | 21 | 9.21+ | .37 |
| AmGnRs b | 19 | 8.70- | .02 | LordAbCsR | 18 | 9.06+ | .47 |
| AmLiqTr | 22 | 8.93+ | .30 | LuthBrM c | unavail | | |
| CapPresrv | 29 | 7.89+ | .57 | MIFNatn c | 43 | 8.69+ | .29 |
| CarnegLq | 1 | 9.06+ | .23 | MassCsM b | 45 | 8.58+ | .16 |
| CashEquv f | 37 | 9.41+ | .59 | MerLyGv bf | 39 | 8.69+ | .23 |
| CshMgtA b | 82 | 9.26- | .09 | MerLyIn bf | 46 | 9.03+ | .07 |
| CashRsM bf | unavail | | | MonMMgt t | unavail | | |
| CentCapCsh | unavail | | | MonMkTrst | 57 | 8.83+ | .03 |
| ColDlvln bf | 26 | 8.55+ | .13 | MonMtA bd | 27 | 9.57+ | 1.59 |
| CompCsMgt | 25 | 8.62+ | .20 | MuniTInv e | 64 | 3.52+ | .03 |
| Currntlnt | 36 | 8.78+ | .38 | MutOmah c | 35 | 9.02+ | .10 |
| CurrIntSnd | unavail | | | NEL Csh c | 56 | 8.68+ | .02 |
| DailyCsh 1 | 24 | 9.20+ | .39 | NatLiqResv | 35 | 8.56+ | .07 |
| DelCshRs f | 54 | 9.01+ | .10 | Oppenh | 20 | 9.29+ | .69 |
| DryfLqAst f | 43 | 8.96+ | .16 | PaineWCs f | 37 | 8.54+ | .08 |
| DryMM GSc af | 45 | 8.53- | .21 | PutDDiv b | 55 | 9.12+ | .13 |
| DryMMkt af | 44 | 8.62- | .11 | ReserveFd | 12 | 9.15+ | .24 |
| EatHowCsh | 21 | 9.08+ | .32 | RowPrP f | 26 | 9.09+ | .20 |
| FedMaster | unavail | | | StPaulMF a | 22 | 8.98+ | .28 |
| FedTxFr e | unavail | | | ScudCsIn f | 29 | 9.10+ | .51 |
| FidCshRes | 56 | 8.68+ | .01 | ScudMRs df | 84 | 9.14+ | .12 |
| FidDlvln c | 59 | 8.96- | .04 | ScudTxF ef | 229 | 4.86+ | .14 |
| FidTxEx e | 79 | 3.95+ | .02 | ShearDDv f | 20 | 9.04+ | .11 |
| FinDlvlnc | 16 | 9.49+ | .34 | ShrtTrmY b | 23 | 8.93+ | .43 |
| FstInvCsh f | 26 | 9.07+ | .23 | StedmnFd b | 7 | 7.86+ | .19 |
| FstVarGv f | 30 | 9.09+ | .33 | SteinroeCRs | 38 | 8.75- | .10 |
| FrklnMny b | 28 | 8.92+ | .13 | TemplnvFd | 41 | 8.83+ | .19 |
| FrklnM II b | 12 | 8.90+ | .01 | TrstCshR f | unavail | | |
| FdUS Govt | 53 | 9.18+ | .30 | TrstShtFed | 34 | 8.22+ | .11 |
| GovtInvTr b | 16 | 9.50+ | .18 | TrstShtFdT | 33 | 8.42+ | .07 |
| GradCshR b | 27 | 8.67+ | .20 | TrstShtGv | unavail | | |
| IDS CsM df | 59 | 9.59+ | .02 | TrstUSTrOb | unavail | | |
| INA Csh b | 38 | 9.04+ | .23 | UnionCsgM | 11 | 9.44+ | .33 |
| IntcapLqAst | 50 | 9.13+ | .16 | UtdCshM | 39 | 9.13+ | .48 |
| JHanCshMg | 21 | 9.07+ | .06 | ValLInSh b | 25 | 9.59+ | .41 |
| JHanCsh II | unavail | | | VangMMT f | 58 | 9.07+ | .09 |
| JohnsCshM | 37 | 9.07+ | .15 | VangMB ef | 168 | 4.85+ | .05 |
| Kemper f | 40 | 9.64+ | .61 | VanMuB ef | 68 | 3.44+ | .07 |
| LegMsCsR f | unavail | | | WebsCshR f | 39 | 9.01+ | .17 |

a-Yield increased by temporary subsidization of expense. b-Actual yield may vary due to net realized/unrealized gains/losses. c-Actual yield may vary depending on account size. d-Change in net asset value during period. e-Invests primarily in Federally tax-exempt securities. f-As of previous day.

SOURCE: NASD

# 6

## Picking the Right Money Fund

*Choosing your fund takes a bit of tailoring.* We've all become burdened by the almost confiscatory tax stance taken by government, and the first two questions I'm often asked are: "Which money funds offer tax-free income?" and "Which funds invest only in U.S. government securities?" The second question is asked by those more worried about economic collapse than about the tax man.

The tax question is handled in detail in Chapter 17, titled, appropriately enough, "Money Funds and the Taxman." As to the government obligations question, let me preface an answer to that one by saying that only money funds follow the most basic of all investment rules, called "sleep" for short.

You should be invested so that you can sleep well at night. We're discounting, of course, other potential sleep inhibitors, such as children, in-laws, and the price of heating oil.

### For the Highly Conservative

If you really feel the world is on the edge of economic collapse, you probably have most of your money in hard assets, such as gold, and are staying only liquid enough to take advantage of buying opportunities. In that case, since the U.S. government should be about the last financial institution to go under, a money fund investing only in U.S. government obligations is probably your best bet. If this kind of conservative investment lets you sleep comfortably, it's worth choosing.

However, if you feel the world will muddle through somehow, a government-only portfolio is probably too conservative for you. It's far and away the most conservative fund stance, which means yields will be as

Top Ten Money Funds for the Past Five Years*

| Rank | | % Yield |
|------|------|---------|
| 1 | Fidelity Daily Income Trust | 7.14 |
| 2 | Kemper Money Market Fund | 7.09 |
| 3 | Oppenheimer Money Market Fund | 6.90 |
| 4 | Reserve Fund | 6.89 |
| 5 | Midwest Income Investment Company | 6.80 |
| 6 | Dreyfus Liquid Assets | 6.78 |
| 7 | Liquid Capital Income Inc. | 6.70 |
| 8 | Columbia Daily Income Fund | 6.68 |
| 9 | Scudder Managed Reserves Inc. | 6.65 |
| 10 | Daily Income Fund Inc. | 6.61 |

*These funds have been in business for at least five years and have been ranked in the top ten highest-yielding money funds for at least one year during the period 1975-1979. Yields represent the average of each fund's yearly performance for the past five years.

much as 1 percent lower than those of the average money fund.

Perhaps a sounder policy would be to diversify, if your savings are sufficient to permit you to do so. Diversificiation, remember, is the safety factor the funds themselves use. Put your absolute-emergency-only savings into an ultraconservative government fund such as Capital Preservation Fund, which invests only in Treasury bills and repurchase agreements collateralized by Treasury bills. Then put your day-to-day cash into a higher-yielding, more aggressive operation.

### Supersafe and High Yield Too

In the government-only category, there are two funds with a rather interesting investment policy you might look into. Half the portfolios of First Variable Rate Fund and Government Investors Trust are invested in relatively high-yielding Small Business Administration, or SBA, loan participations.

## TOP TEN MONEY FUNDS BY YEAR 1975-1979

### 1975

| Rank | | % Yield |
|---|---|---|
| 1 | Fidelity Daily Income Trust | 6.98 |
| 2 | Scudder Managed Reserves Inc. | 6.79 |
| 3 | Dreyfus Liquid Assets | 6.67 |
| 4 | Oppenheimer Money Market Fund | 6.65 |
| 5 | Kemper Money Market Fund | 6.51 |
| 6 | Columbia Daily Income Fund | 6.33 |
| 6 | Reserve Fund | 6.33 |
| 8 | Daily Income Fund Inc. | 6.13 |
| 9 | Midwest Income Investment Company | 6.12 |
| 10 | Money Market Management Inc. | 6.10 |
| | 1975 Average for all money funds | 6.18 |

### 1976

| 1 | Whitehall Money Market Fund | 5.71 |
|---|---|---|
| 2 | Columbia Daily Income Fund | 5.66 |
| 3 | Fidelity Daily Income Trust | 5.61 |
| 4 | American General Reserve Fund | 5.58 |
| 5 | Kemper Money Market Fund | 5.56 |
| 6 | Dreyfus Liquid Assets | 5.50 |
| 7 | Merrill Lynch Ready Assets Trust | 5.38 |
| 8 | Midwest Income Investment Company | 5.28 |
| 9 | Franklin Money Fund | 5.22 |
| 10 | Daily Income Fund Inc. | 5.21 |
| | 1976 Average for all money funds | 5.17 |

### 1977

| 1 | Midwest Income Investment Company | 5.49 |
|---|---|---|
| 2 | Liquid Capital Income Inc. | 5.46 |
| 3 | Kemper Money Market Fund | 5.15 |
| 3 | Reserve Fund | 5.15 |
| 5 | Scudder Cash Investment Trust | 5.07 |
| 6 | Franklin Money Fund | 5.05 |
| 6 | Mass. Cash Mangement Trust | 5.05 |
| 8 | SteinRoe Cash Reserves | 5.03 |
| 9 | Union Cash Management Inc. | 5.00 |
| 9 | Gradison Cash Reserves | 5.00 |
| | 1977 Average for all money funds | 4.87 |

## TOP TEN MONEY FUNDS BY YEAR 1975-1979 *(Continued)*

### 1978

| Rank | | % Yield |
|------|---|---------|
| 1 | First Var. Rate Fund for Gov. Inc. | 7.47 |
| 2 | Fidelity Daily Income Trust | 7.40 |
| 3 | Kemper Money Market Fund | 7.37 |
| 4 | Mass. Cash Management Trust | 7.35 |
| 5 | Midwest Income Investment Company | 7.30 |
| 6 | Rowe Price Prime Reserve Fund Inc. | 7.28 |
| 7 | InterCapital Liquid Asset Fund Inc. | 7.25 |
| 8 | Reserve Fund | 7.24 |
| 8 | Union Cash Management Inc. | 7.24 |
| 8 | Centennial Capital Cash Man. Trust | 7.24 |
| 8 | Merrill Lynch Ready Assets Trust | 7.24 |
| | 1978 Average for all money funds | 6.99 |

### 1979

| | | |
|------|---|---------|
| 1 | American General Reserve Fund | 10.88 |
| 2 | Kemper Money Market Fund | 10.84 |
| 3 | Fidelity Daily Income Trust | 10.73 |
| 4 | SteinRoe Cash Reserves | 10.69 |
| 4 | Union Cash Management Inc. | 10.69 |
| 6 | Reserve Fund | 10.67 |
| 7 | Rowe Price Prime Reserve Fund Inc. | 10.64 |
| 7 | Oppenheimer Money Market Fund | 10.64 |
| 9 | Merrill Lynch Ready Assets Trust | 10.61 |
| 10 | Delaware Cash Reserve Inc. | 10.58 |
| | 1979 Average for all money funds | 10.29 |

Now, as I'm sure you are aware, small businesses aren't exactly paradigms of financial stability. However, *the SBA loans are backed 100 percent by the U.S. government.* What happens is that when a bank lends money to a small business, the SBA, at its own discretion, guarantees 90 percent of the loan's value. The bank then lends the company money at 2 or 3 percent above the prime rate. If the current prime, for example, is 10.5 percent, the bank adds on, say, 2 percent for a loan cost of 12.5 or 13.5 percent.

The bank may later decide to sell that loan. Banks are always buying

**GOVERNMENT-ONLY MONEY FUNDS YIELD VS.
ALL MONEY FUNDS AVERAGE YIELD[1]**

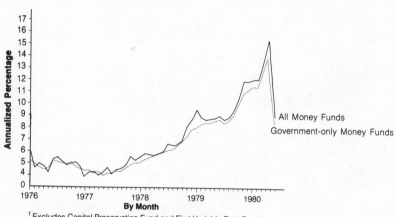

[1] Excludes Capital Preservation Fund and First Variable Rate Fund because they are not typical of Government-Only Money Funds.

## Money Funds That Invest Only in U.S. Government Instruments

One of the first questions many new money fund investors ask is: "Which is the safest money fund?" By that, they mean: "Which fund invests in the safest investments?" The answer is, of course, a fund that, like Capital Preservation Fund, invests solely in Treasury bills. As you can see, this choice of fund portfolio usually means that the investor gives up about 0.5 percent in yield on the average.

We have included in this Government-Only Money Funds Yield average only those funds which maintain a "buy and hold" strategy in U.S. government issues. We have excluded two funds that normally perform differently for specific reasons: Capital Preservation Fund, which tends to have a more actively traded portfolio (and a higher yield), and First Variable Rate Fund, which, like the newer Government Investors Trust, maintains a significant position in government-guaranteed loans that adjust their yields quarterly and thus give the fund a performance less typical (higher yielding) of standard government-only money funds.

and selling loans, although you might not have been aware of it, to adjust their capital position. Participating out, it's called. If the loan is participated out, it's usually the original 90 percent SBA-covered portion that is sold, to yield 1 percent less than the loan rate, or in the above case, 9.5 percent. Getting 2 percent over prime on the 10 percent of the loan the bank still holds plus 1 percent on the remainder, in which it really has no money tied up, makes for an attractive return on the bank's investment.

First Variable Rate Fund, for example, invests heavily in these loans. Since they purchase only the 90 percent covered by the SBA, their portion of each loan is covered 100 percent by the government. The word "Variable" in the fund's name refers to the fact that they invest only in floating rate, or variable interest rate, loans. If the prime drops, the rate drops too, but only at the end of the fiscal quarter. If the prime rises, the rate rises, First Variable's return on that loan remains a constant 1 percent under the prime, and it stays up for a quarter after the change.

Because, by definition, most money fund investments yield *below* the prime, First Variable Rate Fund often yields a bit higher than average. In 1978, it was the top-yielding money fund. And that's with its loan portfolio government guaranteed. That makes it as safe as funds investing in Treasury bills only.

For short-term money, you should note that when rates are rising, First Variable usually has its highest yield in the first month of any given quarter. That's when the fund makes its adjustment to the prime, which, of course, immediately affects the yield.

Yield and safety may not be your only criteria for a money fund. Although money funds, being of the same breed, tend to offer the same services, there are differences in degree and means by which these services are offered. Check them out before you invest.

For instance, the most common minimum for opening a money fund account is $1,000. However, there is a wide range above and below this average figure. Midwest Income Investment Company, for example, requires only $500. Master Reserves Trust requires $250,000. But most funds set a minimum in the $1,000 to $5,000 range.

There are a few funds, such as Merrill Lynch's CMA Money Trust, that have no minimum. There's a catch, of course. You have to have $20,000 invested with Merrill Lynch in some form. Still, if you have a lot of stock or a Keogh plan with the firm, it might be the right approach to open your money fund account there too.

## How to Invest in a Money Fund

### By Mail

Mail your investment check with your application to the address designated on the prospectus, and as soon as the check arrives and is converted to federal funds (up to two days after its arrival), you will be invested.

When mailing your investment, put your own stamp on the envelope. The prepaid mail permits require the postal service to count the envelopes before delivery, a process that may delay the arrival of your investment.

### By Wire

Call the money fund for instructions on how to wire money to the fund, obtain an account number, call your bank and request it to wire the money as instructed (be precise in your instructions), and mail your completed application. Your money should be invested the same day.

The first time you use wire service, you would be wise to go to your bank's main office to arrange for the wire. Most branch offices rarely wire funds, while the procedure is fairly common in the main office.

If you are investing less than $5,000, you will probably be best off investing by check. Larger amounts can make it worth your while to pay wire charges to insure that your money is invested and earning more quickly.

Then there are American Liquid Trust and Alliance Capital Reserves. These two funds really and truly have no minimum initial investment. For that matter, they have no minimum subsequent investment, either. So you could deposit your paycheck or social security check directly to either of these funds, no matter what amount the checks are for.

*The minimum subsequent investment required by a fund is definitely a consideration.* Funds that have no minimum or require only a $100 subsequent investment place no limitations on anyone. However, if you choose, say, Fidelity Daily Income Trust, where a minimum deposit is $500, solely on the basis of the fact that it has been the top performer over the last five years, you may spend a week or two accumulating enough cash to make a deposit.

The Reserve Fund, another money fund in the top ten yielders, requires a $1,000 or larger investment after you have opened an account. So check the funds' minimum subsequent investment requirements and match them against your cash flow before you make a choice. After all, a fractionally higher yield won't do you much good if you regularly have to keep cash lying around until you accumulate enough for a deposit.

### Check the Checking

*The funds' checking feature is one of the most marvelous and underutilized moneymakers around.* The vast majority of the funds allow you to write checks to withdraw money. These checks can be used just like bank checks. But unlike the case with bank checks, your money keeps earning interest right up until the time the checks are cleared.

When I bought my house a few years ago, I remember, I made the down payment with a check drawn on Fidelity Daily Income Trust. The realtor accepted the check readily enough, but he didn't deposit it until the actual closing. Meanwhile, I'd collected $75 worth of dividends on a bill I had already paid. After the closing, we had a lovely celebration dinner—courtesy of my local money fund.

Using a money fund is in many ways like dealing with a bank, or perhaps "second bank" would be a better term, since actually the checks you use are drawn on a bank, the commercial bank at which the money fund keeps its account. One of the subscribers to Donoghue's *Moneyletter,* a writer in Berkeley, California, told us:

> I use a money fund just as I would a savings account at a bank. I have a checking account, and I figure that I need about $400 to cover minimum-balance requirements and my daily check writing. Whenever the amount in my checking account exceeds $700, I shift the excess into my money fund account.
>
> Since I am a free lancer, my cash flows tend to be irregular, so I like being able to get at my money whenever I need it. For example, I had a terrible month last December and had to use money out of my money fund when my car engine blew up. If I'd been in any other investment, I would have been grounded for days or weeks while I came up with the money. Instead, I just paid the $1,000 overhaul bill on a money fund check and had my car right back on the road.
>
> Also, the yield I'm getting on my money will come in handy. I'm getting married soon, and because of the high yield, we can afford to take a nicer honeymoon than we'd first thought. Instead of renting a hole-in-the-wall cottage at Lake Tahoe, we can stay in a decent motel. And it looks like the honeymoon bill will come right out of the money fund.

The truly amazing thing about the checking privilege is that most of the people who have money fund accounts don't use it. On the average, each account writes only two checks a year.

Part of the reason for this is that many funds specify a $500 minimum per check, so people simply assume that's every fund's minimum, which is not the case. Lexington Money Market management, and Fidelity Cash Reserves, for instance, require only that each check be for at least $250. Midwest Income Investment Company requires no more than $350.

Now, $250 isn't that much money these days. Even $500 isn't. Look at your mortgage payments, for instance, and your life insurance premiums, oil bills, car insurance, taxes. . . . The number of bills over $250 each that you pay a year is probably greater than you realize. Add them up. If the total is over ten, merely the dividends earned while these checks clear will get you dinner for two in a good restaurant—free. And meanwhile, there's the fund's high yield on the cash that's parked.

Typical of well-managed moneymaking use of a fund's checking privileges—and how the money ended up doing so—is the money fund account of one of our subscribers, a physician and professor of medicine in Davis, California. His description, representative of how individuals, trying to stay at least even with inflation, have drifted into money funds after being pecuniarily taken advantage of by traditional forms of investing, should be comforting to you if you still feel a little nervous about sailing into previously uncharted financial waters.

> For a long time, I just kept my money in one of the local savings and loan associations, just because that's where my mortgage was. I thought that was what you were supposed to do. I also had a savings account at Bank of America, along with my personal and business checking accounts. Why Bank of America? Well, if you live in California, there's just nowhere else to bank. I mean, with Bank of America, you can deposit at your local bank, and if you're anywhere else in the state, you can just walk into that local office and cash a Bank of America check. I've since learned that's called liquidity, and it's still very important to me, mostly because of what happened when I bought a money market certificate at my savings and loan.
>
> When I bought the money market certificate, the savings and loan was advertising them as "Treasury certificates." At the time, they were advertised as paying 9.75 percent annually.
>
> I bought the certificate for a couple of reasons. First, my stockbroker had given me a "sure thing" investment tip for a new computer manufacturing firm. The stock went up for a while, and things looked good, but then

it started to go down, for who knows what reason. I sold when the stock was back down to my original purchase price, because the broker kept saying, "Just wait, it will go up next week." Needless to say, I've switched brokers. After that disaster, I realized that I'd actually lost money. While inflation had been going up to about 10 percent, my investment had earned zilch. That's when I switched to a money market certificate—at least, at 9.75 percent, I would be close to inflation without risk.

Then a friend told me about money market funds. At the time, they were yielding 12 percent. They sounded as safe as banks, so I decided to jump to the fund and take the money out of the money market certificate.

That's when I found out about liquidity. That is, the savings and loan told me that I'd have to wait until the end of the six month certificate's period or lose most of my interest. I didn't want to lose my interest, so I waited, but I'm sure I lost interest by nòt being able to move into a money fund.

Well, I finally ended up in a money fund. I put about $11,000 of my personal savings in one to begin with and then set up a second account with a smaller balance for my business money. I still have checking accounts with Bank of America, but now I keep only the minimum balances there and all savings money and excess business cash goes right into the money fund. Once a month, I transfer money from my money fund accounts to my checking accounts for bill paying. I use the check-writing service of the money fund, needless to say. My personal credit card payments, since they're so big, are usually made on money fund checks.

Right now, I can't see any reason to use any other savings or investment vehicle. First, my money's probably safer than it would be in a bank, because I invest in one of the funds that's 100 percent in government notes. Second, I get such a nice return that I wouldn't consider entering the maelstrom of the stock market again. Third, I can have access to my money whenever I want it.

And the extra $1,000 I'll have at the end of this year sure is better than a kick in the pants. Now, if it just weren't for income taxes . . .

## Points to Consider Before Selecting a Money Fund

*Minimum Initial and Subsequent Investment*

Checking the directory in the back of this book, you can easily determine which group of funds allows minimum investments of $1,000, though some are lower and still others have no restrictions at all. Subsequent investments are typically in the $100 to $1,000 range, but again, some funds carry smaller or no restrictions.

*Checking Privileges*

The check redemption privilege permits you to withdraw your money simply by writing a check in an amount equal to or exceeding the minimum amount indicated. These checks are, in effect, the same as any bank check. They are drawn against an account which the fund sets up for you.

The checks may be drawn to a third party, such as your landlord, bank, or any other vendor. Many small businesses use these checks to pay all their bills over the minimum requirement. Thus, they can enjoy having daily dividends credited to their accounts until the checks clear.

Checking policies vary from fund to fund. Most funds will provide a certain number of checks, with more supplied on request at no charge. Some will provide an unlimited number of checks to the investor.

If for some reason you do not wish to use the checks supplied by the funds—corporate investors may have continuous-form computer checks, for example—many funds will allow you to print checks at your own expense, as long as they conform to the fund's required format. Another concern of corporate investors may be whether or not the fund will accept a facsimile signature, such as a rubber stamp. Most funds have strict policies against this practice unless the facsimile signature appears on the signature card or is printed by machine.

Some confirmation of check transactions will usually be offered by the funds. Canceled checks are returned on either a monthly, a quarterly, or an as-they-clear basis. Certain funds may return only a confirmation or photocopies of checks. Others will do this only on request.

*Telephone Redemption Privilege*

The telephone redemption allows you to request by telephone that the fund redeem all or part of your investment in at least the amount of the indicated minimum. This privilege is typically used to request that the fund wire the money to your bank account. The standard minimum requirement on a Fed wire is $1,000, though an individual fund may require a larger minimum on a wire transfer.

You may also request a check redemption by phone, but it is usually more efficient to simply write the check yourself. Funds generally will be wired only to the one account designated on your application.

*Exchange Privileges*

Some funds permit you to exchange your shares of the money fund with the shares of another fund, usually an equity or a stock fund. Investors who feel they would rather be in a bond fund or a growth fund or some other fund will often switch their investment using this privilege. Others, feeling they can time the market swings, will use the privilege more aggressively.

The procedure for using the exchange privilege may vary between funds. You should check each fund's prospectus for limitations or restrictions.

*Special Charges*

None of the funds (except the load funds, listed under "Special Purpose" money funds in Appendix A of this book) have a sales charge, or load, though some may charge a fee for services. Charges for check printing, wire redemption, monthly service, one-time setup, subaccounting, and exchange privileges are also indicated in Appendix A. The normal sales charge applied to the exchange privilege refers to a charge for exchanging shares of a no-load fund for those of a load fund.

*Dividend Policy*

Most money funds declare dividends daily and pay, credit, or reinvest dividends on a daily, monthly, or quarterly basis. As long as the dividends are credited directly to your account rather than being mailed to you, the actual dividend policy has no effect on the yield.

# 7

## Your Bank Can Still Make You Money— Sometimes

*By now banks may look like the lemons of the financial world.* Then again, lemons have their uses. You just have to squeeze them. Actually, in the case of the banks, the money funds are already doing the squeezing for you.

Once a cozy monopolistic club providing perpetual care for consumer savings, banks are suddenly finding themselves selling six- and thirty-month investments out in the cold, cruel world of competition. *More than 40 percent of all the money deposited in savings accounts in the U.S. has moved from traditional savings accounts to either money market certificates or money funds since Savers' Liberation Day, June 1, 1978.*

The banks' reaction to this phenomenon was to call upon the politicians. "Protect us, or the housing industry will collapse," they cried. And if the housing industry collapses, you won't be reelected, they implied. "Outlaw money funds. They're really nothing but freewheeling banks in disguise." You see, money funds are what the banks want to be—in 1989. The problem is that the banks don't want anyone else to offer their customers a better deal until they can work out the politics and the economics of offering such a product profitably themselves. The money funds, on the other hand, have not been subject to the same constrictions as the banks. So money funds can offer now what the banks will be able to offer in 1989, when Regulation Q finally expires. By 1989, banks will be able to offer 10 percent on savings accounts—if there are any savings accounts left.

### The Louisiana Money Fund Blues

One state, Louisiana, buckled under the pressure of the banks early in 1980 and declared money funds illegal. The state attorney general ruled

76

that money market funds were "actually engaged in the banking business." Their inroads into traditional banking activities such as check-writing privileges were cited as a leading cause for the funds' being considered banks.

A few weeks following this decision, however, the State of Louisiana decided to reconsider the case. Merrill Lynch Ready Assets Trust (known in the trade as RAT) was allowed to resume selling its fund, at least while the State of Louisiana mulled over the full implications of the ban—and faced the pressure of all the potential litigation it would involve.

The fact is that "people who invest in money funds become shareholders of the fund," as pointed out by Matthew P. Fink, general counsel of the Investment Company Institute, the Washington-based lobby representing mutual funds. That's quite different from simply depositing money in a bank.

Then again, in certain respects it isn't so very different. If you deposit your money in a mutual savings bank, for instance, you become, in fact, a part owner of the bank, though you have no actual shares, such as those issued by a money fund. Nor, for that matter, do you have much shareholder power, as I discovered while trying to cajole my local banker into giving me a lower loan rate because I was, after all, a shareholder and the bank had made a huge profit the year before which I felt it should reasonably share with us shareholders. Still, there are enough similarities so that suits and countersuits stand a good chance of making the financial headlines in the next couple of years.

## Competition Can Work for You

The infighting for your cash among financial institutions won't affect you—except to increase your dividends *if* you play your money right. The effects of this competition on individual banks, however, are apt to be something else. During the eighties the small local bank may be heading the way of the dinosaur. Just look at money market certificates. At the end of April 1980, there were $380 billion of these bank-issued instruments outstanding. Savings and loan associations had more than 35 percent of their *total* deposits in six-month money market certificates. Banks had over a third of their savings deposits accounted for by the same type of certificate. On top of this, heavy competitive advertising keeps selling more and more of these financial leg irons to consumers, who find they are locked in for six months or more while other, better opportunities pass them by unexploited.

*There's a time bomb ticking away in the banks' vaults.* It may have already exploded by the time you read this, although more likely that event is a couple of years away yet. When the explosion does come, be prepared to pick up the good pieces.

The fuse on the time bomb is savers' increasing sophistication. As money market certificates expire and new ones offer lower interest rates than Treasury bills and money market funds, more and more investors are choosing to switch rather than fight. When they get their money back, they simply don't buy money market certificates from the bank again. They put their cash in money funds instead.

The banks, meanwhile, are struggling to strengthen their position through the Federal Reserve and Washington bank lobbies. At one point they tried to hobble the competition from money funds and unit investment trusts with well-timed pressure that led to a Federal Reserve regulation requiring a 15 percent reserve on new money fund assets. Since there had been no reserve requirement previously, this effectively reduced the yields of funds organized after March 14, 1980. By June 10, 1980, the reserve had been reduced to 7.5 percent.

The reserves were finally lifted on July 28, 1980. And what is interesting about this brief skirmish is that with the heaviest regulations in mutual fund history, the money funds still grew over 30 percent in just those four and a half months. You can't keep a good thing down.

About $250 billion of the banks' savings certificates matured in the late summer and fall of 1980. The October 1980 maturities of $98.7 billion alone account for 9 percent of all the savings in the country. For various reasons, including many savers' hidebound traditionalism and plain unawareness of money funds, not all of this cash fled from the certificates. Enough did, however, to further weaken the smaller banks, and even larger ones with 40 to 50 percent of their deposits in savings certificates, through severe disintermediation—that is, withdrawals.

What was the solution to this ebb tide problem? Well, for the ever-increasing legion of sophisticated savers, there was no real problem. They simply continued to go with the flow, lending out their money to the highest available yield. Interest rates were falling. Inflation was indulging in a brief respite—albeit at levels that would have been considered ruinously high only a few years ago. (Remember that before the 1979–1980 run-up of interest rates, the prime rate had never exceeded 12 percent.) Savers had to take advantage of any and every tool to keep from becoming poor more quickly than they wished.

### The War on Inflation

*The Federal Reserve fought its battle with inflation, and inflation won.* Now the saver is learning, out of necessity, to live with it. And that means utilizing money funds, which are essentially a means of investing in inflation.

For the banks and the savings and loan associations, the forthright answer to the withdrawal problem would have been to make their peace with the money funds and learn to accommodate the recently liberated saver understandably anxious to stay afloat. Instead, the banks' initial answer was an attempt to lobby away the enemy.

The Fed's logic, however, didn't support them all the way. For in some respects the money funds are helping certain of the banks considerably, at least while the restrictive Regulation Q remains on the books. The Fed realizes that money funds do tend to drain money from the smaller banks and savings and loans. However, they also place that money in large-scale, high-yielding certificates of deposit with the big money-center banks. It's not that the funds wouldn't buy CDs from the smaller banks because they are trying to drive them out of business. It's that they aren't sufficiently attractive because these CDs are very illiquid. There's really been no after-market of buyers and sellers, until recently.

Not only are the funds forbidden to invest in securities that do not have a secondary, or resale, market, but they have a responsibility to the investors to protect their money as well. The CDs of your local bank or thrift institution may rank high in credit quality. You as an investor, however, can't make that determination. And even if you could, quality alone is not recommendation enough for the money funds. It shouldn't be for you, either. Liquidity is crucial in today's financial world. Since there is no well-established secondary market for your local bank's CDs, they are illiquid and a poor investment.

### Small Bank Sympathy? Sorry

The smaller banks will either have to pin their hopes on the higher rates they will be able to offer with the phasing out of Regulation Q, or they will have to develop a secondary market, with its concomitant liquidity, for their securities, or they will have to merge with larger and better-known banks. Mergers will probably win out in the long run. There are now

14,800 banks in this country. We may well see the wholesale buying out of many smaller banks over the next few years.

Your community banker might feel this to be unfair. And you might well wonder if it wouldn't affect your local economy unfairly. However, let's be honest about this. How do you feel accepting a 5.5 percent savings account when money funds are yielding 15 percent, even if it may help to keep rates down for local businesses? And do you really think you should be underwriting, say, General Motors' borrowing rates with the 8 to 10 percent less interest you are accepting? That's *Robin Hood in reverse*—stealing from the poor and giving to the rich.

The depositors at, let's say, Bank of America might like to think their money is being infused back into their community. In actuality, however, the bank is busy funneling it into more profitable loans overseas.

Lest this all sound as if the banks are about to roll over and play dead for local savers, let me hasten to add that they're not about to send out any funeral announcements. Far from it. Caught between a rock and the Fed, the banks are becoming imaginative marketeers. They're going to get you back one way or the other. Fine. Just make sure, if they do, that they can Sanforize your money as well as anyone else can.

### Goodbye Tacky Toasters

*The banks' first line of attack in the interest battle was to get rid of the toasters*—and the TVs and the electric carving knives and the other blinders designed to keep you from looking at the interest rate figures when you opened an account. What was their new gimmick? Money, that's what. If you're desperate for a toaster, the slower-to-change banks still offer them.

Typical of the new attention-getters is the campaign launched by the Greenwich Savings Bank in New York. The bank gives you a $1,250 finder's fee "when you bring in a friend who invests $50,000 in a 30-Month Money Certificate at the *highest bank yield*." Bring in your wife to open an account and you'll get the reward. Bring in your own money and it's back to toasters.

The reason for the inconsistency is that the banks are already offering that catchy "highest bank yield allowed." They'd really like to offer more. But they can't. So they offer the extra to the finder and let you bend the law for them. Without the finder's fee, the yield of the money market certificate turns out to be 11.51 percent, while the money funds are offering over 16 percent. So it isn't such a great deal. Still, they're trying.

### The Time Bomb Ticks On

Smaller banks are still losing deposits in a flood tide. This is particularly true of thrift institutions like savings and loan associations. At the same time, to a limited extent, they are still issuing mortgages, their way of earning money to pay the interest on CDs and savings accounts. This leads to trouble, a great deal of trouble.

One of the basic maxims of finance is never to borrow short to lend long. Ever since the Depression, however, that's just what the banks have been doing. Up until the thirties, banks didn't issue fixed-rate, long-term mortgages. But they were so worried about falling interest rates as the economy collapsed that they actually forced consumers to accept the now familiar 25- and 30-year fixed-interest mortgages.

The arrangement worked splendidly for many decades. Then suddenly came galloping inflation, and this white knight of bank profits rode off into a red sunset. Mortgages became incredibly unprofitable.

With Savers' Liberation, thrift institutions were free to compete for money at close to money market terms. And compete they did. For a typical example, consider the strategy of the Gibraltar Savings and Loan Association, in Beverly Hills, California. Herbert J. Young, the bank's chairman, set out to carve off a large chunk of the mortgage market by aggressively seeking the new high-interest, short-term money and then flooding the real estate market with loans—a billion dollars' worth, more or less, for starters.

Short-term rates being so high, he reasoned they would fall by the end of 1979. Long-term fixed-rate mortgages would then yield handsome profits. After all, only the short-term interest the bank would have to pay depositors would fall, not the long-term interest the bank would earn.

*Unfortunately, interest rates didn't cooperate.* Short-term interest rates soared through late 1979 and into early 1980. The bank was squeezed into its first loss ever. Its liquidity declined so precipitously that Standard & Poor's downgraded its commercial paper to the point where money funds and other large investors couldn't or wouldn't invest in it.

And this is not to pick on Gibraltar. At the time, 40 percent of all the thrift institutions were suddenly in the red. If the trend continues, it could spell the end of a lot of the smaller savings and loan associations—and of the fixed-rate mortgage.

Meanwhile, Golden West Financial Corporation, the holding company for another California institution, World Savings and Loan Association, is coining money almost as fast as the government is. Under the superstar management team of Herbert and Marion Sandler, the bank had its fifty-third consecutive year-to-year quarterly gain in profits. How come?

It's simple. World more or less stopped issuing mortgages. Instead, most of its new funds were put into high-yielding, short-term investments. It became in essence a money fund, except that the extra earnings went to the owners, not to the depositors.

If the money fund approach is the tack a profitable association takes, while the other savings and loan associations' losses mount, that should tell you something about how to handle your money. It should also alleviate any bank-instilled guilt you may have about the line: "If you don't deposit with us, we won't have mortgage money for your community." The fact is, the future of mortgage money is out of your hands. The future of your money should not be.

### What's in It for You

You can use your bank or thrift institution savings and loan association or mutual saving bank as an investment vehicle. And in these inflationary, high-interest times, its uses aren't limited to the two basic savings plans traditionally offered. But let's start with them.

### Take a Pass on the Passbook

Traditionally, saving through a bank meant a passbook savings account or bank certificates. Savings accounts, like Christmas clubs, vacation clubs, and other so-called clubs which set up regular payments for the undisciplined, are really financial rip-offs in this day and age.

Accepting 5.25 or 5.5 percent interest simply doesn't make sense anymore. The clubs make even less sense. They now offer some interest. But it's ridiculously low. The only reason for using the clubs is that there's simply no other way you can discipline yourself to save. If such is the case, you'll just have to accept the low interest with the rationalization that the difference between what you get and what you should be getting is a "management fee" for forcing you to save.

As to the pure passbook account, you might want to open one in order to establish credit with a certain thrift institution. Many of the thrifts require that you have an account open before you can be considered for a mortgage. Put in a good four-figure amount. As soon as you get the mortgage and have made your first payment, close out the account.

If for some personal reason, or for the convenience of dealing with friends at a local bank, you wish to maintain a passbook savings account, keep the interred amount low. Also, at least make sure you have a day-of-deposit-to-day-of-withdrawal account with daily compounding and no service charges.

A very unlikely scenario is one in which money fund yields drop several points below those of passbook accounts. (But remember, anything can happen in the world of money. Savings accounts may yet become liberated and able to pay market rate interest.) Should this occur, be prepared to switch at least some assets to a bank account. Also be prepared to hear the banks protest that they are unfairly hurt by having to pay 5.25 percent interest when the money market offers only 4 percent.

Back in 1976 when interest rates on the money market fell briefly below those of passbook savings accounts, one enterprising group, the Franklin Money Fund, decided to transfer its assets into savings accounts. Franklin was at the time the only money fund authorized to do this. Being a corporation, however, the fund couldn't legally have more than $150,000 in any one account. So the California-based group opened accounts in savings and loan associations all over the state.

Not only that, but they had numerous accounts with banks offering a full month's interest on funds deposited before the tenth of the month. Come the ninth of the month, they'd fly around to all the accounts not offering this feature, withdraw their money, and deposit it to the banks that did offer the ten days of extra interest. Only a small fund could do something like this. Franklin quickly ran out of savings and loans in which to open accounts.

## SSCs and MMCs Spell L-O-C-K on Your Money

Small saver certificates (SSCs) and money market certificates (MMCs), the other major interest-bearing deposits available from banks, again are really a fool's paradise. True, you can earn close to money market rates. But boy, are you illiquid. New federal regulations place a heavy early withdrawal penalty on such certificates, requiring the complete forfeiture of *at least* ninety days' interest even if you have only been in, say, three days. For example, if you deposit $10,000 on day one and withdraw it on day three, you get back only $9,813. So now it's possible to lose money in an FDIC-insured deposit. You can see why Senator Proxmire, chairman of the Senate Banking Committee, calls it "bank robbery in reverse."

*Banks don't have to give you your money back at all* until the certificates actually mature. Now, this isn't something they exactly put in large print when it comes to promotion. But it's the law. You put your money up for one or two or eight years, and that can be the end of it till the time's up. Even a life-and-death situation does not require the bank to let you have your money, unless the bank is in the mood to settle for just your penalty payment.

Most banks are not refusing withdrawals right now. But a few, such as Long Island Savings, Jamaica Savings Bank, and Roslyn Savings Bank, all in New York, are. As the banks' balance sheets become bleaker, enforcement of this rule could easily spread to your bank, with unexpected, devastating effects.

Consider the case of Stanley Goldin, a professor of medicine in New York. According to a story in *The New York Times*, with his mother suffering from advanced cancer requiring $200 a day in private nursing care, he was first told flatly by Dry Dock Savings Bank that this was not an issue and that early withdrawal of his savings certificate money simply would not be allowed. After much debate, he was finally told he could withdraw $200 a day to pay for the nurse. Never mind that that meant a long daily trip to the bank.

Other customers complained about their treatment at the hands of the restrictive savings certificates. At last, Dry Dock decided not to enforce the discretionary rule.

But the point is, you can't count on this kind of beneficence in case of a real cash crunch. So much for savings certificates—except in the eyes of the super-safety-conscious individuals brought up on the unshakable fact that bank accounts are insured, at least to the best of the FDIC's ability to pay out in the event of a bank failure. What could be safer than savings certificates? these investors may wonder. Perhaps the new Treasury bill certificate, or T-bill accounts?

### The T-bill Masquerade

T-bill accounts represent CDs in the bank's pool of Treasury bills. Here's FDIC coverage plus the backing of the full faith and credit of the United

States government. Right? Wrong. The only connection with a T-bill is that the rate is tied to the T-bill rate.

The bank's implication in calling them T-bills is that they are somehow as safe as T-bills. They are not. These accounts are covered by the FDIC. But it's the bank that holds the T-bills, in its name. You have only a certificate of deposit from the bank itself.

Also, unlike the case when you buy T-bills directly from the government, the interest from a T-bill account at the bank is not exempt from state and local taxes. And buying directly from the government nets you about 0.5 percent more than the bank account does, since the banking institutions are limited to offering a yield 25 basis points above the actual T-bill rate. (One basis point is one hundredth of a percent.) In addition, by buying through the bank, you forfeit ninety days' interest in the event of early withdrawal. Dealing directly, you can sell in an active secondary market anytime you need or wish to.

So what's the advantage of dealing with your bank as middleman? None.

*You can't even trust the Federal Reserve anymore.* On March 1, 1980, the Federal Reserve announced, out of the blue, a limitation on the interest rate banks could pay on the two-and-a-half-year time deposits.

The reason was simple. Money market certificates were too successful, and the Fed was afraid the banks would have liquidity problems if too great a proportion of their deposits were held in these high-yielding instruments.

The March 1, 1980, action placed a temporary ceiling of 12 percent of the thirty-month money market certificates for savings and loan associations and their thrift cousins, the mutual savings banks and the credit unions. Retaining the differential, commercial banks were limited to 11.75 percent. Even with compounding, which is allowed, this effectively put 12.94 percent and 12.65 percent ceilings, respectively, on the certificates. Never mind the fact that the interest was supposedly tied to T-bills, whose rate at the time was 14.65 percent, which would have permitted savings and loans to pay 14.15 percent were it not for the artificial constraints. The unwary saver was soaked again.

Had you bought those bank certificates early in 1980, planning to receive close to Treasury bill rates for a full two and a half years, you could well assume that the government had cheated you out of a truly good deal, making sure you got less than you deserved. No pulling out at this point, either. New federal regulations require a minimum penalty of six months interest for early withdrawal of a thirty-month certificate.

You say you're beginning to feel stiffed by the banks, no matter what you do? Well, cheer up; they even have an investment appropriately called a STIF. Granted, from a spelling standpoint it's short an $f$. Still, it's a more than suitable acronym for the banks' short-term investment funds.

### STIFS Are Just That

STIFs are pooled investment vehicles offered by banks' trust departments. So far so good. However, the Comptroller of the Currency, who regulates them, has set a requirement calling for 30 percent of the pool to be invested in overnight funds, with a total of 80 percent restricted to a maturity of less than thirty days. Not so good. The STIFs cannot extend the maturity of their holdings in a falling interest rate environment the way money funds can. So STIFs become very noncompetitive when interest rates are falling. And because STIFs are trust department vehicles, there are accounting fees to cut into your yield. Stiffed again.

The good news is that STIFs are usually available only to those with trust accounts such as pension and profit-sharing plans. So chances are you won't have to worry about them.

Now, the banks' noncompetitive stance in today's yield hustle is in large part due to the protective legislation they themselves initially sought. Of course, where there's legislation, there's also usually a way around it if you have patient enough lawyers poring through the verbal debris pushed out through the legislative hatch. Loopholes are the life preservers of many an overregulated industry.

### Ah! A Loophole

*The loophole I have in mind here was found lying on a desk at the Casco Bank and Trust Company in Portland, Maine.* In June of 1978, so the story goes, a banker there discovered a way around the federally mandated $10,000 minimum required to participate in the six-month money market certificates of deposit and other types of CDs. These new instruments were immediately dubbed loophole certificates.

Actually, there is some debate among federal regulators as to whether the loophole is a legal or an illegal one. But while the regulators are debating, the banks are making hay.

For the investor, however, in most cases the hay is unfortunately moldy. Yields on the loophole certificates, although they are better than those normally available for other under-$10,000 accounts, are still less than the money funds offer.

Basically, a loophole CD is a standard $10,000 CD that you can purchase for $3,000 or $5,000 or what have you. Let's use the $5,000 for it. The bank gives you a secured loan for the other $5,000.

Secured by what? you may well ask. By the CD, of course. And of course, you have to pay interest on the loan. Although the usual cost is only 1 percent over the CD rate, it means that yields, while much higher than those of the passbook accounts, are inevitably going to be below money market CD yields, since you'll have to pay interest on the borrowed $5,000.

Still, loophole certificates became hot items in the financial markets, so much so that banks even advertised against their own passbook accounts in promulgating the new loopholes. Citibank in New York, remember, headlined its January 9, 1980, message: "If you have money in a passbook savings account, you're a loser."

For $3,000, the announcement explained, you could purchase a $10,000 CD, with the bank lending you the balance. The net yield after charges was 9.7 percent—at a time when money funds were yielding 12–13 percent.

Again, if psychologically you absolutely have to deal with a bank—and if at this stage that's still the case, perhaps you should seek financial counseling—loophole certificates do offer a bit more liquidity than other CDs do. You are allowed to borrow more against them, should you need cash. A minimum of $3,000 must be left in the account until the certificate matures. Additional funds may be borrowed against the loophole certificate, but of course, in that case you have to pay additional interest.

This lends itself to an interesting ploy in the event of an extremely sharp rise in interest rates over a short period of time. We are, after all, entering a period when 5 percent and even 10 percent rate fluctuations over a three-to-four-month span are no longer absurd. They simply happen.

Consider Greater New York Savings Bank's small saver certificate. A variation of the loophole, it's a two-and-a-half-year certificate that allows you to borrow back up to 90 percent of your deposit. The minimum deposit is $5,000, and the bank even gives you checks on which to make your own withdrawals. Shades of money funds again!

Let's say you have $5,000 in your small saver account. Interest rates go up 4 percent, and you wish you could take advantage of the higher rates. You borrow $4,500 from yourself and deposit it in a new account at the new rate. The net loan rate is 1 percent. So you have gained an additional 3 percent on 90 percent of your money. And you're guaranteed you'll earn at least the small saver account rate for two and a half years.

INTEREST RATE "INSURANCE"

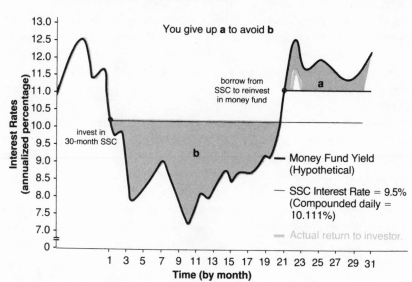

### Interest Rate "Insurance"

A New York-based mutual savings bank has initiated a program tied to its savings plans (either 6-month MMCs or 30-month SSCs), which permits investors to borrow at 1% over the certificate rate simply by writing checks. The program, offered by Greater New York Savings Bank, permits an SSC investor to insure a minimum 9.5% return (actually 10.111% with daily compounding) for the next 30 months. Also, any time interest rates are more than 1% above 10.111% during the maturity period, the investor could write a check for $250 or more and invest in a higher-yielding investment—such as a money fund.

*The bottom line:* If you are invested in an SSC when other rates are below 9.5%, you will earn 10.111% on your investment. When money fund yields are more than 11.111% you can borrow 90% of the SSC and invest in a money fund, effectively earning the money fund rate minus 1%. You trade a little on the upside for a minimum rate you can earn. Not a bad deal.

The ploy is something to consider for part of your portfolio if you hold a certificate and if you are convinced interest rates have reached a two-to-four-year peak.

When all is said and done, there are money-yielding services the banks and thrift institutions can offer the canny. For most people, however, passbook accounts, CDs, and savings certificates simply aren't among them, no matter how much the banks try to persuade you otherwise.

## When to Get Out

*What if you already have time deposits with a bank? Does it pay to bite the penalty and get out?* The answer is yes and no. It depends, as the guru answered his followers when asked how to become rich.

To arrive at a definitive answer, settle down with a calculator the way your banker does. Just plug in the amount you have invested, the number of days left to maturity, and the interest rate at which the deposit was made, and compare the results with the current money market rate. You'll know right away if you are going to earn more or less by leaving your money where it is.

## Big Yields for Big Depositors

For the large-scale investor in the $100,000-plus liquid assets range, banks may on occasion serve as useful conduits for purchasing commercial paper, repurchase agreements, and large-denomination negotiable CDs. However, since most of us don't have that kind of cash lying around, this function of the banks is covered later.

## NOW Accounts Now! Where Were They When We Needed Them?

Probably the best service available through the banks for the average investor is the negotiable order of withdrawal, or NOW, account. Currently available only in New England, New York, and New Jersey, NOW accounts are free checking accounts similar to money funds—except in three major respects. The amount necessary to open a free NOW account is limited only by the minimum balance required by the bank. This can range from as low as $10 to as high as $2,000, depending on the bank's policy. Secondly, there is no minimum amount stipulated for checks written on the account. The money funds normally require minimum check amounts of $500, although some are as low as $250, others as high as $1,000. And now the bad news. The yield of the NOW accounts is limited by law to 5 percent. Additionally, there are service charges if your account drops below the minimum balances.

Still, there is definitely a place for a NOW account in almost anyone's money management plans, assuming, of course, that one lives in a region where these accounts are permitted. For the rest of us, NOW accounts are on the way. They will be available nationwide in 1981.

Basically, a NOW account should be used to complement your money fund account. Set aside a monthly day on which to pay your bills—say, the third Wednesday of each month. On that day, make out your checks. (Actually, the negotiable orders of withdrawal aren't checks. They look like checks, work like checks and are accepted like checks. Everybody calls them checks. But they're not checks.) Balance your book. Mail the checks on Thursday, and with the help of the post office, they won't be cashed until the following Monday.

On Friday (or Thursday if you want to be careful), have your money fund wire the total amount of all the checks to your bank. You're covered, and you have now earned an extra day's dividend on your money fund account. In addition, since most of the checks won't actually be cashed until much later in the week, or even the following week, you earn an extra 5 percent from the bank of the float. Of course, checks over $500 should be written directly on your money fund account.

Some banks are lenient enough to let you simply deposit a money fund check on Monday rather than having the money wired in. (My bank does, though somebody there may stop me from doing so after reading this book.) In that case, you earn an extra three, possibly four day's dividend on the money fund float.

I know all this doesn't sound like much—a few dollars here, a few dollars there. But month after month, it adds up. Over a decade it could add $3,000 or $4,000 to the average family income. The choice is yours. Could you use a few thousand dollars?

The strange thing is, NOW accounts are really a minor part of banking even in those states where they are allowed. The money in the average checking account turns over 150 times a year, that in NOW accounts only 20 times a year. When the banks finally give people a good deal, hardly anyone takes advantage of it.

NOW accounts are quite often not altogether free, by the way. Where banks commonly make their money on these accounts is on the minimum balance. Bankers have calculated that an account needs a $2,000 minimum balance in order to fully defray the bank's costs. In a competitive market, however, few institutions can afford to require a four-digit minimum in exchange for free checking. Most require a $300 to $500 minimum. But there are enough banks offering no-minimum-balance, really free NOW accounts to make shopping around worthwhile. Just watch out for any hidden fees or monthly service charges.

Looking for hidden charges is an important part of money management. Looking for hidden profit potential is just as important a part, if usually a more neglected one.

### The Big Payoff

*A bank can offer you a 5, 10, or even 15 percent overnight tax-free return on your money.* And it can do so during a period of double-digit interest rates. The banks don't advertise the fact. Some banks are less likely to cooperate in the unorthodox venture than others. However, if you are in a position to avail yourself of this superbly profitable ploy, by all means use it.

The stratagem involves two key essentials. One is that you have excess cash, such as a large bonus or inheritance for which there is no foreseeable immediate need. The other is an old mortgage at one of those now-ridiculously-low-seeming rates of yore, say anywhere below 7 or 8 percent.

Banks, in case you aren't aware of the fact, can sell your mortgage to a third party. It's a negotiable instrument—and a perfectly legitimate way for a cash-starved bank to raise money. Of course, if your bank sold your, say, 6.75 percent mortgage in a market where mortgage interest rates were running 14 percent, it would have to do so at a huge discount, and it would take an awful beating.

You, on the other hand, can offer the bank more for it and still make a tidy profit. If you have, say, $10,000 principal outstanding on a 6.75 percent mortgage, and you walk into the bank and tell the people in the mortgage department that you'd like to buy it back for $7,500, they may laugh in your face. More likely, they'll say they couldn't afford the loss—and call you back the next day to inform you that after a most unusual loan meeting, they've decided perhaps they could let you have the mortgage for $8,500. Whether and how you negotiate is up to you. But a $1,500 reduction in debt is a tax-free gold mine.

Oh, I know, the standard persuasion is to be as far in debt as possible during inflation. And yes, the interest on your mortgage is tax deductible. But toward the end of a mortgage term, most of what you are paying back is nondeductible principal.

Also, the interest earned on your hypothetical $8,500, if that amount was invested instead of being used to pay off the mortgage, would be taxable. The $1,500 (or more) just vanishes before the taxman even knows about it. It's a discounted debt and nobody's business. Instant interest at a phenomenal rate. Discounting your mortgage is probably the single best way there is to profit from your bank.

In summary, then, the seven banking rules for you are:

1. Avoid passbook accounts unless their yields exceed those of money funds.
2. Never put your money in gimmicky accounts such as Christmas or vacation clubs.
3. Remember that savings certificates and money market certificates are a fool's paradise—definitely not for you if you wish to remain liquid.
4. T-bill accounts at the bank aren't T-bills. They are not, as implied, backed by the full faith and credit of the government. Stay away.
5. Don't stick your neck in a loophole CD unless you're convinced that interest rates have peaked and won't go higher for at least two years.
6. Use a NOW account to pay all your small bills if the bank's required minimum balance for free checking is less than $200.
7. When interest rates are high and you have cash on hand, as well as an old low-interest mortgage, buy your mortgage back at a discount—and a huge profit.

# 8

## How to Make Money from Your Stockbroker—At Last

If banks are fighting money funds, brokerage firms, finding that funds bring in new customers and money, have greeted them with open arms. Almost. Since money funds pay no commissions, they may not be your broker's favorite investment vehicle. But the broker is savvy enough to realize that building up good customer relations can lead to other profitable business in the future. Besides, all the brokerage firms are doing it.

### Give Your Broker Another Chance

With or without cynicism about brokerage firms' past performance, the fact is that about half the money invested in money funds, some $40 billion or more, is in stockbroker-managed funds. If you severed relations with Wall Street after the stock market's sour seventies, now may be the time to renew them.

Like the other money funds, broker-sponsored funds charge no commissions, although some firms, spotting a golden-egg-laying goose, have decided to at least give it a small squeeze. In a Smith Barney brokerage account, for instance, there is a $5 redemption fee, and Bache charges $2 for the same services, but only if the money fund investment is part of a brokerage account. If you deal directly with these funds, there is no redemption charge. The rationale for the policy is to cover accounting costs. My rationale would be to switch brokers to one that is more competitive. Personally, I use a broker which has no accounting charges for its account-executive-handled money fund.

### Stockbrokers' Money Funds—Flexibility Is the Key

*There is a very valid reason for having your money fund account with a stockbroker.* That reason is flexibility. And it's why most brokerage firms are happy to open a free money fund account for you even though there are no commissions involved.

In a money fund brokerage account, the investments are actually maintained in the street name (an old term derived from the fact that the funds are registered to the name, or address, of the brokerage firm itself).

Let's say you are dealing with Merrill Lynch. Not only is Merrill Lynch the biggest brokerage house in the country, but its money fund, Ready Assets, represents almost 18 percent of the outstanding investments in all money funds. Your investment in Ready Assets would be in Merrill Lynch's name to your benefit.

This gives you complete telephone flexibility. If you want to purchase a T-bill or stock, you merely call up your broker and ask to have the appropriate amount transferred from your money fund account to your cash margin account. If you're buying stock, make sure the transfer doesn't occur until after 3 P.M. on the stock's settlement date—that is, the day you actually have to pay for the stock, not the day you bought it.

Settlement dates are a holdover from the old send-the-check-by-mail days. The settlement date is usually five days following the purchase date. So you get five days' free dividends on your money fund while actually owning the stock.

Dealing directly with money funds does not provide this convenience. Money funds will wire money only to *your* bank account. This is a safety feature written into their rules. There is, after all, a risk in telephone redemption—how can anyone prove you wanted the money wired to, say, a broker? With the wire-to-bank-only restriction, should someone get hold of your identification and call the fund for redemption, the worst they could do would be to wire it to your bank account. If you didn't know about the transaction, it would show up on your statement, and the money would remain in your account until you personally withdrew it.

Of course, you could have a nonbrokerage account, write a money fund check for the right amount, and mail it to the broker. You could even wait until the settlement date to mail in the check and draw as much as ten or twelve days' extra interest. This, however, would definitely be bending the law. Chances are the broker would refuse to execute your stock orders without cash in hand after your first few forays into check kiting. Still, many brokers will open an account or make a deposit for you the day you give them a check—*before* the funds are actually withdrawn from your checking account.

## Money Market Unit Investment Trust—Like an MMC, Only Better

*A unique and useful money market instrument offered by brokers is the (CD) unit investment trust.* Almost all brokers sell unit investment trusts (which invest in CDs) even if their own firm doesn't issue them, which is most often the case, since currently only Merrill Lynch and Dreyfus actually underwrite these unique instruments.

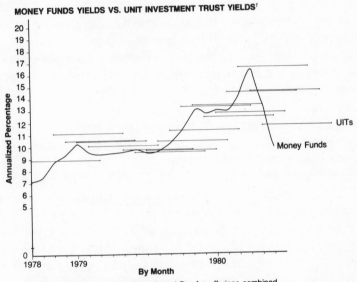

MONEY FUNDS YIELDS VS. UNIT INVESTMENT TRUST YIELDS[1]

[1] Averaged by month. Merrill Lynch and Dreyfus offerings combined.
Portfolios often consist of Euro$ CDs.

Unit investment trusts which invest primarily in CDs are actually 6-month money funds although they do not have checking privileges or other conveniences. Money fund yields in the above chart are represented by a smooth-flowing line since they are variable rate investments. Once you have bought a unit investment trust, the rate you will earn is fixed if you hold for the full 6-month term. We have, therefore, represented the unit investment trusts as straight lines. As you can see, there were many times during 1979–1980 when unit investment trusts would have earned you more than money fund investments, although this was not always true. It is true, however, that the unit investment trusts always outyielded money market certificates issued at the same time.

Your money has to be in the right place at the right time to participate in a unit investment trust, unlike a money fund, which you can buy at any time. Usually when they are in vogue, new trusts are issued once a week.

Rarely, however, are unit investment trusts issued if the market can't provide them with a return better than 12 percent.

For example, the sponsoring broker goes out and buys $300 million or so worth of CDs—Eurodollar CDs, Yankee CDs, representing deposits of foreign banks in their New York branches, and sometimes foreign CDs, such as deposits in London banks like National Westminster. He's buying quality CDs, but with a more aggressive stance than that taken by most money funds. There is a slightly higher degree of risk involved in dealing with overseas funds, although most professionals consider the risk from these well-diversified pools far from substantial. With some $10 billion in unit investment trusts currently outstanding, it's obvious many people consider them a prudent haven in their pursuit of higher earnings.

Once the sponsoring firm has bought these hundreds of millions of dollars' worth of CDs, it sells shares in the asset pool, usually over a period of a few days. Denominated in $1,000 units, the shares are redeemed in six months.

So far the unit investment trust sounds pretty much like a money market certificate from the bank. But there are differences—profitable differences in certain parts of the interest cycle.

• First, the minimum investment is a $1,000 unit rather than $10,000.

• More important, unit investment trusts when issued carry a yield up to 2 percent higher than that of money market certificates.

• Third, you can withdraw your money from the pool at any time during the first four months of the unit investment trust's life, and you can do so in $1,000 units, so you don't have to redeem at once as with a bank CD. Your entire investment. This means flexibility. You're locked in only for the last two months, and some trusts will now even waive that constraint.

### Riding the Yield Curve with as Little as $1,000

The redemption feature can also be used to increase your yield dramatically during a period of declining interest rates. Because the pool actually rises and falls in value with the tide of market interest rates, your shares also rise and fall in value. At the end of their six-month term, the shares will be worth their original $1,000 plus, of course, the interest, in the form of dividends. In the intervening period of time, however, there's extra cash to be made.

*A yield curve is a profitable roller-coaster,* previously limited in its use to large-scale professional money managers and institutional investors with million-dollar Treasury bill portfolios. With the availability of unit investment trusts, the price of admission to the interest-plus-capital-appreciation yield curve ride has been reduced to only $1,000.

Essentially, riding the yield curve entails getting out of a fixed-term investment before it is due and reinvesting immediately in a new instrument. It's done during a general interest rate decline.

Consider $10,000 put into a unit investment trust. As interest rates decline, the shares will increase above the initial $10,000 value. However, as the unit investment trust comes closer and closer to maturity, the increase above $10,000 will begin shrinking until at maturity it is again worth $10,000—plus accrued interest, of course. Your investment increases in value because overall yields have dropped, so your fixed-interest high-yielding investment is worth more—until it is redeemed at $10,000.

There are two forces at work here—the overall decrease in interest rates, which adds to the value of your $10,000 investment, and the encroaching maturity date, which tends to bring the investment's worth down to its $10,000 face value. At the midpoint in the life of the trusts, these forces are as much on your side as is theoretically possible.

To ride the yield curve, then, you sell your unit investment trust at the end of the three months and buy a new six-month unit investment trust, or T-bill, or whatever you desire to buy. You sell that in three months, and so on.

Thus, instead of falling down a series of steep declining-interest steps, your money slides gently down the yield curve, earning more than would otherwise be possible. All it takes is a simple telephone call every three months. There are no transaction costs to cut into your profit.

On the up escalator, please note, riding the yield curve does not work. If interest rates are rising and you sell your unit investment trust at the midpoint of its term, rather than receiving more than your original $10,000 back, you accept slightly less than face value for it. In a rising interest rate environment, it pays to hold the unit investment trust to maturity. So if you are expecting interest rates to fall and they rise instead, simply hold the trust to maturity, and you will earn the stated rate of return.

### Making Government Agencies Work for You

*U.S. government agency obligations are another form of money instrument available from your broker.* These instruments, such as Federal Farm Credit and Federal Land Bank bonds, are usually not direct obligations of the United States government. Instead of being backed by its full faith and credit, they carry an implied guarantee backed by the government's "moral obligation" to pay. Of course, morality being what it is in government today, such a guarantee may leave a little to be desired. Still, these instruments are considered almost as safe as Treasury bills.

The question is, why, if they are only *almost* as safe, would an investor consider them? Your broker will point out that their yield is slightly higher than the return on T-bills. Considering the safety and relative liquidity of agency obligations, this additional profit does make them attractive. Also, some of them have an investment minimum of $5,000, though most are $10,000, like T-bills.

On the negative side, unlike T-bills, not all agency obligations are exempt from state and local income and property taxes. This is an important consideration if you live in a high-tax state.

The real value of agency obligations for many people is that they are offered in bearer form. T-bills are dealt with on a book-entry basis—by computers. You never receive a piece of paper like the old savings bond or today's filigreed stock certificate. Somewhere far over the rainbow a little machine enters the transaction when you purchase a T-bill and removes it when you sell. You never have anything physical to run through your fingers, feeling your riches tangibly. Agency obligations confer upon you a debenture certificate.

This might not seem so special to some of us in today's electronic world. But many people still feel more secure exchanging their money for something tangible rather than a remote set of digital impulses.

More to the point, for some, is the term *bearer form*. Unlike a stock certificate, which represents a registered form and has your name on it, the government agency debenture certificate has nothing on it to indicate who the owner is. Owning a bearer bond is like owning cash, cash that is constantly earning interest—even though the issuer doesn't know where to send the interest until you clip and deliver the attached coupons, instructing the debtor where to forward your money.

Now, if the wheels in the back of your head are beginning to spin with thoughts like "untraceable," "no tax," and "what a great way to hide illicit funds," then you understand why T-bills are no longer offered in bearer form. Agency obligations are among the few money market instruments still available to larcenous souls seeking to hide illegal funds from the government (which is certainly not to imply that all investors in these instruments are crooks).

### Bonds with Floating Rates

*Floating-rate bonds were the precursors of money market funds.* Issued by banks, they are nevertheless traded on the bond exchange rather than being sold directly to savers at the banks themselves. The interest rate of these bonds is tied to money market rates. The yields are adjusted every six months to bring them into line with the market. Floating-rate bonds, such as those originally issued by Citibank, were quite popular a few years ago. With the development of money funds, however, the bonds have taken very much a back seat, serving no real purpose for the average investor.

### How to Buy a T-bill

*Both your broker and your banker charge more or less the same $25 to $30 fee for purchasing a T-bill for you.* Usually the fee is $25. But in most cases it's more efficient and profitable to make this kind of investment through the broker rather than the banker, particularly if you have an established money fund account with the brokerage firm. The reason is time. You can easily buy and sell by telephone, no questions asked.

It's possible to buy and sell by phone through a bank as well, but consider two facts. First, you would have to keep your money in a savings account, low-yielding though it is, until you actually purchase the T-bill. You would not be accumulating the kind of earnings you would in a money fund. Secondly, there's the matter of psychology. You expect your broker to be there ready to help you with your investments when you call. It's a service he offers. Banks offer that service too. But how many of us are really comfortable calling up a bank to ask for investment service?

If you buy and sell T-bills with any frequency, and unless you do so in million-dollar quantities, it usually pays to purchase them through the Federal Reserve auction rather than on the open market. True, on the open market you can put your cash to work no matter what business day it is. But you'll end up paying the asking price, plus commission. That means fractionally lower yields. Better to leave the cash in your money fund account and tell your broker you want to participate in the original auction. This gives you the best price and interest while you wait.

Comparing the Return on a $10,000 Investment in a T-bill Vs. an MMC

| When the T-bill discount rate is: (%) | The MMC interest rate will be: (%) | You earn: MMC*: | You earn: T-bill[+]: | T-bill–MMC= $ Difference |
|---|---|---|---|---|
| 7 | 7.75 | $387.50 | $366.27 | –$21.23 |
| 8 | 8.25--comm'l banks | 412.50 | 420.62 | + 8.12 |
|   | 8.50--thrifts | 425.00 | | + 4.38 |
| 9 | 9.25 | 462.50 | 475.48 | + 12.98 |
| 10 | 10.25 | 512.50 | 530.83 | + 18.33 |
| 11 | 11.25 | 562.50 | 586.70 | + 24.20 |
| 12 | 12.25 | 612.50 | 643.07 | + 30.57 |

*Interest earned on an MMC is fully taxable. These interest calculations do not take daily compounding of interest into account.

[+]Interest earned on a T-bill is exempt from state and local taxes. These interest calculations assume investment of the discount at the same rate.

T-bills and the money market certificates offered by banks are often confused with each other. This is no accident. The confusion being to the banks' benefit, they subtly encourage it. This in part explains why savers have been choosing money market certificates over T-bills at a ratio of fifteen to one, despite the fact that T-bills are nearly always a better deal (over 9 percent), paying a higher return and being more liquid.

Another reason savers fall into the lower-than-good-for-you yield trap is simply lack of adequate investor information. That problem you will no longer have after reading this book.

### T-bills—A Way to Avoid State and Local Taxes

*A six-month $10,000 T-bill will earn you more than a money market certificate will* under current conditions. In a high-tax state, the net yield difference will be even greater, since the T-bill interest, besides being safer, will not be subject to state and local taxes.

With $50,000 to invest, you would earn at least $425 more by buying a T-bill. In fact, the more money you have to invest, the greater the advantage of T-bills becomes, even counting the service charge paid to your bank or broker.

Fine, you say, but what exactly is a T-bill? Most of us have at one time or another purchased savings bonds. But T-bills, aren't they strictly for banks and coupon-clipping millionaires?

It's true that the T-bills' minimum denomination is $10,000. And ten years ago, $10,000 might have seemed a lot of money. Today it will hardly buy a car if you want such optional extras as tires. So forget about T-bills being just for the big boys. Even if you don't have $10,000 in cash right now, there will be times when you do have. Knowing what to do with it then is essential.

Consider simply the equity in your house, for example. Far too many people, when they sell a house or collect on an insurance policy or some other five-figure fund, simply put the money in a savings account until they need it. After all, it's only for a few weeks. What's the difference? Plenty.

So even if you're not in a position to purchase T-bills currently, consider the future, yours and Uncle Sam's—yours because you're going to need to make every extra dollar you can on capital, Uncle Sam's because that's who you're lending money to when you buy T-bills. Selling T-bills is the Treasury's second most important way of raising money for the government. (Its most important way is printing money—in quantities out of all proportion to the economy. But that's another horror story.)

By buying T-bills, you essentially lend your money to Uncle Sam for three months (91 days), six months (182 days), or twelve months (360 days). Anything over a year in term is a Treasury note (with a maturity of from one to seven years) or a Treasury bond (with from five to thirty-five years to maturity).

T-bills are currently issued in $10,000-minimum denominations. But until 1970, you could buy one for $1,000. Then the Treasury found that an increasing number of small investors were purchasing the bills in order to garner the attractive interest, which was running 2 percent above that available on other savings media at the time. Wanting to get rid of the financial riffraff, the Treasury raised the ante to $10,000.

Actually, the Treasury's press release gave a more acceptable reason for the action, quoting George Romney, then secretary of Housing and Urban Development: "The outflow of savings from Savings and Loan Associations, Mutual Savings Banks, and other thrift institutions has aggravated the shortage of mortgage funds and contributed to a serious decline in housing production. To avoid a serious, growing housing shortage, it is essential that we discourage the outflow of funds from mortgage lending institutions. This Treasury action should substantially improve our housing outlook."

Translation? Screw the little guy. Someone has to put money in the bank, and we certainly can't expect the sophisticated investor to be foolish enough to cut his yields just to keep the thrifts afloat.

Here, at least, is one place where inflation has helped the average saver. Ten thousand dollars just isn't that much anymore. Of course, if too many people start buying T-bills, the Treasury will probably raise the minimum to $25,000.

But for now it's $10,000, with $5,000 increments available—that is, $15,000, $20,000, and so on. If you have $12,000 to invest, for instance, you can't put it all into a T-bill. You can buy one $10,000 T-bill, putting the additional capital into, say, a money fund until you've accumulated enough for a larger-denomination T-bill.

### Buying T-bills at a Discount

*Probably the hardest adjustment to make in buying T-bills is getting used to the fact that their yield is quoted at a discount rate.* So the actual yield is always greater than the yield at which the T-bill is issued.

Discounting means that you don't really put up, in this instance, the full $10,000 to buy a T-bill. Consider a one-year T-bill issued at 12 percent interest. Your actual cost is roughly $8,800. At the end of the year, you collect $10,000. The difference, $1,200, is your interest. And it's more than the 12 percent face interest at which the bill is sold. The discount rate always understates the true value of return on a Treasury bill, something you should keep in mind when reading advertisements for competitive investments that claim to offer yields as high as or higher than those of the T-bills.

The true rate of return on a T-bill is called the coupon equivalent rate. In the case of your $8,800 investment, this means a return of 13.64 percent discounted—or an actual 13.83 percent annualized. The difference comes about because, for accounting purposes, the discounted yield is figured on 360 days, the annualized yield as if interest were earned for 365 days—and please don't ask about leap years! What counts is that the true yield of your 12 percent T-bill is actually over 13.50 percent. Not only that, but you get to leave the extra $1,200 in your money fund and thus earn even more on your total $10,000 investment.

This is a trick the Treasury plays on you so the banks can quote the T-bill yield on their six-month money market certificates (based on the lower discount rate) and disguise the fact that the T-bill actually always pays a greater real return. As Romney's press release stated, this is another ploy to support the banks—at your expense.

Since you can buy T-bills maturing in only a month on the secondary market, it's unlikely that you will enter actively into buying and selling them as an in-and-out trader, one who tries to profit from day-to-day fluctuations. At least, I'm assuming you probably wouldn't attempt such a venture until you'd acquired a fair amount of experience. However, if you decide to watch the T-bill tables in your newspaper—most of the major ones, including the *Wall Street Journal,* carry them—the discount feature of this instrument produces a real anomaly in the world of buying and selling. It's the only market I know of where the asking price is always lower than the bidding price.

This is because the prices are quoted in terms of yield, not in terms of the actual dollar amount to be paid. For example, the bid price may be 13.09 and the asking price 12.88. I'm asking you, in other words, to buy my T-bill at a dollar amount that will mean a yield of 12.88 percent if you hold the bill to maturity. You, on the other hand, feel that particular yield isn't high enough. You want 13.09 percent. Your bid quote is numerically

higher. But it's less in actual dollars. Remember, dollars are always sub-
tracted, or discounted, from $10,000 until the appropriate yield is reached.

Only a government obligation could be so complicated. Don't lose
sleep over it, however. Just remember two things. A T-bill's true yield is its
coupon equivalent rate, not the discount rate. And if you haven't developed such a feel for the T-bill quotes that you can explain them without
having to think about how to do it, don't speculate.

Oh, it's possible to profit from such speculation, all right. Speculation
in federal instruments can produce profits—and, needless to say, losses—
of such staggering proportions as to make the go-go stocks of the sixties
seem like archconservative investments. There will be more on that, for
the curious and for those in a position to speculate, in Chapter 14, "The
Advanced, Aggressive Money Market Portfolio."

### Repos for the Pros

*Repurchase agreements (repos) are a more esoteric investment vehicle
available from your broker.* Stockbroker-issued repurchase agreements are
not even confined to the $100,000 or greater minimum your bank re-
quires, although they are rarely traded for less. Also, you really have to be
a first-class—read "profitable"—customer before a broker will extend his
repurchase agreement services to you. It's really an accommodation.

Repurchase agreements from a broker tend to yield more than those
from a bank. The bank can always borrow cheaply from the Fed funds
market, the pool of money used by banks to lend their temporarily excess
funds to other banks. These bank-to-bank loans are unsecured. After all, if
your banker can't trust his fellow banker, whom can he trust?

The broker, not being a banker, is of course excluded from this source
of capital. He borrows his short-term funds through what are referred to as
call loans, overnight loans secured by the firm's portfolio of securities (and
yours if you leave them in the street name). The rate of the call loans is always higher than the Fed funds rate. Since the broker's normal access to
funds requires him to pay a higher interest rate than the bank's, he will
perforce do the same for you.

There is perhaps a last word that should be spoken on dealing with
brokerage firms. When some of the big names started crumbling in the sixties, Wall Street decided it needed some kind of sign, a shingle that could
be hung out, modeled on the impressive "Insured by the Federal Deposit
Insurance Corporation" insignia that banks sported. The Street came up

with SIPC, the Securities Investor Protection Corporation. This organization is your protection against fraud or a member firm going under. It does not guarantee the safety of either your interest or your capital.

A broker would not tell you otherwise—although some brokers have been accused of implying it. This is not to scare you away. For in many cases, as I've noted, it really pays to have a broker—even if you don't buy any stocks. A broker can not only execute orders, but get you information you need quickly. Do remember, however, that he's part of the financial shark pool. When it comes to investing, the only person you can really count on to make the most profitable decisions is yourself.

As you make those decisions, remember the four keys to profiting from your stockbroker's money market:

1. Use telephone flexibility for instant switching from money funds to stocks, bonds, T-bills, and other investments.
2. Buy unit investment trusts to increase your profits, and ride the yield curve when rates are falling.
3. It's more efficient and profitable to buy a T-bill from your broker than from your bank.
4. If you're a big customer ($100,000 and up), use your clout to buy repurchase agreements for short-term funds.

# 9

## Money Market Services from Your Insurance Agency and Other Places You Never Thought to Look

*Everyone is getting into the money fund act, and your insurance company is running with the herd.* Mutual of Omaha, New England Life, and John Hancock agents are already selling shares of their money market mutual funds. Equitable Life Assurance, Prudential, and a number of others are standing in the wings to see how the act goes over with the public.

"We figured it only logical for the insurance industry to enter the money market business," says Donald Day, head of NEL Cash Management, New England Life's fund. And with their large number of salesmen, the insurance companies have a real advantage over independent money funds, which depend primarily on advertising to attract new customers.

But what do the insurance-company-sponsored funds offer you that the other funds don't? In essence, very little. After all, the fact that they have a large sales force already in the field doesn't mean higher yields, and it doesn't otherwise affect your bottom line.

Still, the insurance funds are competitive. Their agents receive no commissions on fund sales. They handle the product to help keep their foot in the door. The salesmen knows the average household, even in these times, has a lot of idle dollars. By providing an extra service, they might pick up commissions on other sales.

### Mostly Comforting Convenience

Again, from your point of view, this adds very little to the good things in life. However, there is good reason for some people to use insurance-sponsored funds. There's something comforting about getting a piece of the rock or some other symbol. If you deal regularly with your insurance agent, you might overcome any hesitations you may have about investing

106

in something as unfamiliar as money funds by going through him.

Also, given enough capital, it might be possible to set up an automatic dividend-withdrawal plan to pay for your insurance policies out of the parent-company money fund. Then you would be combining convenience with interest up to the minute your bills are due.

There's another way you can put your insurance company money market mutual fund to use, which involves no real risk and could give you a substantial return. Your insurance policies, as I mentioned earlier, probably have a cash value upon which you can borrow at low rates, as low as 5 and 6 percent. When their money fund is paying more than that, you may want to draw on your cash value and invest it in your insurance company money fund account. When interest rates fall back below the interest rate on the cash value policy loan, repay the loan to the company with a money fund check.

This can pay off very well. For example, had you used the ploy in 1979, with the average money fund earning 10.55 percent and policy loans costing, say, 5 percent, you'd have made an easy profit of 5.55 percent. On, say, $20,000, that would have meant $1,110 found money. Not bad for an essentially riskless arbitrage, as the professionals would call it.

Now, you could play this game with any money fund, of course. But somehow it seems easier and safer if you do it with your insurance company's money fund.

And the prime consideration still lies in the answer to an all-important question: How do the funds perform compared with what else is available? An insurance-company-sponsored fund may well be right for you—but only if its yield is as high as what you could get from another fund. For that matter, don't limit yourself to funds. Look around at alternative investments.

*One alternative investment not to look at is savings bonds.* Ever since Franklin D. Roosevelt bought the first defense bond on May 1, 1941, these instruments, now renamed savings bonds, have been a mainstay in the government's attempt to stay afloat—at your expense. Oh, originally the bonds not only served a patriotic purpose but were actually a decent savings plan. Today they will drive you to the poorhouse in OPEC style.

And yet one household in every three owns savings bonds. The average holding is an astounding and depressing $3,500 of diminishing capital. Savings bond buyers may be taking stock in America, but they're giving away their future to pork-barreling politicians with bottomless pockets.

Now, however, it appears that even these "investors" are waking up at last. Through most of the seventies, as inflation bled the consumer, savings bond sales flowed on uncauterized. But in the first quarter of 1980, redemptions abruptly began to exceed sales. Five billion dollars ran out of savings bonds in the course of a few months.

Considering the fact that savings bonds represent almost 10 percent of the entire national debt, the exodus left Washington feeling poorly. "Something has to be done to arrest this flood of redemptions," exclaimed Jesse L. Adams, deputy national director of the Treasury's United States Savings Bonds Division.

Have they ever thought of raising the interest?

Actually, yes, they've thought of that. Congress usually assumes that the small investor should underwrite the government. After all, he's always done so before, quite docilely. But the Treasury knows a little more about how to balance the books, and Treasury Secretary G. William Miller, testifying before the marvelously nomenclatured Senate Finance Committee's Subcommittee on Debt and Taxation, has requested that interest restrictions be lifted entirely.

*If that occurs, savings bonds may, and I repeat may, become an excellent investment* for the small saver, especially under those circumstances where tax deferral is beneficial. Taxes on EE bond interest, for example, are not due until the bonds are cashed in, eleven years after their purchase.

Then again, when the Department of the Treasury came out with the new HH bonds, it decided to slap on an early-redemption penalty, locking you in for ten years. It took away more than it gave.

So don't hold your savings waiting for a miracle on the savings bond front. But do keep your eyes on the market. Something favorable may develop. Today there's no such thing as the right investment for a given situation. There's only the right investment for a given situation at a given time.

At the moment it can safely be said that savings bonds don't have anything right about them. Stay away.

### Buying Direct from Uncle Sam

The pros and cons of Treasury bills—never to be confused with savings bonds—have already been discussed in this book. But there's one more facet of Treasury bill investment to explore here, and that is buying them directly from the Fed. A lot of people are curious about the process. Their underlying feeling is that it must somehow be more profitable to deal directly with the source than through a middleman. It really isn't in this instance, unless you are retired and live in a city where a Federal Reserve bank is located.

In that case, the weather being pleasant, and you having time to spare, standing in line at the Federal Reserve may be an enjoyable way to spend a Monday morning. I can't think of any other occasion when it would pay for the average saver to buy directly. The reason is simple—time again.

*You can buy T-bills directly from the Fed by mail.* The first thing to do is call up the Federal Reserve bank in your district and ask to be placed on the mailing list for auctions. Request applications for the purchase of T-bills as well.

When it comes time to buy your T-bill, you must include a certified

## TREASURY BILL PURCHASE COSTS

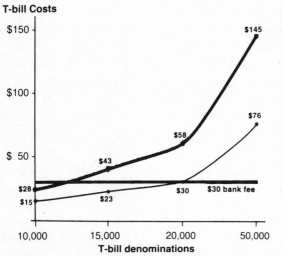

**T-bill Costs**

$150 — $145

$100

$76

$58

$ 50 — $43

$28 — $30 — $30 bank fee

$15 — $23

10,000   15,000   20,000   50,000
**T-bill denominations**

**T-bill Purchase Costs**
(all figures at 15% interest rate)
**Direct by Mail**
Cost = 6-day interest loss on full T-bill value and 4-day interest loss on discount
**Direct in Person**
Cost = 3-day interest loss on full T-bill value and 4-day interest loss on discount
**Bank**
Cost = $30 fee (estimate)

**Treasury Bill Purchase Costs**

Treasury bill (T-bill) purchase costs are often neglected, but as the chart above shows, they *can* be significant. Each of the three methods of T-bill purchase is illustrated: through a bank (which typically charges a constant fee), direct in person (the "fee" is the interest you lose on your withdrawn money for seven days), and direct through mail (here also the "fee" is lost interest, but for ten days). As you can see, the direct costs increase with the size of the T-bill, and the mail purchase always costs more than in-person purchase.

In general, buying your T-bill from a bank will be cheaper than direct purchase, and the larger the T-bill, the more important it becomes to compare direct purchase costs.

check for $10,000, or whatever available denomination you wish to purchase. The check must arrive at the Federal Reserve by Monday, which is auction day. Along with it, you include an application for a noncompetitive bid, which means you accept the average interest of that particular series of T-bills.

You can also make a specific competitive bid. This might yield you slightly higher interest. It might also mean the Fed's returning your money because your bid was not competitive enough. In that case, during the interim, which could be a couple of weeks, your money would be earning no interest.

The T-bills auctioned on a given Monday are actually issued on the following Thursday, which is when interest begins to accrue. And therein lies the problem with buying directly from the Fed. Let's say you are buying a six-month T-bill. In order for the post office to have a sporting chance of delivering the check to the Fed by Monday morning, you have to withdraw the money from your bank or money fund by the preceding Thursday. If you waited until Friday, the check might not make it on time, and then, in addition, it might take another week or so for the Fed to return it to you, and you'd be losing interest all the way.

Even by mailing off that check on Thursday, you will be losing interest Thursday, Friday, Saturday, Sunday, and the Monday of the auction. Then, since the T-bills aren't actually issued until Thursday, you will also receive no interest on Tuesday or Wednesday. That's seven days' worth of interest lost before you even start.

At the T-bill's maturity, the same thing occurs. The check is mailed out on Thursday. You'll be lucky to receive it by Monday. Another five days shot.

No, better to buy through your broker or banker and suffer the small ($30 average) commission.

To mention a last money-costing complication, after the auction the Fed mails back the excess of your discounted $10,000 T-bill. If your T-bill cost $8,800, they mail you back $1,200. This money floats around, back and forth, not earning a cent. Dealing in the secondary market, not only do you start earning interest immediately on the $8,800, but the $1,200 can continue earning a daily high dividend in a money fund.

But what about wiring money to the Fed? you ask. Surely that wouldn't take so long. True. If you have an open account at the Fed, you can wire money directly to it. But in order to make sure the money is there on Monday morning, you still have to wire it on Friday. The Fed doesn't post, or count, its incoming money until 3 P.M. And the auctions are held in the morning. Plus, of course, you have wire fees.

*Keeping an eye on the auctions even though you aren't purchasing directly can be profitable,* however. The rate posted on Monday will indicate what the money market certificates issued on Thursday are going to yield. That advance notice gives you three days to make an investment choice between a money market certificate and a T-bill. Normally the choice is obvious. You want the T-bill. But in the event of a sudden drop in interest rates, a six-month money market certificate might offer a more attractive yield, albeit at the expense of liquidity.

The money market certificate rate changes on Thursday, when the new T-bill rate is actually first put into effect. With, say, a 1 percent or greater drop to come in the T-bill yield, you could buy from your bank on Tuesday or Wednesday a money market certificate issued at the previous Thursday's rate, thus yielding more than the new T-bill. It doesn't happen all that frequently, but it's something definitely worth checking before you invest. A week before this writing, for instance, the money market certificates briefly offered almost 2 percent more than T-bills were offering. For the preceding twelve months they had offered considerably less return than T-bills were yielding.

Where else can we look for a profitable nook for our money? How about the finance company, for starters?

### Forget the Finance Company

*Finance company notes and debentures can be dangerous investments for the average saver.* On the whole, you won't be confronted with commercial paper issued directly by corporations unless you deal through a broker and in large dollar volume. Paper issued directly by finance companies, however, is not so rare. In fact, it is often advertised in the newspapers. With all the other available income possibilities for your money, I see little need for investing in finance company obligations. There is no guarantee of return on them except for the issuer's good faith. There is neither any actual insurance, as there is with a bank, nor any implied insurance through diversification, as there is with money funds. I'm not saying going with a finance company may not be a good investment, nor am I saying that the yields may not be above average. But you really have to know and trust that finance company. Do you?

*Employee thrift plans have the benefit of forcing regular saving.* If the employer also adds to the kitty, the plan is usually too good to pass up. It may well be a better investment than a money fund. But check on how the money is being invested. Should it be in savings bonds or other low-yielding investments, it's time to talk to your employer about changing the plan's focus.

Don't be afraid to approach him on the subject. Many employee thrift plans have been left to run themselves as they always ran in the past, simply because they did well then. Forgotten in the rush of changing times, they just keep rolling lugubriously along. Your employer will usually be glad to implement changes if they're good ones. Remember, the better the thrift plan does, the better he looks in the government's eyes as well as yours.

For instance, recently I did some consulting for a firm that had a guaranteed-return contract with an insurance company, which yielded 9 percent. That was certainly a good deal in the past. When interest rates shot up, however, something had to be done. So I helped to set up a plan with a top-performing money fund. As long as the money fund yields were above 9 percent, that's where the employees' savings would be channeled. If the fund's yield fell below 9 percent, why, then the money would be shifted back to the insurance company's guaranteed-return contract. It's like having a 9 percent yield floor.

### Hidden Assets Checklist

- Ask your insurance agent about his company's money funds and the applications to borrow on the cash value of your insurance at about 5 percent.
- Dig out those old savings bonds and see if you want to cash them in to invest at higher rates elsewhere. Patriotism has its limits.
- Buy your T-bills direct from Uncle Sam with your broker's or your banker's help.
- Avoid investing in finance company notes.
- Check out your employee thrift plan. If your employer is chipping in a percentage *plus,* the plan is earning a good return and it's a good deal.

# 10

## The SLY System—The Key to Conservative, High-Yield, Low-Risk, Commission-Free Money Market Investing

### Why Most Systems Don't Work

Have you ever wondered why all those people who start with nothing and make a million dollars in six months with a "system" write books explaining their secret? If you had a sure way to make a million, would you share it with anyone who plunked down fifteen dollars for your book? Really now.

Unless, maybe, you could make even more money that way—without screwing up the system, of course. There are, in fact, systems, and then there are systems. Aside from such crucial details as whether they work or not, some systems can be disseminated to the public without self-destructing.

Take some of the popular systems for leveraged real estate investment, for instance. If you followed the rules and pyramided your equity, and every other reader of the books did the same thing, there would still be plenty of investment opportunities around for everyone. The universe of real estate investment—that is, the number of possible investments—is so large that the effect of everyone's following the same investment pattern would distort the overall dollar-and-cents results very little.

Then consider a horse race. Now, I'm not recommending handicapping systems to anyone. Far from it. It's just that betting at a track is a perfect example of a small universe that could easily be distorted by a system—if such a system could ever be developed. Since the odds on a horse race are a product of the betting pattern, if there were a system, and if it worked, and if someone wrote a book about it, and if most people at the track used the system, why, then everyone would lose. The odds would drop to even. The track and the government would take their cut and you would win—

with a return of, maybe, 85 cents on each dollar bet.

Most people who buy a system rarely act. They buy a dream. There's security in the dream of someday—and no risk.

### Why the SLY System *Will* Work for You

*The SLY system* is going to make you money, more money than you're making now. And it will let you sleep at night while doing it. The SLY system won't turn you into a millionaire in six months, unless, of course, you start with $950,000+. But it will make your money *work as hard as you do.* It will consistently yield more than you'll earn by simply putting your money in the bank, or in Treasury bills, or in any other single money market instrument.

The system works in one of the largest statistical universes created by man—that of the dollar. Here is a universe so huge—and it's expanding all the time, as even astronomers would not debate—that even if everyone followed the SLY system, the consequent distortion would be minimal.

Again, most readers won't act. So the system's influence will be less than minimal, except to those who do follow it. They will be that much better off because of it. So be SLY. Put your money into high-interest gear.

### What's So Sly About SLY?

The words behind the initials stand for what you really want for your money. First of all is *safety,* as I've remarked before. In today's turbulent and uncertain world, there is no absolute safety. But with all the rip-offs, pyramid schemes, scams, government-sponsored inflation, and other devious deprivations to separate you from your money, you at least want to make sure you have the best possible chance of getting your capital back. A 50 percent return on your investment really isn't that great if you don't get the investment itself back. As Will Rogers allegedly said, "I am not so much concerned with the return *on* my money as with the return *of* my money."

Then there's *liquidity.* Liquidity is a crucial investment component in these fast-turning times. An investment without liquidity is like buying a dead horse. The smell lingers, but there isn't much you can do about it.

Still, a truly safe and truly liquid investment whose yield is *less* than the rate of inflation leaves you safe, liquid—and broke. You need all three ingredients: safety, liquidity, and yield.

Fine, you say, I'll buy that. But where do I get those three good things?

Well, you get your three factors with about ten minutes' reading a week. And yes, there's much more to the system than simply safety, liquidity, and yield, because in the economic turmoil of our now-you-see-it, now-you-don't politicized world, there no longer is a "best" investment. There is only a best investment for the moment, even though the money market deals in fixed-income investments, ones that guarantee a specific rate for a specific term.

Whichever way interest rates are heading, up or down, there will be no more quiet years when interest rates hold steady. And you need to know

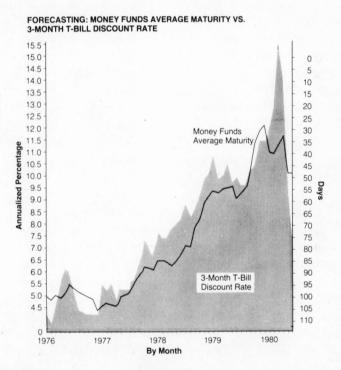

FORECASTING: MONEY FUNDS AVERAGE MATURITY VS. 3-MONTH T-BILL DISCOUNT RATE

## Putting $80 Billion of Their Money Where Their Mouth Is

That's what money fund managers were doing in the spring of 1980. And their opinion of interest rates' future direction was expressed in their average maturity. When the funds' average maturity shortens (decreases), it's an excellent bet that interest rates will rise. Conversely, when the average maturity lengthens (increases), it's a sure sign that interest rates will decline and the money funds are locking up the current high yields now, before those rates decline. So keep an eye on the money fund average maturity for a preview of things to come.

## MONEY FUND LISTING AND AVERAGE MATURITY INDEX

| Net Assets ($ mill) | Fund | Valuation Method | Average Net Yield (%'s) | | | Portfolio Holdings (%'s) | | | | | | | |
|---|---|---|---|---|---|---|---|---|---|---|---|---|---|
| | | | 30-day Ending 4/2/80 | Month Ending 2/29/80 | Average Maturity (days) | U.S. Treas | Other | Repo's | C.D.'s | Banker's Accept | Comm'l Paper | Euro C.D.'s | Other |
| | **GENERAL PURPOSE** | | | | | | | | | | | | |
| $92.1 | American General Reserve | 3 | 14.6 | 12.5 | 30 | - | 3 | - | 4 | 26 | 67 | - | - |
| 237.0 | American Liquid Trust | 1 | 14.2 | 11.6 | 23 | - | - | 13 | 5 | 82 | - | - | - |
| 711.1 | Capital Preservation | 1 | 14.0 | 12.3 | 20 | 83 | - | 17m | - | - | - | - | - |
| 271.5 | Cash Mgmt Trust | 1 | 15.7 | 12.9 | 10 | 6 | - | 40 | 19 | 3 | 25 | - | 13 |
| 34.1 | Centennial Cash Mgmt | 1* | 14.0 | 8.2 | 16 | - | - | 29 | - | - | 71 | - | - |
| 247.1 | Columbia Daily Income | 1 | 14.0 | 12.5 | 26 | - | - | 5 | 1 | 45 | 49 | - | - |
| 468.0 | Delaware Cash Reserves | 4 | 16.0 | 13.3 | 26 | - | - | 4 | 32 | 2 | 26 | 33 p | 3 |
| 2,963.1 | Dreyfus Liquid Assets | 3 | 14.3 | 13.1 | 36 | 6 | - | 7 | 35 | 11 | 14 | 27 p | - |
| 81.7 | Eaton & Howard Cash | 2 | 14.9 | 13.0 | 16 | 11 | - | - | 8 | 1 | 80 | - | - |
| 166.6 | Federated Money Mkt | 2 | 14.3 | 12.3 | 34 | - | 1 | - | 7 | 25 | 32 | 23 p | 12 |
| 670.8 | Fidelity Cash Reserves | 3 | 14.3 | 13.5 | 26 | - | - | - | 10 | 3 | 15 | 24 p | 51 |
| 2,785.0 | Fidelity Daily Income  h | 4 | 14.2 | 13.3 | 29 | - | - | - | 33 | 37 | 30 | - | - |
| 83.7 | Financial Daily Income | 2 | 15.2 | 13.0 | 16 | - | 9 | - | - | - | 91 | - | - |
| 125.9 | First Investors Cash Mgmt. | 1 | 14.8 | 13.4 | 21 | 10 | 6 | 6 | 14 | 58 | 6 | - | - |
| 280.5 | First Variable Rate | 1 | 14.1 | 13.1 | 60b | 55 | 45f | - | - | - | - | - | - |
| 155.5 | Franklin Money Fund | 1 | 15.1 | 12.9 | 24 | - | - | - | 16 | 77 | 7 | - | - |
| 293.4 | Fund/Govt Investors | 4 | 13.9 | 11.7 | 54 | 26 | 74 | - | - | - | - | - | - |
| 31.7 | Government Investors Trust | 2 | 14.7 | 13.7 | 45b | - | 34f | 66 | - | - | - | - | - |
| 330.3 | IDS Cash Mgmt | 3 | 14.6 | 13.3 | 43 | - | - | - | 12 | 25 | 54 | 4 p | 5 |
| 97.4 | John Hancock Cash Mgt Trust  h | 4 | 14.7 | 12.8 | 20 | - | - | - | 2 | - | 95 | - | 3 |
| 43.8 | Johnston Cash Management | 4 | 14.7 | 12.8 | 49 | 5 | - | 6 | 5 | 2 | 82 | - | - |
| 883.7 | Kemper Money Market | 1* | 15.3 | 13.3 | 21 | - | - | - | 11 | - | 58 | 31 p | - |
| 43.5 | Lexington Money Market | 1 | 14.5 | 12.7 | 26 | 30 | - | - | 7 | 7 | 61 | - | - |
| 150.5 | Lord Abbett Cash Reserve | 1 | 14.7 | 12.6 | 21 | - | - | - | 19 | 10 | 71 | - | - |
| 211.5 | Lutheran Brthd. Money Mkt. n | 4 | 13.8 | 12.9 | 25 | - | - | - | 6 | 12 | 25 | 36 p | 21 |
| 259.6 | Mass Cash Mgmt Trust | 1 | 14.5 | 13.0 | 24 | 6 | - | - | - | 2 | 85 | 13 p | - |
| 101.1 | Midwest Income | 1 | 12.4 | 10.9 | 27 | 10 | 46 | 25 | 19 | - | - | - | - |
| 95.4 | Money Market Mgmt | 4 | 14.1 | 12.5 | 29 | - | - | - | 9 | 41 | 29 | - | 21 |
| 10.2 | Money Shares, Inc. | 3 | 13.5 | 11.9 | 31 | 32 | - | - | - | - | 68 | - | - |
| 83.1 | Mutual of Omaha | 4 | 15.2 | 13.4 | 31 | - | 3 | - | 1 | 4 | 86 | 2 p | 4 |
| 219.3 | NEL Cash Mgmt Acct | 4 | 14.2 | 13.1 | 39 | - | - | - | 9 | 41 | 32 | 18 p | - |
| 121.5 | Putnam Daily Div Trust | 1* | 14.6 | 12.0 | 28 | 7 | - | - | 26 | 31 | 36 | - | - |
| 1,788.0 | Reserve | 1 | 14.2 | 11.3 | 21 | - | - | 11 | 2 | 2 | - | 83 p | 2 |
| 1,049.4 | Rowe Price Prime Res | 2 | 15.3 | 12.6 | 27 | - | - | - | 29 | 5 | 40 | 26 p | - |
| 154.4 | Scudder Cash Inv Trust | 3 | 14.7 | 13.3 | 21 | 33 | 7 | 1 | 8 | 3 | 48 | - | - |
| 461.3 | Scudder Mged Reserves | 2 | 14.2 | 9.1 | 51 | 22 | 4 | 1 | 7 | 8 | 57 | - | 1 |
| 19.5 | Selected Money Market | 4 | 14.5 | 12.6 | 33 | - | - | - | 20 | 24 | 51 | - | 5 |
| 20.1 | Short-Term Yield Securities | 1 | 14.9 | 12.8 | 23 | - | - | - | 8 | - | 88 | - | 4 |
| 290.4 | SheinRoe Cash Reserves | 3 | 14.3 | 13.1 | 31 | - | - | 1 | 6 | 22 | 55 | 16 p | - |
| 287.6 | Union Cash Mgt., Inc. | 2 | 15.4 | 13.4 | 20 | - | - | 4 | - | - | 36 | 42 p | 18 |
| 109.7 | United Cash Management | 2 | 15.7 | 13.7 | 18 | - | - | - | 1 | - | 63 | - | 36 |
| 26.5 | Value Line Cash | 1 | 14.5 | 13.3 | 39 | - | - | - | - | 5 | 95 | - | - |
| 297.5 | Whitehall Money Mkt | 3 | 14.7 | 13.1 | 28 | 17 | - | 2 | 14 | 21 | 46 | - | - |
| 16,854.1 | Average Yield | | 14.54 | 12.59 | | | | | | | | | |
| | **STOCKBROKER/GENERAL PURPOSE** | | | | | | | | | | | | |
| 523.0 | Alliance Capital Reserves | 3 | 14.7 | 12.8 | 23 | 5 | - | 1 | 36 | 8 | 47 | 3 p | - |
| 864.3 | Cash Equivalent Fund | 1* | 15.5 | 13.6 | 19 | - | - | - | 10 | - | 61 | 29 p | - |
| 2,751.1 | Cash Reserve Mgmt | 1 | 15.3 | 12.5 | 19 | - | - | 10 | 3 | 6 | 73 | 8 p | - |
| 475.5 | Current Interest | 3 | 14.3 | 12.9 | 32 | - | - | - | 9 | 37 | 54 | - | - |
| 1.885.1 | Daily Cash Accum. | 3 | 15.1 | 13.6 | 18 | - | - | - | 8 | 5 | 86 | - | 1 |
| 501.2 | Daily Income | 3 | 15.6 | 12.3 | 41 | 20 | 16 | 6 | 32 | - | 25 | - | 1 |
| 254.1 | Gradison Cash Reserves | 1 | 13.1 | 11.7 | 31 | - | 3 | 3 | 22 | 58 | 14 | - | - |
| 196.3 | INA Cash Fund, Inc. | 3 | 15.5 | 13.4 | 15 | - | - | - | 11 | - | 86 | 3 p | - |
| 3,493.4 | InterCapital Liquid Asset | 4 | 14.0 | 13.1 | 33 | 8 | - | - | 46 | - | 46 | - | - |
| 76.4 | Legg Mason Cash Reserve Trust | 4 | 13.1 | 12.6 | 24 | - | - | - | 5 | 36 | 46 | - | 13 |
| 882.3 | Liquid Capital Income | 1 | 14.5 | 12.6 | 20 | 19 | 24 | 5 | 15 | 11 | 5 | - p | 21 |
| | **Merrill Lynch** | | | | | | | | | | | | |
| 1,951.9 | CMA Money Trust | 1 | 14.3 | 12.3 | 27 | - | 23 | 2 | 48 | 14 | 13 | - | - |
| 139.8 | Merrill Lynch Govt | 3 | 13.6 | 12.1 | 17 | 100 | - | - | - | - | - | - | - |
| 10,189.2 | Merrill Lynch Ready | 1 | 14.9 | 10.7 | 33 | 23 | 9 | 4 | 47 | 13 | 4 | - | - |
| 1,477.0 | MoneyMart Assets | 1 | 14.4 | 13.1 | 22 | - | - | 5 | 7 | 19 | 48 | 21 p | - |
| 1,351.8 | National Liquid Reserves | 3 | 14.0 | 13.2 | 26 | 7 | 1 | - | 5 | 8 | 66 | 13 p | - |
| 540.8 | Oppenheimer Monetary | 3 | 15.2 | 13.2 | 26 | - | - | - | 3 | 5 | 92 | - | - |
| 2,238.6 | Paine Webber Cashfund | 1 | 14.3 | 13.0 | 31 | 6 | 5 | 2 | 21 | - | 66 | - | - |
| 1,733.9 | Shearson Daily Dividend, Inc. | 3 | 12.4 | 13.5 | 31 | - | - | 2 | 10 | - | 2 | 86 p | - |
| 481.3 | Webster Cash Reserve | 3 | 14.0 | 12.2 | 26 | - | - | 2 | 22 | 5 | 57 | 13 p | - |
| 31,989.0 | Average Yield | | 14.39 | 12.71 | | | | | | | | | |

**MONEY FUND LISTING AND AVERAGE MATURITY INDEX** *(Continued)*

| | INSTITUTIONS ONLY | | | | | | | | | | | | |
|---|---|---|---|---|---|---|---|---|---|---|---|---|---|
| | **Dreyfus Service Corp.** | | | | | | | | | | | | |
| 107.0 | Dreyfus Govt Series | 4 | 14.1 | 12.5 | 24 | 76 | - | 24 | - | - | - | - | - |
| 1,047.1 | Dreyfus Money Market | 4 | 14.3 | 13.4 | 32 | 9 | - | 4 | 36 | 8 | 17 | 26 p | - |
| | **Federated Securities** | | | | | | | | | | | | |
| 1,430.7 | Federated Master Trust | 4 | 13.9 | 13.1 | 32 | - | - | 1 | - | - | 99 | - | - |
| 820.3 | Money Market Trust | 4 | 14.1 | 12.9 | 32 | - | - | 3 | .18 | 43 | - | - | 36 |
| 2,245.7 | Trust/US Govt Secs | 4 | 13.3 | 12.0 | 42 | 16 | 60 | 24 | - | - | - | - | - |
| 192.1 | Trust/US Treasury Obligs. | 4 | 14.1 | 12.5 | 30 | 67 | - | 33 | - | - | - | - | - |
| | **Fidelity Money Market Trust** | | | | | | | | | | | | |
| 87.6 | Government | 3 | 13.7 | 12.6 | 12 | 76 | - | 24 | - | - | - | - | - |
| 122.1 | Domestic | 3 | 14.8 | 13.3 | 23 | - | - | 8 | 15 | 52 | 25 | - | - |
| 19.9 | International | 3 | 14.5 | 13.9 | 11 | - | - | - | - | - | - | 30 p | 70 |
| | **Shearson Loeb Rhoades Inc.** | | | | | | | | | | | | |
| 467.4 | FedFund | 3 | 13.3 | 12.2 | 23 | 56 | 35 | 9 | - | - | - | - | - |
| 2,089.6 | TempFund | 3 | 14.3 | 13.3 | 27 | 6 | - | 1 | 24 | - | 68 | - | 1 |
| 513.2 | Mer Lynch Institutional | 3 | 14.5 | 13.2 | 28 | 8 | 8 | - | 41 | 36 | 7 | - | - |
| | **Salomon Brothers** | | | | | | | | | | | | |
| 690.6 | ILA Government | 4 | 13.6 | 12.6 | 55 | 12 | 63 | 25 | - | - | - | - | - |
| 1,481.3 | ILA Prime Obligations | 4 | 13.9 | 13.2 | 39 | - | - | 14 | 2 | 30 | 54 | - | - |
| 11,314.6 | Average Yield | | 14.02 | 12.89 | | | | | | | | | |
| $60,157.7 | Total - All Funds | | 14.31 | 12.73 | | | | | | | | | |
| | Yield - 10 Largest Funds | | 14.21 | 12.85 | | | | | | | | | |
| | Average Maturity (wtd by assets) | | 44 | 40 | | | | | | | | | |

**Valuation Methods**

1. Constant NAV, mark-to-market
2. Variable NAV, mark-to-market
3. Pennyrounding
4. Amortized Cost
* Applied for #3 (Pennyrounding) valuation

where to put your money with each shift in interest rates so that it earns the best return while remaining safe and liquid.

## Tracking Interest Rate Trends

*How to predict interest rates is the key question.* Yet it is almost impossible for an individual to forecast interest rates. Some pundits have been able to do it for a while—even, in the case of the current majordomo of interest prediction, Henry Kaufman of Solomon Brothers, for a few years. But overall, one of the major problems in attempting to control the economy has always been an inability to accurately foretell interest rate trends. If the government can't do it at all, and the Wall Street wizards only for a little while, then you may well ask how you're supposed to do it.

The answer is simple, and to figure it out, all you have to do is be able to read a figure that you can find in the financial section of many major newspapers, including *The New York Times,* (New York) *Daily News To-night, Washington Post* and *Washington Star, Chicago Tribune, Los Angeles Times, San Francisco Examiner, Boston Globe, Detroit News, Miami Herald* and *Miami News,* and *Tallahassee Democrat.* This figure is called the *average maturity index* of money funds and it will give you the most accurate prediction available regarding what interest rates are going to do in the near future.

The *average maturity index of money funds* is essentially a figure that represents the consensus on the future direction of interest rates from some of the smartest and most high-powered money fund managers in the country.

This average maturity of money funds figure has been an amazing precursor of interest rates to come. And since the fund managers who are responsible for it are putting over $80 billion of their money where their mouths are, you can feel confident in using this figure as a guide in how to invest *your* money in a money fund. Or, looking at it another way, why not put their hard work to work for your money?

To do this, look in any of the above newspapers that carry a table of money fund yields. In the same table, you should find listed the *average maturity* of the money funds. This figure represents the money fund industry average. The average maturity for all funds can also be found in Donoghue's *Money Fund Report.*

### How the Average Maturity Index Works

The average maturity index moves *opposite* to future interest rates. When it *rises,* interest rates can be expected to *drop.* If it stays in a *narrow range,* interest rates will remain more or less the *same.* An index reading that is *declining* indicates interest rates can be expected to *rise.* Finally, the *faster* the average maturity changes, the *sharper* the change in interest rates will be.

On the whole, if the average rate of maturity fluctuates within a five-day range—for example, between 40 and 45 days—interest rates will be relatively *stable.* If the average rate of maturity for all the money fund investments *jumps* suddenly from 45 to 55 days, you can expect interest rates to begin *declining* rapidly. If, however, the average rate of maturity for the money funds suddenly *drops* from 40 to 32 days, you can expect interest rates to *climb.*

Because of the size of many money fund portfolios—billions of dollars—it takes a few weeks for a dramatic change in the average maturity of a money fund investment portfolio to be felt. So a shift of three days in the average maturity in any one week, say from 45 to 42 days or from 45 to 48 days, is considered significant. If the average maturity continues to increase or decrease by as much as three days for two weeks in a row, this is an important shift and it means the money fund managers think that interest rates will either rise or fall soon.

## How You Can Use the Average Maturity Index to Predict Interest Rates

For example, if the money funds' average maturity decreased from 48 to 45 days, as they did when I was writing this book, you could expect the fund managers felt interest rates would continue to rise. In the week following this period, if the average maturity shortened to 42 or 41 days, you could feel very confident the fund managers definitely expected interest rates to continue to rise. On the other hand, if, during this same time, the average maturity increased from 45 back up to 48 days, it would mean the fund managers were not sure what interest rates would do and it would be better to wait at least one or two more weeks before assuming that interest rates were on the rise.

To take the opposite example, if the money funds' average maturity increased from 48 to 51 days, you could conclude money fund managers were expecting interest rates to fall. The week after this, if the average maturity increased to 54 days, you could safely assume the money fund managers were betting that interest rates would decline. If, however, as in the above example, the average maturity shifted direction during this week and began to shorten, say from 54 back to 51 days, you should hold off for a week or two before concluding which direction interest rates were taking.

Watching the average maturity is the *only* way you can know exactly what the professionals in the field think interest rates will be in the near future.

Essentially, a well-managed money fund operates so that when interest rates look as if they are going to decline, the maturity of the investments the funds holds is extended beyond its average 43 days to 60, 70, or 80 days—even, in some cases, to 120 days. That way the fund locks in the current high interest rates and maintains a higher return than it would achieve by buying new paper in a declining-interest-rate market.

On the other side of the coin, if the managers feel that interest rates are going to rise, the funds try to keep their average maturities quite short. That way they have cash on hand to invest when the new higher-interest-bearing paper is issued.

Of course, not even the money fund managers are right all the time, but their track record in the past has been so good that you can feel confident this system will work reliably for you and your money. Listen to what these money fund numbers can tell you about your money and always remember to be SLY.

### The Proof Is in the Pudding

To give an example using the average maturity index, in November 1979, with the prime at 15.75 percent, the general press was saying, "All right, this is it. Interest rates have peaked and will soon decline." For the following ten weeks, however, the index fluctuated between 40 and 36 days. Then it dropped even lower.

At the time, the funds, with some $50 billion of their money on the line, said interest rates would not decline. They didn't. Instead, the prime crept up a full point to 16.75 percent a few months later, pulling all other interest rates with it. And the average maturity index remained on the increasing-interest-rate side of the scale even after that lofty prime was reached. This was at a time when people were again saying, "No, it can't go on." So it went until the prime nudged the unimaginable—20 percent.

Following the popular news commentators, you would have locked yourself into long-term money market investments when the prime reached 15.75 percent. Following the index, you would have waited, increasing your yield by around 4 percent. The pros know.

So forget about the Dow Jones averages or Standard & Poor's. For dealing in the money market, what you need to follow is the average maturity of money funds. Then juggle your money among the various instruments available to maximize yield as a function of interest and the duration of your deposit.

You'll want to start by parking your money in a safe, liquid, yet high-yielding money fund while you look over some of the preferred strategies for the future, using the index to guide you. The interest rates in the examples used here may not correspond to the interest rates behind the strategy, but they are just as valid, and just as profitable, no matter what the current interest levels are—and profit is, after all, the name of the game.

### When Rates Are on the Rise, Stay Short and Liquid

*Let's assume the average maturity index is declining two to three days each week—which means that interest rates are going to rise. Let's also assume* the going investment rate is 12 percent (it would be reflected in the discount rate on Treasury bills, which you will find listed in the financial section of your newspaper every week). What should you do?

Well, if interest rates are rising, money funds are probably yielding about the same as Treasury bills. Actually, money fund yields may be a little lower, since money fund yields tend to lag, or follow, T-bill yields. As the rates rise, the yield of both the T-bills and the money funds will rise too. So you have a choice of investing in a liquid money fund currently yielding 12 percent, a more restrictive money market certificate yielding the same, or a six-month Treasury bill yielding a discounted 13.1 percent. Yet another alternative would be a unit investment trust, which at this time would probably be yielding about 13.5 percent for six months, since these vehicles invest in more aggressive portfolios than Treasury bills.

Which do you choose, then? Well, comparing the Treasury bill with either the money fund or the money market certificate, clearly the Treasury bill is more profitable at the moment. However, comparing it with the unit investment trust, the Treasury bill's yield is lower. So if you're willing to accept a bit more risk, you should go with the unit investment trust. After all, comparing it with the money fund, you find you would have approximately 13.5 percent coming for the next six months on the unit investment trust, while the money funds are yielding only 12–12.5 percent.

But remember, you think *interest rates are rising*. So you put your money in the money fund after all. It has a slightly lower initial rate. But its rate will rise with the increasing rate of return for the marketplace. The money market certificate, T-bill, and unit investment trust rates won't do that. Thus, you are better off putting your money into a money fund and waiting. Next week's unit investment trusts, Treasury bills, and money market certificates will all be yielding higher rates. That will be true for each subsequent week until interest rates peak. So there's no reason to lock in those rates yet.

### Waiting for the Peak

You'll keep your cash in a money fund until you see that interest rates have leveled off. Then you'll decide how much of your money you can lock up, and you'll buy T-bills or unit investment trusts with it. In the special case where T-bill interest rates are hovering at 9 percent or below, however, an argument can be made for buying money market certificates. The extra half of a percent paid on money market certificates—purchased through a thrift institution, not a bank, however—makes them attractive in that particular instance.

This is also a good time to open an account in one or more of the superyielders that came to the fore in the spring of 1980. As rates approached the peak, three funds—Scudder Managed Reserves, Putnam Daily Dividend Trust, and Cash Management Trust of America—showed unusually low yields; and when interest rates began to fall, the same funds posted yields of 20 percent and more. The reason? They were reflecting in their dividends the full impact of short-term money market yield shifts. As rates fell, they passed on the increase in portfolio market value faster than the majority of funds, which valued their under-sixty-day securities at cost. Consequently, these funds, which were "bums" when rates were rising, were "winners" during the period of rapidly falling rates in April and May

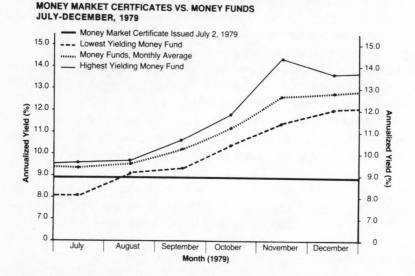

**MONEY MARKET CERTFICATES VS. MONEY FUNDS**
**JULY-DECEMBER, 1979**

- —— Money Market Certificate Issued July 2, 1979
- - - - Lowest Yielding Money Fund
- ······· Money Funds, Monthly Average
- —— Highest Yielding Money Fund

*Month (1979)*

**Money Fund Vs. Money Market Certificate: How You Could Have Improved Your Return**

The above chart illustrates the impact of a decision to invest in a money market certificate rather than a money fund on July 2, 1979. The $10,000 MMC would have earned 8.903%, or $445.15, over its 182-day term while the average money fund would have returned $548 on $10,000 over the same period. You could have improved your yield by an average of $102.85 during the last 6 months of 1979 if you had invested in a money fund instead of an MMC. To have accomplished this, you would have had to believe the economists who predicted a rise in interest rates over the period. You would have received the benefits of both instruments had you left your money in a money fund until money market certificate rates peaked in late October and then bought a 6-month MMC.

1980. You should keep an open account in one of these superyielder funds, then switch your money into it temporarily as the descent of interest rates begins plummeting.

### The $49 Billion Blunder

In July 1979, the choice for investors was between a 9 percent money market certificate and a 5.5 percent saving account. Obviously, the money market certificates looked good. (Unit investment trusts weren't available at the time.) To a lot of people, people with a combined $49 billion in savings, in fact, it looked as if the money market certificates were definitely the way to go, and that's where they put their money. People locked themselves in at 9 percent for six months, sat back—and watched interest rates rise while their return didn't.

When they redeemed their certificates in January 1980, interest rates were already at 13 percent. Had they invested in a money fund, they would have averaged 11 percent instead of 9 percent, and they could now have bought Treasury bills yielding 13.1 percent.

By accepting the current yield in a rising market and allowing the money fund rate to take your money along for a ride on the interest curve, then buying Treasury bills at or near the peak, you receive a much more substantial return. True, in the example given, the 9 percent return seemed to be a high yield at the outset. But as soon as three months later, it certainly was not. Don't be fooled by high numbers. What counts is *how an investment stacks up against current return.* Interest rates change very rapidly these days. So keep your options open.

### At the Peak—Spreading Your Risk

On the other hand, don't expect to always be able to make your investment at the very peak. As interest rates fall, however, you'll get another shot at those high yields you saw on the way up. Remember, they have to come down from a peak, even if the overall cycle is up. Let's say, for example, you've been watching a 13 percent yield go to 13.5 percent, and you begin to think, well, maybe I should invest now, but I'll wait a little longer. And the yields go back down to 13 percent. You can still pick up that 13 percent as it goes past you again. That's the time to lock up interest.

The trick in money market investment is being right 90 percent of the time. Nobody is right 100 percent of the time. You can't buy the curve. You can't have it all. What you want to do is to get most of it.

## Keeping Your Options Open

Okay, but let's say, for a further example, that you were wrong, that 13.5 percent turned out not to be the top, and interest rates continued to rise. Had you stayed in a money fund, your yield would automatically have risen. And you could have liquidated without a penalty any time you wanted to. If you had wanted to get out of something like a unit investment trust, on the other hand, your $1,000 share would have been worth less than you paid for it. You might have gotten out at $990 per share. As for a money market certificate, well, you couldn't have gotten out of that at all, because you'd have ended up taking a really substantial interest penalty—and some banks simply do not allow early withdrawal. Even a Treasury bill you'd have sold for less, because of the interest rates going up.

Conversely, suppose you were wrong, and you got into a money fund, and interest rates fell instead of rising. Well, then you could have changed your mind immediately and said, Okay, interest rates have fallen; I'll buy the unit investment trust or the Treasury bill now, before interest rates fall further.

## When Rates Are Declining, Go Long

*What do you do when interest rates are going down?* Let's suppose the money fund average maturity index plus everything you read in the financial news indicates that interest rates are about to decline. At a certain point, you become convinced that the decline is going to be a long one rather than just a dip in an otherwise rising yield curve. The choices for investment, then, are the same. But the strategy is different. First let's look at the money funds. As interest rates fall, their yields will tend to fall more slowly than those of direct investments in the money market. Remember, in the case of a money fund you're buying part of an already existing portfolio, one that has locked in higher-than-market rates for months to come.

If you buy a unit investment trust, on the other hand, and interest rates fall, your shares will appreciate, but those shares must be sold during the first four months of their term in order for you to take advantage of that appreciation. If you don't sell within that time, they must be held till their full six months' maturity.

**CASHING IN ON THE MONEY FUND "LAG"**

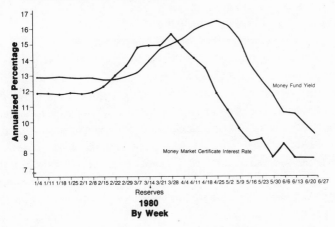

## You Can Win Even When Interest Rates Are Declining

"If you missed the peak interest rates, Merrill Lynch and Fidelity are still selling it." That's what I told a group of corporate cash managers in April 1980. You see, as interest rates fall, money funds hold on to the previously higher yields longer and appreciate (increase in value) as well. In fact, the "superyielders" yielded over 20% while interest rates were falling. This "holding on to yesterday's yields" effect gives you some extra time to make your decisions and to see if rates are really falling or will rally (rise) soon.

Money market certificates are really not a viable investment unless the market rate is below 9 percent. Even then, you're trading that extra half of a percent for liquidity, so be sure you don't need the liquidity. Rarely should money market certificates exceed half of your total money market investment, even under the best of conditions.

Treasury bills offer some unique profit potentials as interest rates decline. They're also very flexible. You don't have to buy the six-month Treasury bill. If you're not really convinced interest rates are going to decline over a full six-month period, there are three-month Treasury bills to be considered. And if you're convinced that a long, steady decline lies ahead, there are one-year Treasury bills to fit the decline.

### Riding the Yield Curve

The real beauty of T-bills in a declining interest environment is their adaptability to the very profitable technique that large institutional investors developed to ride the yield curve.

*Riding the yield curve for fun and profit,* that wonderful way to increase your take, is an essential part of your operations when the market is in a declining interest mode. So let's review it. The greatest appreciation in the value of your securities in a declining interest period occurs halfway through to maturity—not at their actual maturity. This is because, while the value of your investment appreciated to match the current yield, it must return to par when it matures.

The strategy of riding the yield curve, then, is quite simple. Buy a one-year Treasury bill and sell it after six months. Or buy a six-month Treasury bill and sell it after three months. In each case, purchase a newly issued T-bill as the old one is sold. The securities are continuously replaced on a three- or six-month basis. There are no real transaction costs other than the small charge the bank or the broker makes, and the return is greater than the stated yield of the underlying securities.

## The $1,000 Yield Curve Ride

Unit investment trusts also lend themselves to riding the yield curve. Their yield will be higher than that of T-bills, their safety fractionally less.

But what if your expectations prove wrong, and interest rates don't fall, but continue to rise. Well, with a money fund investment, the yield will rise along with the general level of interest rates. The Treasury bill will decline in value for a while and then rise back up to par. As it is simply held to maturity, no capital is lost. The interest earned is the original discounted rate for the whole period of retention. By holding it to maturity, you eliminate market risk at the cost of slightly lower interest.

Basically, as long as you are not forced to sell out because of a liquidity problem, the interest *loss*—the difference between the T-bill's fixed yield and its current yield—is twice as great for a one-year Treasury bill as for a six-month bill. Conversely, if you've guessed right, the additional *gain* on a year bill will be twice that of a six-month bill.

## The Conservative Approach

*The key to being wrong safely is protecting yourself.* This is where diversification comes in.

- *Put part of your money market investment in safety,* with a capital S. That means either Treasury bills or money market certificates, the option being exercised by that crucial 9 percent yield threshold. Below 9 percent, it's money market certificates from a thrift institution paying the quarter of a percent differential. Above 9 percent, it's T-bills.

- *Put another part of your investment in a money fund for liquidity.* That's liquidity with a capital *L*.
- *Put the last part of your money into the higher-yielding unit investment trusts.* If none are available at the time of your initial investment, add this amount to your money fund until a new unit investment trust makes its way down Wall Street.

The MMCs and T-bills can be avoided entirely when general rates are over 9 percent. The confident investor should substitute unit investment trusts.

Such a money portfolio maximizes your yield while eliminating any substantial credit risk. It won't make you rich overnight. But it will let you get poorer more slowly than the rest of the population. And don't forget, for every story about millionaires made in the stock market, real estate, or precious metals, there are tens of thousands of untold stories about the people who took the same route—to poverty. So don't be sorry—be SLY.

### Applying the SLY System: A Case Study in Strategies

In order to see how to apply the SLY system to your finances, let's first make some assumptions about what financial alternatives you have available and how they will be affected by fluctuating interest rates. We will use the money fund average maturity index to predict interest rate trends.

To keep the example simple, let's assume interest rates rise to a peak and then fall off at the same rate as they increased. In the real world, the change would be more erratic. However, the principle is the same and the results will show the effect of this interest rate fluctuation on your return for five different basic investment strategies.

*Fixed Income Investments Throughout the Interest Rate Cycle*

Again to simplify the example and show you the basics, let's limit our investments to four instruments: money funds, unit investment trusts, and three- and six-month Treasury bills. (The reason I'm leaving out money market certificates—MMCs—is that you would always choose the higher-yielding unit investment trust over a money market certificate whenever interest rates are above 10%. Small saver certificates have been omitted because under most circumstances, you would not enjoy the required liquidity if you locked up your money for such an extended period.)

## For the Conservative Investor

### What to Do When Interest Rates Are on the Rise

1. Invest in money funds.
2. Never invest in anything else—you'll lose higher yields tomorrow.
3. Borrow at fixed rates to invest at higher rates. Make sure there are no prepayment penalties in the loans.

### What to Do When You Think Rates Are About to Peak

1. Put 25 percent of your portfolio into unit investment (CD) trusts, if available. Put 75 percent of your portfolio in treasury bills (MMCs) if rates are under 9 percent.
2. Keep 50 percent in normal money funds, as opposed to superyielders.
3. Put 25 percent into a superyielder like Scudder Managed Reserves, Cash Management Trust of America, Putnam Daily Dividend Trust—the funds with superyields in a falling rate environment.
4. Wait for the peak.

### What to Do When Interest Rates Peak

1. Move another 25 percent of your portfolio from your money funds into unit investment (CD) trusts.

### What to Do When Interest Rates Are Falling

1. Keep investments in superyielders.
2. Add to unit investment trust holdings.
3. Sell unit investment trust holdings three months after buying them if they can be sold at a profit.
4. Reinvest in unit investment trusts, if still available, or invest in superyielders.
5. Move back into a 75 percent "money" fund 25 percent unit investment trusts profile. (Check First Variable Rate fund for yield. If it's high in the first month to a quarter, move into this fund.)

### What to Do When Interest Rates Begin to Climb

1. Move back into a 100 percent money fund position.
2. Shift money out of superyielders quickly.

## For the More Confident Investor (When the Choices Are Clear)

*How Your Money Market Portfolio Should Look*

| | Money Funds | Unit Investment Trust* | Superyielders† | Money Fund Average Maturity Index |
|---|---|---|---|---|
| | | Percent | | |
| Rising rates | 100 | — | — | Shortening (decreasing) |
| Approaching peak | 50 | 25 | 25 | Shortens faster |
| At peak | 25 | 50 | 25 | Begins to lengthen (increase) |
| Falling rates | 25 | 60 | 15 | Continues to lengthen |
| At bottom | 75 | 25 | — | Starts to shorten |
| Rising rates | 100 | — | — | Continues to shorten |

* The ultraconservative investor should substitute T-bills if desired. If UITs are not available, then use T-bills (over 9%) or MMCs (under 9%).

† Scudder Managed Reserves; Putnam Daily Dividend Trust; Cash Management Trust of America. *Avoid* in rising market; *use* only in falling market.

*Four Investment Strategies to Improve Your Return*

As you can see in the first chart, all the money market investment strategies are the same when interest rates are rising. When interest rates rise, you should *invest all your available money in money funds,* because their yields, though lower at the time of purchase than other money market investments, increase each day, while the others remain fixed. For example, if you invested in a unit investment trust when money funds were yielding 11.5%, the former would remain at 11.5% while the money fund yield would be free to climb to 11%, 12%, 13%, and on up. The monthly average yield for a money fund over a period of rising interest rates, then, is higher.

FIXED INCOME INVESTMENT IN INTEREST RATE CYCLE

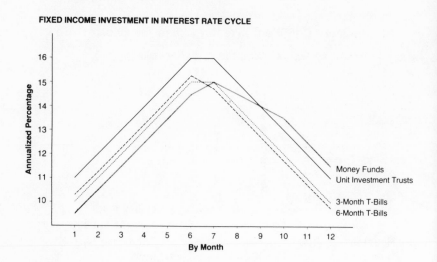

Money Funds
Unit Investment Trusts

3-Month T-Bills
6-Month T-Bills

*Strategies at the Peak of the Interest Rate Cycle*

This is the point at which choices must be made. Let's assume interest rates have peaked for a while (see second chart); here are the options you have open with, say, a $20,000 savings base.

*Strategy A:*   *Invest all your available money in a money fund. Your average yield will be 12.58%.*

*Strategy B:*   *Invest all your available money in a money fund as interest rates rise. After interest rates have peaked, invest 75% of your portfolio in a three-month Treasury bill and keep the remainder in the money fund. When the Treasury bill matures, reinvest those funds in a money fund, since it will be paying a higher rate of return than T-bills. Your average yield will be 12.84%.*

*Strategy C:*   *Invest in a money fund as interest rates rise and then, if you feel more certain that interest rates are falling and will continue to do so for at least six months, buy a six-month Treasury bill with 75% of the portfolio. Leave the balance of 25% in a money fund to keep your finances liquid. Your average yield will be 13.22%.*

*Strategy D:*   *Invest in a money fund as interest rates rise, and when they peak, invest 90% of your money in a six-month unit investment trust (the CD variety). Again, keep the remaining 10%*

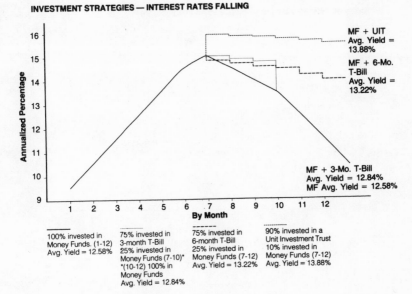

INVESTMENT STRATEGIES — INTEREST RATES FALLING

MF + UIT
Avg. Yield =
13.88%

MF + 6-Mo.
T-Bill
Avg. Yield =
13.22%

MF + 3-Mo. T-Bill
Avg. Yield = 12.84%
MF Avg. Yield = 12.58%

By Month

| 100% invested in Money Funds. (1-12) Avg. Yield = 12.58% | 75% invested in 3-month T-Bill 25% invested in Money Funds (7-10)* *(10-12) 100% in Money Funds Avg. Yield = 12.84% | 75% invested in 6-month T-Bill 25% invested in Money Funds (7-12) Avg. Yield = 13.22% | 90% invested in a Unit Investment Trust 10% invested in Money Funds (7-12) Avg. Yield = 13.88% |

in a money fund for liquidity. Your *average yield will be 13.88%*.

Strategy D gives you an additional $260 over Strategy A for the six months during which interest rates are declining. Note that, since we are talking about a $20,000 portfolio with a minimum of 10%, or $2,000, liquidity at all times, you can invest only 75% of your total investment capital in a T-bill. With T-bills, remember, you are limited to an initial $10,000 minimum and subsequent multiples of $5,000. On the other hand, you can buy $18,000 worth of unit investment trusts at $1,000 each and still keep your $2,000 liquid.

### Riding the Yield Curve: The Final Strategy

Strategy E:  *Invest your available cash in money funds when interest rates are on the rise. When they peak, buy $18,000 worth of unit investment trust units. Again, keep $2,000 in a money fund so you will stay liquid. Sell the unit investment trusts at a profit three months later as interest rates decline. Reinvest the money in yet another unit investment trust. If interest rates continue to fall, do the same thing in three months, again selling at a profit. Your average yield will be 14.38%.*

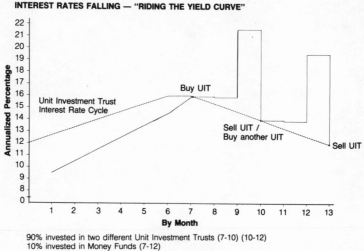

INTEREST RATES FALLING — "RIDING THE YIELD CURVE"

90% invested in two different Unit Investment Trusts (7-10) (10-12)
10% invested in Money Funds (7-12)
Average Yield = 14.38%

*Strategy E* will give you a profit in two ways: (1) because interest rates
have fallen, you can sell the unit investment trusts at a profit; (2) you can
reinvest your money before interest rates decline further. (Note: Unit investment trusts are not always available, in which case you should substitute six-month Treasury bills. Six-month Treasury bills will perform in the
same way as unit investment trusts and will yield about 1–1.5% less—still
a very profitable investment strategy.)

### How Did You Do?

|  | Yield | Dollar return on $20,000 | Investments used |
|---|---|---|---|
| Strategy A | 12.58% | $2516 | Money funds only |
| Strategy B | 12.84% | $2568 | Money funds, 3-month T-bill |
| Strategy C | 13.22% | $2644 | Money funds, 6-month T-bill |
| Strategy D | 13.88% | $2776 | Money funds, 6-month unit investment trust |
| Strategy E | 14.38% | $2876 | Money funds, 6-month unit investment trusts, riding the yield curve |

*Conclusion:* By using *Strategy E* and making two phone calls over the
year, you earned an extra $360, or $180 per phone call.

# 11

## The Beginner-to-Intermediate Money
## Market Portfolio

Five hundred dollars used to be the minimum you needed to open a money fund account. And that amount limited you to one of four funds. Now the fund competition has heated up, and two funds, Alliance Capital Reserves and American Liquid Trust, have eliminated entirely the minimum requirement for the initial deposit. They do still, however, require that any checks written against the account be a minimum of $500.

These money funds represent the only viable strategy for a small starter account. They certainly beat keeping your money in a thrift-institution passbook savings account earning 5.25 percent.

Another alternative is pooling your money with friends or relatives to purchase a higher-yielding T-bill. That's the old investment club idea. Beware of it.

By pooling your money, you can enter into one of the most illiquid investments ever. For instance, if a member of the pool died, the whole investment would be tied up until his will was probated. Not only would you have no access to your money, but the money itself might end up earning much less interest than it should—or, for that matter, no interest at all if the estate took years to settle. Now, that's an investment problem in which you don't want to become embroiled.

### Where to Start Small

There are four funds available to those with only $500 or less to invest: American Liquid Trust, a subsidiary of Travelers Insurance Company; Alliance Capital Reserves, operated by the brokerage firm of Donaldson, Lufkin and Jenrette; the Midwest Income Investment Company in Cincinnati (with low—$350—minimum checking privileges); and the California-based

Franklin Money Fund. All are good funds with a solid track record. When it comes to choosing the one for you, it's just a matter of checking which has the highest current yield—unless you live in California.

The Franklin Money Fund has a special relationship with California's Security Pacific Bank. You can use any of the bank's 435 branches as a depository for your Franklin Money Fund cash. If there's a branch near you, you can deposit directly to the bank for next-day credit at the fund. It probably wouldn't hurt your standing at the bank, either.

### The Starting Gate for Most Investors

*Most of the individual investors in money funds are in the intermediate-portfolio category* of $1,000–$20,000. With a portfolio of that size, where does one begin? Well, as mentioned in the chapter on strategy, "The SLY System," the first thing to do is to park your money in a fund. This gives you time to make the right personal investment decision, resting assured that your money is earning high interest meanwhile.

Your basic strategy should be that of the SLY system, but with a few of the money management fillips described earlier in the book added to it. For instance, once your money fund savings base is $5,000 or more, almost all your bills should be paid with money fund checks. Certainly your mortgage payments, taxes, and other regular bills over $350 should be paid that way.

But you should also consolidate your other payments so they can be paid with a dividend-earning money fund check as well. Consider how you use your credit cards, for example. Most of us have several of them—usually several more than we need these days. Try to use one exclusively rather than diversifying your payments among your card collection. By doing so, and by charging wherever possible, you should be able to pay your monthly credit card bill with a single dividend-earning check.

### Getting It All Invested

*Another use of your money fund is in rounding out individual investments.* Let's say you have $14,000 which you wish to invest in T-bills. It can't be done, since T-bills are sold in $10,000 minimum denominations with $5,000 increments.

So you buy one T-bill and put the remaining $4,000 in the money fund. If you're a more aggressive investor, you might then buy four units of a unit investment trust when one becomes available. Either route will earn you more money and keep you more liquid than buying a money market certificate will.

As an intermediate investor, you'll definitely want to ride the yield curve whenever the market is in a declining interest mode. But stay liquid in a money fund as rates increase. There are, of course, special investment priorities that often require being particularly flexible and keeping your money dry when you aim your guns at inflation. I'm continually getting letters inquiring about what to do in particular situations.

*Let me share a few of these letters of inquiry with you, and some answers,* to help forestall any future problems you might encounter. S.F., of Burlington, New Jersey, writes:

> I would like some information on money market certificates. I have a Keogh plan that has CDs paying 8 percent for eight years. This doesn't seem like a lot right now, and I'm looking for a better return to keep pace with inflation.

Okay, S.F., let's assume that money funds are earning 13 percent, which is their current rate. If the Keogh plan has had these 8 percent CDs for more than six months, it's going to lose six months' interest if the certificates are redeemed early. Six months' worth of interest on, say, $10,000 at 8 percent would be $400. If the plan could earn 13 percent through a money fund—that is, 5 percent more—it would take ten months to recoup the loss, after which time the plan would earn 13 percent clear, or whatever the money fund was paying by then. Now, getting out of a short-term certificate would probably not make sense, considering the penalty. But accepting a low 8 percent yield for another seven years does not seem prudent.

### What About European CDs?

T.M., of West Islip, New York, has an interesting question.

Dear Mr. Donoghue:
Many funds are heavily invested in Euro CDs. The freeze on Iranian accounts and the threatened economic war on Russia make me very nervous about investments in these instruments. Does this situation present any danger to portfolios, and if so, what can be done about it?

Actually, T.M., only about a third of the money funds invest in Eurodollar CDs or are permitted to invest in Eurodollar CDs. If you're worried, you can identify the funds investing in Eurodollar CDs very quickly by checking the chart in our *Moneyletter*. You can also check the *Money Fund Directory* [Appendix A reprints the latest available copy] to see which funds are authorized to invest in Eurodollar CDs. The *Money Fund Directory* list covers all the funds entitled to make such investments, even though they may not currently have any such holdings. Personally, I would not be particularly concerned about any fund that had only 5 or 10 percent of its investments in Eurodollar CDs. But those with 80 or 90 percent socked away overseas are certainly not ones with which you would be comfortable.

Incidentally, the only precedent I know of for what you're worried about, a case where a country actually put an embargo on someone else's money, involved deposits made in a branch of Citibank, then called the National City Bank, in St. Petersburg, Russia. The bank closed one night in St. Petersburg and tried to open the next day, after the revolution, when it was the National City Bank in Petrograd. It didn't work. The money could not be transferred back to the United States after the revolution. The courts, however, settled in favor of the depositors, and Citibank made good on every dollar. While it's not an excellent precedent, nor a very clear precedent, it is the one precedent that exists in the field.

### Money Fund Switching

L.F., of Arlington, Virginia, writes:

> I've noted your report in *The New York Times* giving the various rates several of the funds pay. I am interested in learning whether, by following their recent yields, there is a way of mathematically forecasting the approximate future yield the next month or the next week and, by switching among a few of the funds, obtaining a higher yield. You've been dealing with the funds as a specialty and might have an answer. Thank you.

Well, L.F., what you're trying to figure out is something we've been trying to figure out too. The best advice we can give you is that the shift in the average maturity of the funds gives a good indication of future yields in general. [See the discussion of the average maturity index in the preceding chapter.] It is also true, incidentally, that if you see a fund that presently has a substantially lower yield because interest rates have been generally rising, causing a lot of temporary capital depreciation in the fund, this may offer a real buying opportunity. As the fund's holdings mature and interest rates stabilize, this fund should offer above-average yields for some time.

A case in point is Scudder Managed Reserves, which is often pretty hard hit because it uses mark-to-market valuation. This method of valuing a fund tends to make for wide swings in yield. Scudder's seven-day yield has been known to drop as much as 7 or 8 percent in the face of a 100-basis-point, or 1 percent, increase in overall interest rates. Then, the following month, its yield doubles to 16 or 17 percent as it recovers that temporary loss. The time when Scudder has a particularly low yield may be the best time to invest in this fund, to take advantage of the typically higher interest it offers for the following couple of months as interest rates moderate.

### Following Money Yields

R.B., of San Diego, California, notes:

> The thirty-day yield of the money funds, as reported in *The New York Times* and based on your reports, suggests that there is something wrong in the way the yields are calculated. For example, it is difficult to believe that the yield on Scudder Managed Reserves could drop from 16.6 percent on November 28 to 13 percent on December 12. Fidelity Daily Income only dropped from 16 percent to 14.2 percent during the same period.

As I've said, Scudder Managed Reserves tends to move in more dramatic shifts from week to week as it reflects all of its appreciation or depreciation of net asset value. It's not a mistake—unless you fail to take advantage of this anomaly.

### Foreign CDs

The following comes from D.P., of St. Clairsville, Ohio:

> I've just reviewed a profile report on money market funds containing essential information *except* with respect to Euro funds denominated in Swiss francs, West German Deutsche marks, and the Canadian dollar. I'm seeking the customary information on their availability and the procedure in obtaining them.

D.P., I don't know of any funds that invest in foreign currencies. All the investments the money funds make in either foreign banks or foreign branches of United States banks are denominated in dollars. An additional currency risk is not something the funds are particularly anxious to take on.

### Donoghue's Money Fund?

F.T., of Claremont, California, writes:

> My wife and I, eighty and seventy-six years old, respectively, and in excellent health, have a sum of $5,000 to reinvest by mid-December. We are very much interested in your *Money Fund Report,* and we would like to know the details about making this kind of investment with your organization.

You can't invest with us, F.T., because we do not handle accounts, have a fund, or offer specific investment advice. We sell only information and ideas. The actual implementation is up to you.

### Of What E. F. Hutton Speaks

C.C., of New York City, asks:

> Is a money fund the same as what is called a "money management fund" by the stockbrokerage houses? My broker is with E. F. Hutton, and he told me his firm accepts deposits of funds for "management" and pays interest on such deposits equal or superior to savings bank time deposits. What is your opinion of this?

Yes, it's a money fund. In E. F. Hutton's case, the fund is called Cash Reserve Management, and it has well over a billion dollars in assets. In general, it's an excellent fund.

### Keeping Your Money Fund Investment Liquid

L. R., of Detroit, writes:

> If I invest in a money fund, and if I need money, how long will it take to get it?

If you have checks, you can write out a check and deposit it right into your bank account. If the bank won't clear the check without waiting a week or ten days, you can call the fund and have them wire the money to you within twenty-four hours.

### Who Do I Pay to Invest for Me? No One

M. R., of Maplewood, New Jersey, asks:

Do I have to pay someone for handling money fund transactions?

No. Money funds are no-load investments. There are no commissions for handling transactions. But you should read a fund's prospectus to see if there are any charges for services such as checks and wire privileges. Probably there won't be. But, as with all investments, you should verify every pertinent detail.

### Quoting an Exact Return

B. A., of Los Angeles, writes:

What is the exact return I would get on $10,000 invested in a money fund for one year?

Money funds do not guarantee an exact return. If you want exact return for a year, you have to invest in a Treasury bill. Money funds do, however, float upward with interest rates, and you would find, if you invested in one, that any time you were not satisfied with those interest rates, you could have your money back and go into another investment immediately.

### Higher Yields for Larger Investments?

I.D., of Methuen, Massachusetts, queries:

If one were to deposit $100,000 or more, would the interest rate be higher than on the minimum deposit?

No. It would be exactly the same as on the minimum deposit, because the SEC requires that mutual funds treat all investors equally.

### Money Fund Qualifications as Profit-Sharing Plan Investments

T.K., of Palatine, Illinois, writes:

Please advise me if there is a money market fund that complies with the Internal Revenue Service rules for a small corporation's profit-sharing retirement plan which will have annual contributions in the $12,000 to $18,000 range. The number of employees is six to eight, their ages are fifty-one, twenty-six, twenty-five, twenty-four, twenty-three, and twenty-two. The plan would probably be in effect until they were fifty-nine and a half years old. Our year end is January 31. So please reply quickly.

T.K., all the money funds qualify for a profit-sharing plan. And you'll find that most money funds will be glad to help you and set up separate accounts for each employee under what is known as a subaccounting service. There is normally no charge for this service. In effect, you have one master account and several subaccounts. So each employee's share is kept separately. However, fifty-nine and a half years is as much as thirty-seven and a half years from today for one of your employees, and you may find that money funds aren't the only places you want to keep your money during that time. The nice thing about a money fund is that when you decide the profit-sharing plan should invest in something else, you can easily move your money out of the fund. It's also a very safe investment—one which no one could criticize you for investing in—thus excluding you from any personal liability for losses under the new ERISA laws.

### Evaluating a Funds Portfolio

S.R., of New Orleans, writes:

> I've sent off for a number of brochures of money market funds which had a 10-percent-or-over rate of return in the last two or three months, but I need some guidance. I'd like to know if the raising of interest rates by the Federal Reserve and subsequent tightening of the money supply will affect the money market in general and Treasury bills and notes in particular. I'm also wondering if a fund which invests primarily in Treasury bills and notes would be superior to one which has a diversified portfolio in corporate bonds and commercial paper in addition to government securities. Will Fannie May and Ginnie May be affected by the high interest rates?

Well, there are quite a few questions here. First of all, the general tightening of the money supply, the actual tightening of credit, and the raising of interest rates by the Federal Reserve will have the tendency to drive interest rates even higher. In fact, many people believe that interest rates will continue to rise until they hit the inflation rate, which is now running 18 to 20 percent. [They indeed did just that in the period following this query and response.]

Will they affect the market in general? Certainly they will. All interest rates will move up. Treasury bills and Treasury notes will certainly move up. However, that's the yield on new issues of Treasury bills and notes we're talking about. The sales value of older ones will actually decrease temporarily, because they were issued at a lower rate.

Overall, Treasury bills tend to have the yield at the bottom level of the money market. Commercial paper and the certificates of deposit of major banks tend to yield a bit more. So if you invest in a fund that only purchases government debt, you'll find that it will yield probably 50 or 100 basis points—that is, 0.5 to 1 percent—less than a money fund with a more aggressive portfolio.

As to corporate bonds, most money funds will not buy them unless they are within a year of maturity. And there aren't many of those around. Ginnie Mae and Fannie Mae will certainly also be affected by high interest rates. All money market investments will be affected by high interest rates. However, Ginnie Mae and Fannie May securities are two examples of securities that money funds do not hold.

### Do "Prudent Men" Invest?

S.V., an attorney in Orlando Beach, Florida, questions a legal point:

> I wonder whether the courts consider money market funds to be reasonably safe investments for the average prudent personal representative of an estate.

Yes. Very much so. As a matter of fact, the Comptroller of the Currency has strongly encouraged bank trust departments to take advantage of the flexibility and safety of money funds instead of putting money in savings accounts in their own banks. The beneficiaries of that advice, of course, have been the widows and orphans of the country. Currently there's more than $10 billion worth of bank-trust-department money invested in money funds. So it must certainly be considered to conform to the prudent-man rule.

### Using "Out-of-Town" Money Fund Checks

> Could you kindly advise if your latest records include the existence of any New York-area money fund allowing check-writing privileges below $500. I am aware of the same in other places such as Fidelity in Boston, but

I have in mind some parties looking askance at checks drawn on an out-of-town bank, with crediting delays involved.

That's signed E.L., of New York City.

We've had this same question asked by many investors in various locales. A good way around this problem is to have your fund checks imprinted with your name, local address, and telephone number. That's what most neighborhood vendors look for. They don't normally look at the location of the bank itself. I've had very little trouble cashing out-of-town money fund checks.

For those of you looking for an opportunity to increase the float on checks that you use to pay bills by mail—and no one notices on which bank such checks have been drawn—note that most funds clear their checks through either Boston or New York. That's why some astute investors choose to use Kemper Money Market Fund, which clears its checks through Kansas City; Midwest Income Investment Company, which clears its checks through Provident Bank in Cincinnati; Capital Preservation Fund, which clears through the United California Bank on the West Coast; or Columbia Daily Income Company, which uses a bank in Portland, Oregon. It takes checks from these funds several extra dividend-paying days to clear through their more remote banking locations.

Lastly, for those dealing with our friends north of the border, J.C., of Bermuda, has a pertinent question:

### Canadian Money Funds

Do you know of any Canadian money funds? There are some tax advantages to our doing business with a Canadian money fund.

Yes, there is one, the AGF Money Fund of Toronto. Actually, it's the only Canadian money fund there is. And the reason there's only one is that most Canadian banks and trust companies offer checkable savings accounts with interest rates as high as those of money funds. Money funds are simply not necessary in Canada, since there is no restrictive Regulation Q, as in this country.

# 12

## Fund Switching—Keeping Your Money Profitably in Tune with the Market

*The key to profitable investing is that hoary old chestnut "Buy low, sell high." And as Will Rogers used to say, "If they don't go up, don't buy 'em."*

While it's obviously not possible to be right all the time, using the average maturity index to track interest rates enables you not only to buy low and sell high in the money market, but to switch into equity, or stock, funds at times when you can profit more from them than from money funds. And it must be working. About 20 percent, or $400 million, of mutual fund sales in June 1980 were accounted for by exchanges or switches between funds.

It's almost axiomatic that when interest rates decline, stocks go up. They do so because with lower interest rates it's cheaper to carry inventory, cheaper to buy new equipment, and cheaper to expand business in general. To boot, with low interest rates the public has more money to spend. And spend it they do. So, overall, corporate profits, and subsequently the stock market, tend to rise.

In that stage of the economic cycle, when interest rates are declining and equity prices are rising, switching into a diversified stock fund makes a lot of sense. The trick is to eliminate any possible commissions and minimize your paperwork.

### Playing Both Sides of the Street

*The best way to jump back and forth between the money market and the stock market is to invest in a mutual fund group that has both types of funds under its management umbrella. If all the funds in the group are no*

**SWITCHING TO AVOID LOSSES MEANS GREATER YIELDS**

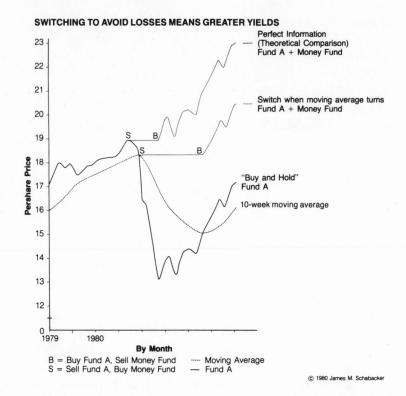

B = Buy Fund A, Sell Money Fund     ---- Moving Average
S = Sell Fund A, Buy Money Fund     — Fund A

© 1980 James M. Schabacker

This chart shows the additional yield you could have earned by the switching strategy: switching *out* of the fund when the ten-week moving average of per share values declined and switching *back into* the fund when the average increased. Two telephone calls over a seven-month period could have improved your return significantly. As you can see from the chart, most of the benefits would have been available with perfect information from a very simple system. With professional advice, directly or through a newsletter service, you could have made money. With a "buy and hold" strategy over the same period, you would have barely broken even.

loads, as they should be, switching by mail or telephone becomes a simple, inexpensive proposition.

To give an example, if you use Financial Daily Income Shares as your money fund, you can switch into any one of the specialized equity funds of Financial Programs Inc., the parent organization. These include Financial Industrial Fund, Financial Industrial Income Fund, Financial Dynamics Fund, and Financial Bond Fund.

You'll find all the funds that currently have a switching arrangement with a money fund listed in Appendix A of this book. You'll also find charted there such fund-choosing considerations as whether or not the funds permit telephone or mail switching, and what the costs are, if any.

*Remember, frugality is the lost key to financial success* in this country. Don't pay for any service if you can get the equivalent service free elsewhere. Why pay an 8 percent load to get into a fund even if there are no charges for future switches?

If you are switching often, telephone action becomes almost mandatory. The beauty of telephone switching is its instant nature. For example, you can call the Dreyfus toll-free 800 number and have them immediately exchange your money fund shares for bond fund shares, or vice versa. In a world where interest rates sometimes fluctuate half a point or more a day, speed in switching can be a crucial factor in maximizing your return.

It would not surprise me to see almost all the funds offering telephone switching, or even a direct-transaction link-up to your home computer, within a few years. Meanwhile, to stay on top of the ever-changing fund services, you can procure an updated version of Donoghue's *Money Fund Directory* whenever you need it.

### Updating Switching Advice

Every investment adviser claims he has a system for market timing, for knowing when to invest where. You can enlist the help of one of these advisers, you can devise your own system, or you can subscribe to any of a number of switch fund advisory newsletters, most of which are priced under $100 a year—a real bargain if you have more than a few thousand dollars to invest.

My own favorite source is the *Switch Fund Advisory,* published by Jay Schabacker. Over the thirteen months ended July 31, 1980, his recommended portfolio was up 41 percent. The tables and graphs used in this section are from this newsletter; for further information about *Switch Fund Advisory,* contact our offices in Holliston, Massachusetts 01746.

Jay's approach is fairly simple to follow and easy to use. He limits his initial analysis each month to those no-load mutual funds that have a money fund offering switching or exchange privileges with their equity fund. Load funds with similar features are treated separately.

Ranking the performance of the mutual funds by fund category, he gives a very clear overall view of where the "hot" funds have been for the past months.

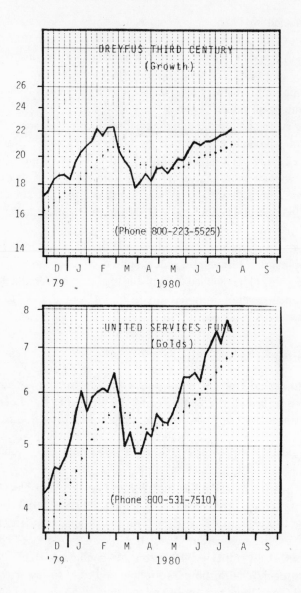

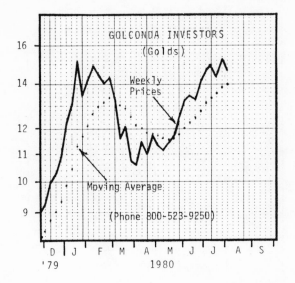

Let's see how his analysis works. For instance, we might decide that, in addition to keeping an eye on our money market investments, we would like to review gold funds and long-term growth funds in more detail as potential alternatives to our money fund investment. So we turn to Jay's table ranking the no-load mutual funds by category and performance. From his breakdown we can readily see that the gold funds have performed so spectacularly this past year that they probably should have been in everyone's portfolio. We can also see that Third Century, a Dreyfus fund, has been the top performer among the funds oriented toward long-term capital growth. Third Century permits telephone switching in $500 minimums too.

The *Switch Fund Advisory* graphs the cumulative performance of the funds, providing a most useful tool in evaluating their growth and potential. For instance, from the moving averages we see that our two gold funds are obviously both on the upswing. If we're thinking of switching to them, we should buy when the moving average shifts up. By the same token, we'll sell when the moving average moves down. The graph for Dreyfus Third Century shows that this fund appears to be at the end of an upswing. So we might wait another month before reviewing this fund again.

Current Yield and Performance Record of Mutual Funds
As of June 30, 1980

| Perf. Rank | Last Mo. | Mutual Fund Category | 1 Mo.% Perf. | 6 Mo.% Perf. | 12 Mo.% Perf. | % Current Yield | Total % Return |
|---|---|---|---|---|---|---|---|
| 1 | 1 | Gold funds | +10.9 | +30.1 | +124.0 | 2.6 | +126.6 |
| 2 | 2 | Long-term growth | + 4.3 | + 7.6 | + 26.5 | 2.7 | + 29.2 |
| 3 | 3 | Maximum capital gains | + 4.1 | + 4.0 | + 16.7 | 2.5 | + 19.2 |
| 4 | 4 | Growth with Current Income | + 2.2 | + 3.5 | + 12.3 | 4.8 | + 17.1 |
| 5 | 5 | Balanced funds | + 3.1 | + 5.9 | + 8.0 | 5.5 | + 13.5 |
| 6 | 6 | Income, stocks &/or bonds | + 2.2 | + 3.5 | + 0.7 | 8.3 | + 9.0 |
| 7 | 8 | Income, stocks only | + 0.7 | + 2.5 | + 3.1 | 5.0 | + 8.1 |
| 8 | 7 | Bonds, non-tax-exempt | + 0.5 | + 1.1 | - 4.8 | 10.8 | + 6.0 |
| 9 | 9 | Tax-exempt bonds | - 0.1 | - 3.8 | - 11.6 | 6.6 | - 5.0 |
|  |  | S&P 500 Composite | + 2.7 | + 5.8 | + 11.0 | 5.4 | + 16.4 |
|  |  | Dow Jones Industrials | + 2.0 | + 3.5 | + 3.1 | 5.9 | + 9.0 |

Note: Total % Return is the summation of last 12 Mo.% Perf. and the % Current Yield.

© 1980 James M. Schabacker

No-Load Mutual Fund Rankings by Category and Performance

| Perf Rank | Fund Name | Min. Inv. | Tel./ Mail | Fund Group | Assets (Mil $) | Share Nav | 1 Mo.% Perf. | 6 Mo.% Perf. | 12 Mo.% Perf. | % Yield | Total % Return |
|---|---|---|---|---|---|---|---|---|---|---|---|
| | | | | Objective: Golds | | | | | | | |
| 1 | United Services | $ 500 | NA | United Services | 52 | 6.84 | + 8.4 | +35.4 | +135.9 | 5.2 | +141.1 |
| 2 | Golconda | 500 | NA | Golconda | 4 | 14.15 | +13.3 | +24.7 | +112.1 | 0.0 | +112.1 |
| | | | | Objective: Long-Term Growth of Capital | | | | | | | |
| 1 | Third Century | $ 500 | T | Dreyfus | 62 | 23.27 | +6.2 | +12.0 | + 50.5 | 1.3 | + 51.8 |
| 2 | Cap. Opportunities | 300 | M | SteinRoe | 44 | 17.37 | +8.8 | +16.5 | + 43.0 | 1.5 | + 44.5 |
| 3 | New Era Fund | 1000 | T | Price (Rowe) | 310 | 18.78 | +7.7 | + 9.6 | + 40.4 | 2.8 | + 43.2 |
| 4 | Energy Fund | 100 | M | Neuberger | 272 | 21.13 | +4.7 | +12.5 | + 36.8 | 3.2 | + 40.0 |
| 5 | Number Nine | 500 | T | Dreyfus | 57 | 9.83 | +5.2 | +13.6 | + 37.3 | 1.8 | + 39.1 |
| 6 | Capital Shares | 500 | T | Bull & Bear | 29 | 10.38 | +5.0 | + 5.8 | + 32.4 | 1.7 | + 34.1 |
| 7 | S.R. Stock Fund | 300 | M | SteinRoe | 138 | 16.65 | +4.4 | +11.1 | + 25.5 | 2.8 | + 28.3 |
| 8 | Manhatten | 500 | T | Neuberger | 47 | 3.52 | +1.7 | + 3.2 | + 24.8 | 1.4 | + 26.2 |
| 9 | Scudder Common | 500 | T | Scudder | 125 | 12.51 | +2.2 | + 4.3 | + 17.7 | 3.4 | + 21.1 |
| 10 | Four Square Fund | 0 | M | Eaton & Howard | 6 | 9.04 | +2.1 | + 6.5 | + 14.3 | 3.5 | + 17.8 |
| 11 | Morgan (W.L.) Growth | 500 | M | Vanguard | 191 | 9.30 | +1.6 | - 1.8 | + 9.7 | 3.4 | + 13.1 |
| 12 | Growth Stock Fund | 500 | T | Price (Rowe) | 844 | 12.13 | +3.1 | + 0.9 | + 6.9 | 3.6 | + 10.5 |
| 13 | Windsor Fund | 500 | M | Vanguard | 639 | 10.17 | +2.9 | + 4.6 | + 5.3 | 5.1 | + 10.4 |

© 1980 James M. Schabacker

### How Do the Mutual Fund Families Feel About Switchers?

There are two schools of thought on switchers. On the negative side, some fund groups are concerned about the impact of switching on their portfolios. A fund that has long-term growth as its objective, for example, may be unduly influenced by switchers. Its assets may begin to swing widely, causing it to have to buy and sell part of its portfolio at less than ideal market times. Remember, if there's a heavy spate of selling by the fund's shareholders, the fund in turn must sell its holdings in order to come up with the cash to cover the redemptions. Many portfolio managers then rebel at such maneuvers, feeling they can't do their job properly under such circumstances.

On the other hand, mutual fund managers also recognize that in today's turbulent times there is no one best investment for everyone. They have to offer investors a wide variety of alternatives, and they have to live with the fact that those same investors will want to exercise the alternatives by switching.

*Mutual fund managers are now talking about "lifetime money management,"* in which the concept of switching plays an increasingly important role. The mutual fund industry has come to appreciate the changing roles of the funds and is working to provide investors with the services they want.

The one fly in the ointment for both investors and fund managers is the aggressive switcher, who dances to the beat of a different drummer. He's hard to predict, and that can cause problems.

How do the funds deal with this problem? Well, Fidelity, for instance, limits switching to five transfers a year—which is plenty—to minimize the disruption caused by superswitchers. Limits like this should not discourage you from switching, however, as its benefits can be substantial. Besides, when you have used up, say, your Fidelity switches, you can move into the Fidelity money fund and then, with a check, move on to the Dreyfus or the T. Rowe Price family of funds to start over with a clean slate. Where there's a will, there are relatives.

# 13

## Long-Term Alternatives—Sometimes They Make Sense

*At today's high interest rates, there's always the temptation to lock into the yields* of some five-year Treasury notes or long-term corporate bonds. That's fine—if you are absolutely sure inflation is completely under control.

Realistically, the probability of such a monumental economic occurrence as getting inflation under control is pretty slim—about equivalent to, say, the establishment of the Moscow Stock Exchange. Oh, there will be ups and downs. By the time you read this book, as a matter of fact, interest rates may well have plummeted from their early-1980s highs and thus have begun another ascent. Remember the old saying "What goes up must come down."

However, when applied to inflation and interest rates, the maxim should really read: What goes up must come down and go up again, and down, and up. . . . Remember President Ford's WIN (Whip Inflation Now) buttons? Inflation did subside after the buttons flopped. But it came right back again a few years later, stronger than ever.

As unhappy a circumstance as it is, inflation will be with us through the eighties and probably well beyond, unless the world suddenly comes to an end. In either event, long-term money market investments really won't hold their own against swollen interest rates. Interest rates are always below the inflation rate. When one rises, the other rises even more, while long-term investments plummet in investors' attempts to equalize yields.

But when it comes to money, there's always a way to make more by finding the exception to the rule. In the case of long-term alternatives for your cash, there are two such exceptions.

### Picking the "Flowers"

*Sometimes it pays to take the lowest possible yield.* The coyly named flower bonds are a case in point. Geared toward funerals, not weddings, these are special, old low-coupon government bonds that sell at a substantial discount from their face value. The 3.5 percent flower bonds due in November 1998, for instance, sell at 75 (100 is the face value) for a sterling actual yield of 5.56 percent—this at a time when money funds are paying 16 percent. Who needs that kind of return? An estate, that's who.

Flower bonds are accepted at face value for purposes of paying estate taxes if they are owned by the decedent at the time of death. In other words, every $750 worth of bonds owned by the decedent will pay $1,000 worth of taxes. For potentially large estates, these low-yielding long-term investments may make good financial sense.

### Seeking the Common Bond

Surprisingly, there are still other places for long-term bonds in financial planning. True, the bond market is in turmoil. And you may well say, "So what? I've never even seen a bond, and I'll probably never own one."

Actually, you may have done so and not realized it, since most company pension funds buy bonds as part of their investment. More important, now is the time to find out about bonds if you're not familiar with them. For many people, they represent an exotic investment available only to the rich. But they're a subject that should be of particular interest to parents with children who might be heading for college sometime within the next ten years.

At the moment the situation is so horrendous in the bond market that the current joke on Wall Street is: "How do you recognize a cowardly bond trader? He's the one who's volunteering to fight the Russians in Afghanistan." Now, when markets (and the jokes about them) are that bad, a few lucky people—or are they smart?—tend to make a lot of money. Your children could.

### Inflated Money, Deflated Bonds

Let's take a look at what's happening. More than anything else, the problem is that new bugaboo, inflation. Government reassurances and predictions aside, it's simply out of control. Over the long term, either this infla-tion will be brought under control or we will face an economic collapse not unlike that of the inflation that swept through Europe earlier in this cen-tury. In my opinion, it's an even-odds toss-up as to which happens.

If the end does come, those who have invested in gold, diamonds, and real estate may well come out ahead of the crowd. However, contrary to all that has been written about becoming rich during inflation, the holders of these real assets could also fare as poorly as, or even worse than, the rest of the population in the case of a true economic collapse.

Consider real estate, for instance. A lot of money has been made by small speculators in realty investment—and a lot lost. At the moment, many of those who have chosen to make their fortunes in housing may be facing their own financial Waterloo. As interest rates and costs rise, their properties begin to incur a negative cash flow. In plain English, they lose money. And because they have built their pyramid on borrowed money, the losses feed on themselves as quickly as the profits once did.

Fine as investments for engagement or anniversary rings, diamonds are almost impossible for the inexperienced to deal in purely as financial prop-erties. We simply don't know enough about them. Quality, the all-impor-tant consideration, is a highly subjective element, and even dealers are un-able to agree on it among themselves. In addition, as an individual, you are buying diamonds at retail and selling at wholesale. Read that sentence again. Does it seem backward to you? Well, it explains why the dealers are the ones who profit.

There is, of course, gold. I would never discourage anyone from buying gold coins. As the ultimate inflation hedge, the precious metal is hard to beat. While gold can be a high-risk investment, many financial advisers counsel keeping ten percent of your investible money in gold. And the easi-est way to invest in gold without restricting your liquidity is to invest—in no-load gold funds. Which brings us back to the disaster area on Wall Street.

Bonds are basically IOUs issued by a corporation or by the U.S. Trea-sury. They are backed either by the corporation's assets or, in the case of Treasury bonds, by the full faith and credit of the United States govern-ment. They are issued for specific time periods with a fixed rate of inter-est. And therein lie the bonds' current woes.

Consider the General Motors Acceptance Corporation bond issued a number of years ago at what was then the quite good interest rate of $7\frac{1}{8}$ percent per $1,000 bond. Would you buy it today? Certainly not, even though GMAC is a highly rated company. That is, you certainly wouldn't if it paid only 7⅛ percent. And neither would anybody else. Yet it's a high-quality bond with an active market, simply because there are always some investors who have to sell. There is an estate to be liquidated, for instance, or the bond owner needs the money to buy a new house, and so on.

In order to get someone to buy that 7⅛ percent bond in today's high-interest environment, however, the seller must be willing to part with it for considerably less than $1,000. As I write this, in fact, that bond is selling for $620. Such a bond is known as a deep discounted bond, and it means, in this instance, that for only $620 you can buy a promise from GMAC to pay you $1,000 when the note becomes due in 1990. Meanwhile, the corporation will pay you 7⅛ percent interest, or $72.50 annually. Did you notice that $72.50 is 7⅛ percent of the original $1,000 value of the note? At the $620 price let's say you paid for it, the yield is actually 11 percent. Plus you're making an extra $380, on top of the interest, in cold-cash capital gains at the end of ten years. Your $620 investment would show a gain of $1,105 by 1990. Altogether, you'd have $1,725 by then. So where's the catch?

Glad you asked. The catch is that plenty of people who bought these bonds when they were originally issued thought they were as great a deal. But they hadn't counted on interest rates skyrocketing the way they have. If interest rates continue their climb, the value of these bonds will continue to decline.

In 1990 they will be redeemable at their full $1,000 value. But a lot of people can't wait. They need the money now.

That's why I mention your children's college education. Let's say you have an eight-year-old child who will be ready to go to college in 1990. And let's say you've been saving $500 or so a year since that child was born, and, for the sake of keeping the numbers simple, you have $6,200 put away so far. You buy ten GMAC bonds for that amount, knowing you will not have to touch the money until the child goes to college.

### You Trade Liquidity for Yield

*The key is not needing to spend the money* until then. Even if the bond market continues its decline for a while—and the bond professionals themselves can't call the bottom and top of the market—you're still assured of having $17,250 from this one investment in 1990 when it's time for your child to start garnering a sheepskin.

There are two or three more points to consider. If you purchase the bonds in your child's name under the Uniform Gifts to Minors Act, or UGMA, the income tax liability should be close to zero. That means your child gets to keep almost all of that $17,250. One should note, however, that it also means you have given the money irrevocably to your child.

Secondly, to really make the most of the money, you should take the $6,200 and buy into a money market fund account in your child's name before investing the money in the bonds.

Once the account is open, you buy the bonds, and you are then able to deposit the semiannual dividend checks to the high-interest money market account. In this way the $6,200 should grow to approximately $20,000 in ten years.

Considering inflation, you should also continue to add $500 or so to the account annually, if possible, in order to really be able to finance an education. As the money accumulates in the account, more discounted bonds can be purchased every few years.

There are some bonds coming due every year, and that includes top-rated U.S. Treasuries. So whether your child has two years or twelve to go, you can find a bond that will mature at the same time your child's bills do. You can even buy bonds due for four consecutive years if you want to try to cover the entire cost of a college education over the time it takes to get a degree. Deep discounted bonds may not be the perfect way to save for a college education in this unpredictable world, but at the moment they may well be one of the best deals available for that purpose.

For another tack on long-term investments, look at money funds. Oh, I know, they invest in short-term money. But nothing in the financial world is static. In the midst of all the interest turmoil, along comes James Benham, founder of the original Capital Preservation Fund, with a new investment vehicle called Capital Preservation Treasury Note Trust. Specializing in U.S. Treasury notes with maturities of from 13 to 48 months, the fund is designed to capitalize on interest-rate fluctuations by locking into the high yields of the swings' peaks.

With its long-term orientation, the fund pays its dividends quarterly. It does not offer check-writing services. Though so new as not to have a real track record by which to judge its performance, Capital Preservation Treasury Note Trust has all the earmarks of a winning long-term money market investment.

# 14

## The Advanced, Aggressive Money Market Portfolio: Not for the Fainthearted

If the old saying "It takes money to make money" is a truism, nowhere is it more applicable than in the money market. While with the advent of money funds the small and the intermediate investor have been given a really profitable break, it's still the large investor who has the most options. The reason is simple. The larger investor can afford to avail himself of high-risk situations, which in turn can provide astronomical yields. He can also survive what would otherwise be devastating losses—on part of his savings.

### For the Well-Heeled Only

Even the most well-heeled investor should follow the three-part breakdown of his investment money into the categories of safety, liquidity, and yield. But once above the intermediate level, investors should add a fourth category, *R,* for the *radical* stance, to their investment strategy. (Oh, I know, the slogan should somehow be SLYER, or the preferred SLIER, but are you going to quibble over an E in an acronym if it's going to make you a bundle?)

### Who Qualifies?

*The radical ploys that can earn you 200 percent, 300 percent, or even more in the money market* are a lot easier to describe than the advanced investor himself. What exactly separates an advanced investor, so called, from an intermediate one? Where do you draw the line? At $20,000 in savings? $50,000? Or $100,000? That's a nice round number.

Personally, I prefer to define the break as a ratio of money, or a percentage. That way the cutoff moves along with inflation. After all, a decade ago someone with $10,000 in savings would have been considered reasonably well off. Today $10,000 is barely enough to buy a new car and the tankful of gas to drive it home.

The best description of the upper-income individual I've come across is the one stating that you've reached this financial status when more than half your earnings come from investments. Now, there's a nice neat definition that remains reasonably constant even during a dollar collapse.

To parallel this concept, one could also say that you're a large, or advanced, investor once your savings base exceeds three times your annual salary. In other words, if you're earning $20,000 a year and have $60,000 in the bank—or hopefully, by the time you've read this far, parked in a money fund—why, then you're in a position financially secure enough to utilize the more aggressive strategies of advanced moneymaking.

At the same time, if you're earning only $10,000 a year, you can begin to utilize these more advanced investment strategies with a savings base of only $30,000. And of course, if you're in the $50,000-per-annum category, you should have $150,000 socked away before you put into effect any high-risk strategies.

The reason for this proportional salary-to-savings cutoff for the advanced investor is, to put it quite simply, the high risk involved in truly aggressive investment. You must be able to sustain some capital loss without its affecting either your sleep or your economic security. If you lose the equivalent of six months' salary in a week and that's your entire savings base, you're back to square one. If it's only part of a three-year savings base, on the other hand, you have both a tax deduction and the income to offset it.

*Never take the high-risk-strategy route if you're undercapitalized.* Such a move could set your quest for security back years, not to mention destroying your morale. So count your pennies before you leap into the volatile world of superyields.

### Leveraging Your Investments with Futures Contracts

The way to really dramatic yields is through leverage. Leverage is one of the greatest financial tools ever devised for creating wealth, and also one of the riskiest. That's why you need the SLYR approach. The R, the fourth segment of your savings base, will be out on a limb of the money tree—a very long limb, in fact, one that has been known to break for even the shrewdest of speculators. But that precarious position is worth the risk—if you're in an advanced, aggressive investment position and can afford to take that risk.

*You can buy a million dollars' worth of T-bills with only $5,000.* That's one example of the kind of ploy the large-scale investor should take advantage of. But before you run those figures through your calculator and come up with the idea that a 10 percent T-bill is going to yield you $100,000 interest on your $5,000 investment, let me hasten to add that you don't get a cent of interest on that million-dollar T-bill.

Where you make the money is on the interest-rate fluctuations of the marketplace. For what you have either bought long or sold short is not actually a million-dollar T-bill, but rather the right to buy or sell that bill at some specific date in the future. You'll never really do it, however. What you will do is make money through the rise and fall of the potential value of that bill as the interest rates bob around. Essentially, the transaction treats money as a commodity like wheat or coffee, which, in fact, it is—the universal commodity, perhaps, the one in which all others are measured, but a commodity nonetheless.

It's not only T-bill futures that the sophisticated investor can use to soup up his yield machine. There are other financial futures to be dealt in as well, including Treasury bonds, GNMA, or Government National Mortgage Association, securities, and commercial paper. All these except the commercial paper contracts, which don't trade even $100 million a day, are large-scale, very liquid operations. Let's take a brief look at them and what they have to offer.

### Getting Acquainted with Ginnie Mae

The GNMA, or Ginnie Mae, contracts are traded on both the American Commodity Exchange and the Chicago Board of Trade. The basic contract calls for delivery of $100,000 worth of GNMA paper yielding 8 percent.

When the contracts were devised, 8 percent was good interest, and no one really expected it to go much higher. Adjustments have obviously been made in the general money market since then. But a commodity needs a fixed reference point. A financial commodity needs two. In this case, those two constants are the amount, $100,000, and the interest, 8 percent. They allow a third, variable factor, the actual yield, to fluctuate with the marketplace without the computations and bookkeeping becoming impossibly complicated. (As you'll soon see, they're not too simple, as it is.)

Ginnie Maes are quoted in the archaic $\frac{1}{32}$ form, in which each $\frac{1}{32}$ rise is worth $31.25 per contract. The normal trading limit is $\frac{24}{32}$, or $750 a day. That is, a GNMA future is not allowed to go up or down more than $750 a day. Of course, in an active market with wild interest rates, the rules change—which is fine if you're on the winning side, not so good if you're losing.

*That $750 represents a 25 percent yield—or loss—on the average $3,000 margin* currently required. Margins may vary from broker to broker and from time to time. But a 25 percent overnight yield is not atypical, even after commissions, which currently range from $35 to $100 per contract, depending on how good a customer you are (commissions are negotiable, remember), whether or not your transaction is a day trade (in which you buy and sell on the same day), and who your broker is.

Let's look at a CBT, or Chicago Board of Trade, futures transaction for July 15 and the following day, July 16, 1980. The September Ginnie Mae contract, that is, the one which would deliver a collateralized depository bank receipt or a certificate representing $100,000 at 8 percent to you in September—for which you would have to fork up the full trading value at that time unless you sold the contract beforehand, as most speculators do—was quoted as follows in the *Wall Street Journal:*

| | Open | High | Low | Settle | Chg | Yield Settle | Chg | Open Interest |
|---|---|---|---|---|---|---|---|---|
| Sept | 75-05 | 75-19 | 74-26 | 74-25 | −28 | 12.126 | +.176 | 13,366 |

The following day, the quote read:

| | Open | High | Low | Settle | Chg | Yield Settle | Chg | Open Interest |
|---|---|---|---|---|---|---|---|---|
| Sept | 75-07 | 76-18 | 75-06 | 76-11 | +1.18 | 11.813 | −.313 | 13,197 |

What do the figures mean? Well, the open, high, and low categories are pretty obvious. Those are the price at which the contract first traded that day, its highest price, and its lowest price, respectively. The opening, which was $75\frac{5}{32}$ on July 15 and $75\frac{7}{32}$ on July 16, may seem excessively low on a scale of 100 (100 being par, or the value at which a Ginnie Mae is normally redeemable). But remember that the fixed interest rate on this basically hypothetical security is 8 percent. Since it never varies, the actual price of the security swings with the prevailing interest rate. With rates close to 12 percent, an 8 percent security is only worth in the neighborhood of 75.

Instead of a closing price, a settlement price is listed. There are two reasons for this. First of all, there might be, and in fact usually are, dozens of trades at the last minute—the last second, actually. Which one is the very last? That's impossible to determine. So the exchange averages out the prices at which all the last trades occurred and thus determines a settlement price.

Another reason for having a settlement price instead of, for instance, a high-low range of closing prices for the last few minutes of trading has to do with that crucial factor, the velocity of money. Unlike stocks and bonds, for which you have to wait five business days after the sale for the settlement date, when you actually take possession of your money, interest rate futures settle daily.

In the example we're looking at, one September contract bought at the close of July 15 and sold at the close of trading on July 16 would have netted you the change, or 1.18—that is, $1 + {}^{18}\!/_{32}$, with each $\frac{1}{32}$ worth $31.25, for a total of $1,562.50. Now, there you have an example of a more than 50 percent return overnight—if you'd placed your money on the long side and bought a contract. If you'd been wrong, on the other hand, and sold short, you would have been out the same amount.

Since interest rate futures settle daily, you can instantly take your $1,500 profit and run. You can shift it, along with your $3,000 margin deposit, immediately into your money fund account. For that matter, if you are convinced that interest rates are going to continue to drop, you can deposit just the $1,500 profit and hold on to your Ginnie Mae future itself for another day, or another week, or whatever, withdrawing the profit each day. It's a dangerous way to live, but it's possible. And we are, after all, talking about a high-risk, superhigh-yield investment for only a small fraction of your savings base.

The yield figures, 12.126 on July 15 and 11.813 on July 16, are actually irrelevant except for charting and keeping track of interest rates. They represent what the marketplace thinks would be a good return for the real-world 8 percent Ginnie Maes in that future September.

The open interest represents the number of contracts outstanding, on a given day, in the particular month involved. In this case, on July 16 there were 13,197 September contracts outstanding, which is 169 fewer such contracts than there were the day before. In dollar amounts, what those figures mean is that traders were holding some $131,970,000 worth of

September Ginnie Mae futures, having liquidated another $1,690,000 worth to take a profit—or a loss.

### Talking Turkey on Trading T-bills

*Trading in T-bill futures is an abstraction to yet a higher degree.* Prices are quoted in terms of the abstract IMM—International Money Market of the Chicago Mercantile Exchange—index. Par is, as usual, 100. And the quote is simply the difference between the actual T-bill yield and 100. If the yield for a given month is 7.95, for instance, you know at once that the price should be 92.05 (100 − 7.95 = 92.05). The index is strictly an arbitrary one, but it's easy to work with.

Each .01 movement of the index is equivalent to $25 going into or out of your savings, based on the $1,000,000 represented by a contract. With a daily limit of .50, the rise and fall can mean a $1,250 gain or loss in one day on a single contract. If trading gets hectic, the limit is expanded to allow even greater price fluctuations.

The longer-term T-bonds are quoted in $\frac{1}{32}$ increments, and the overall operation of their market parallels that of GNMA trading, although, befitting their stature as the safest of securities, the T-bond contracts trade at a lower nominal interest rate. For instance, at a time when GNMA futures were listed as yielding 12 percent, T-bonds for the same month were quoted at 10.5 percent. The difference is a matter of no great importance to the trader, since he is attempting to profit from the change in the securities' underlying value as expressed in futures contracts. One of these days, however, someone watching the ratio is no doubt going to come up with a trading system based on it.

Now, it's not my intention here to give you a complete introduction to trading interest futures. That would require a volume or two of its own. Still, if you might be dealing in such futures, there are some fundamental trading principles of which you should be aware before you even go beyond this page.

### Futures Fundamentals

First, you should familiarize yourself with any commodity in which you are thinking of investing. If you're planning on trading in T-bill futures—and there's a psychological magic in wheeling and dealing in million-dollar amounts—start reading everything you can find about them, not only in

the futures contract, but in the real world as well. High among your perus-
al priorities should be the Money Rates listing in the *Wall Street Journal,* a
daily compilation of the key U.S. and foreign interest rates. Alongside it
you'll find a column giving the latest prognostications, gossip, and trend
analyses of the money markets.

*There are several key trading rules to keep in mind* as you prepare to
take the plunge into the risky world of futures. To begin with the absolutely crucial one, never start trading interest futures until your savings base
has reached the advanced investor's level. Even then, do not trade in such
a volatile market without accepting the idea of losing every cent in this
portion of your portfolio. Hopefully, that will not happen. But you need to
be prepared for the worst. The flip side of the superhigh-return coin simply
has to be superhigh losses.

Savvy investors, of course, will minimize their chances of loss wherever
possible. To this end, you'll want to work out your strategy before you invest. Trade this strategy, using the average maturity index for your direc-
tion-of-interest-rates predictions, on paper for at least three months, to give
yourself a feel for and a familiarity with the market. Then, and only then,
trade for real. Slowly. And stick to your system. Changing systems in mid-
trade, so to speak, almost always leads to a string of unexpected losses,
particularly if you shift and shift again.

Speaking of losses, the classic rule in trading is to cut your losses and
let your profits ride. It's a very hard rule to follow. For hope truly springs
eternal in the trader's heart—and his heart is usually in his throat while
he's participating in this volatile market. That's true for even the biggest
traders. Consider the $1.7 billion assets of the Greater New York Savings
Bank teetering on the financial high wires as I write this. The bank took an
exceptional loss of $40 million early in 1980 on Ginnie Mae trades. In view
of the explosive interest rise in the money market at the time and the
bank's size, perhaps such a loss should be attributed simply to bad timing.

But looking at it more closely, we see that it was greed combined with
a failure to follow the cut-your-losses rule that did it. At one point, the
bank's commitment to Ginnie Maes was $3 billion, which was almost twice
the bank's assets. And the Ginnie Maes involved were the genuine notes,
not futures. As for the second mistake, the cut-your-losses rule was violat-
ed in the worst possible way. According to the records, instead of selling
out early and cutting its losses, the bank actually kept adding to its position.

Even the big boys, you see, make mistakes. But that doesn't mean you have to.

As a private futures investor, of course, you will be thinking of the margin requirement, not the amount it controls, as the sum invested. Unlike such supersized investors as banks, most of us, after all, would find it rather difficult to develop a savings base where the $1 million face amount represented by a contract was a mere fraction of our total worth.

## Know When to Hold 'Em and When to Fold 'Em

There are two more basic rules for you to follow besides the original classic. First, don't be in the market all the time. When things look only average or uncertain, stay out. Even a sure bet isn't a sure bet in interest-rate futures. So all you need to really stack the deck against you is uncertainty. Second, don't overtrade. If things are going well, don't start buying all the contracts you can get your hands on. As sure as there are interest rate futures, you'll trip. So don't be greedy. Even as an advanced investor, you should settle for a gain of 300 to 400 percent a year on the high-risk sector of your portfolio—and be happy.

# 15

## Special Investment Problems and How to Solve Them

Money, as you well know by now, isn't the same for everyone. Quantitatively, investors who have more of it have more opportunities to increase their savings base. But it's not only the amount of money they have that influences their investment decisions. In order to maximize benefits for their special needs, investors may find themselves in situations that call for managing their resources differently than the general public might.

### Where Women's Liberation Really Counts

*The largest share of personal wealth in this country is actually controlled by women.* Yet the financial markets take little cognizance of the fact. Many women are not yet able to operate in the money market the way a man does. Financially speaking, women are still—let's face it—second-class citizens. And unless women make a few extra maneuvers with their money, they will remain so, at least under current conditions.

The credit rights of women, one of their master keys to the world of financial growth, have been equalized—on paper. But there's nothing automatic about it. A woman must manipulate the market in order to be recognized as an equal. Here's one place where money funds can be used to yield more than simply above-average dividends. They can yield above-average credit ratings too, as we'll see in a moment.

### No Credit Where Credit Is Due

In and of themselves, money fund holdings do little for your credit rating. Even running up thousand-dollar debts makes you a more acceptable credit risk than having $20,000 or $30,000 cash in a money fund. Why? Simply because there's no outside verification of your fund holdings for a cred-it bureau or a potential creditor to call upon. Sure, you can bring in a statement or your latest dividend check. But that's not the same as the in-formation-seeker's calling up a bank and speaking to someone in charge, or getting a nice computer printout from a credit card company indicating how far it's let you run up your bills. Your word alone often isn't good enough, particularly if you're a woman.

Of course, credit discrimination is against the law these days, and has been since President Ford signed the Equal Credit Opportunity Act in 1974. At most banks you'll find a sign to that effect right next to the plac-ard announcing that your savings are insured up to $100,000. Neither the law nor the sign, however, assures you of anything unless you take a stand. Fight for your money—or lose it slowly to inflation.

It may sound absurdly elementary, at this point, to stress that if you are a woman, *you must have a bank account in your own name.* Yet most married women have only a joint account with their husband. A joint ac-count won't do, although the credit laws are supposedly remedying the drawbacks of that type of account for credit-rating purposes right now. What you need is an account in your name alone. Psychologically it makes a big difference to both you and your broker.

This doesn't mean eliminating joint accounts for married couples. There can be real advantages to these too, depending on how the family fi-nances are handled. But that account in your name alone may be the key to credit should you, for instance, suddenly become widowed. Without it, your financial world might well come to a sudden standstill. The bills, how-ever, most certainly would not.

Bills, even the relatively small ones, such as those you run up at the grocery store, should always be paid by check from your account. It's even more important to pay the large bills, like, say, the one for the second car, by check. If the family needs a second car, buy it with your own money. If you don't have enough money for it, ask your husband to channel some of his through your account. Then you pay the bill and flowing through your account is the first step in establishing your independent financial standing. That goes for the small bills too, of course. In the case of a detailed credit investigation, if you couldn't show that you'd earned enough for the car, that particular maneuver would be only marginally helpful, but you have to start somewhere.

The next step in establishing your credit is to *get yourself a credit card as soon as possible* if you don't already have one. Then charge everything that can be charged. But do be cautious about what you buy. Your new-found credit doesn't mean newfound money. A credit card is a wonderful way to build up your credit rating—or destroy it.

Does it sound contradictory for me to say that you should charge everything you can after I've said you should pay for everything you can by check? It's not really contradictory. It's complementary—or should I say compounding? For you'll be paying your credit bill by check. So a $100 purchase, for example, will actually show up twice on your credit record—once on your charge card statement and once on your checking account statement. You're not spending any more money, but you are generating a better credit record.

After you've acquired these two basic credit tools, what's your next move in improving your standing in the world of finance? Well, you can use a money fund to paint a rosier picture of your financial situation for your local banker at the same time that it's earning you more on your money than his bank can pay you.

First, you need to determine the closing date on your checking account. That's the date each month on which your account is balanced prior to the statements being mailed out to you. Just look back at your past months' statements and see when the last check entered was debited. On the 6th, the 15th, the 21st of the month? The actual date itself doesn't matter. It will be consistent for your account. If you write checks infrequently—and by now you know you shouldn't—the next time you're at the bank, simply ask which day of the month the statement for your particular account is closed.

Once you know the closing date, deposit a large money fund check directly to your checking account two days before this date. On the closing date, write your money fund a check on your bank account. Vary the amount of the checks from month to month, and sometimes withdraw two or three smaller checks instead of the large one. Overall, you'll lose only three or four days' interest on your money fund cash.

But that seems like just spinning wheels, you say. The money is simply rushing back and forth in a lot of senseless activity. Well, there's a lot of activity, yes, but it's far from senseless. The money involved remains the same, but your average monthly checking account balance now includes the savings in your money fund as well. For credit records, you look as if you're spending a lot more money every month than you really are. Rather than being a small, inactive saver, you are now a large, active one. Guess who has the better credit rating?

Building up a solid credit rating puts any woman on an equal financial footing with a man. From there on in, the game plan is the steps in asserting your rightful financial position.

### New Money for Your Old Age

*Retirement poses another specialized money management problem.* The future of social security is very much in doubt. It won't disappear. But you may find that by 1990 you have to be seventy-five to start collecting, or that the payments are greatly reduced, or . . . You fill in the negatives. There are more than enough to choose from. That leaves the private pension fund—if you're fortunate enough to have one—to take out an income for your golden years.

Of course, the private funds have their own problem, and that's the 10 percent inflation. As J. Anthony Forstmann of Forstmann-Leff Associates, a firm managing some $1.2 billion worth of private pension fund money, put it in a *New York Times* interview: "The pension system in this country is a phony promise. You can't run inflation at this order of magnitude and have the promise survive. The standard of living of retirees has to decline rather dramatically."

Consider a fixed pension for someone retiring in 1980. By 1985, each dollar of pension would have a purchasing power of only 62 cents if inflation averaged 10 percent. If the same inflation rate continued through the decade, then by 1990 that dollar would be worth all of 39 cents. Whatever you do, don't plan to live too long after you retire. For should you survive twenty-five years, that dollar wouldn't be worth even a dime.

If you are retired now, or about to enter that state of bliss, your options are somewhat limited. Obviously, your funds should be earning the maximum money fund rates whenever possible. At the moment, you can't have your social security checks deposited directly to your money fund account the way you can with your bank account. However, as inflation boosts the size of the social security payments, the checks will begin to approach the minimum required for deposit by most money funds, and just such a direct-deposit system will no doubt be devised.

The banks can be expected to fight such a plan vigorously. Still, with at least a show of emphasis on consumer concerns by the government, the banks' resistance should be overcome. Look for the availability of direct deposits of social security checks to money funds by 1984 (an election year) if not before. And take advantage of the plan as soon as it makes its winding way down to the end of the bumpy road of legislation.

Automatic withdrawal plans are already available from the funds. You can have a monthly check sent to you covering the dividends earned by your savings. Let's say you have a $50,000 saving base in a money fund yielding 12 percent. An automatic monthly check for $500 can be sent to you. As overall interest rates fluctuate, of course, your monthly check will be more or less than $500. However, representing only dividends paid out, this arrangement leaves your capital untouched.

An alternative would be to have a fixed-amount monthly check sent to you. Assuming the same figures, $50,000 savings and a 12 percent yield, $500 could be withdrawn automatically each month. As long as interest rates stayed above 12 percent, you would then actually be adding to your capital even while receiving the $500 monthly payment. Below 12 percent interest, however, you would be eating into your savings base.

On the whole, under this last kind of plan, you would be better off simply writing yourself a check for $500 each month instead of having the fund mail you one, because then you would be earning money until your check cleared. When the fund mails you a check, the days it spends in transit represent lost dividends.

At the time of this writing, some funds are contemplating using automated clearing houses that would electronically deposit money directly in banks on a same-day basis. Keep your eyes open for this feature and take advantage of it as soon as it arrives—if it's to your benefit. It will mean losing those three or four days' dividends that accrue while the check you write yourself clears. So be sure it's really to your advantage.

It's certainly to the money fund's advantage. An electronic transaction costs the fund about a nickel. Writing and processing a check costs just as much plus postage.

In the case of either dividend withdrawal or fixed-amount withdrawal, there is one limitation to take into account. The amount involved each month must equal or exceed the fund's minimum check requirement.

*If you are retiring in the more distant future, there are several money market approaches to building up a nest egg.* One new wrinkle is combining money fund management with an insurance annuity. Now, if there's one basket you don't want to put your eggs in during inflationary times, it's a fixed-income annuity. The annuity funds I'm talking about are a different breed, however.

Annuities have been offered by insurance companies for a long time. They allow you to defer all taxes on the dividend income until the annuity is terminated. At that point, of course, you have to decide what to do about all those tax-deferred dividends.

But the real problem with these annuities has always been that you earned a fixed rate of return, say 3 or 5 percent—ridiculous in this day and age. Now, however, money fund managers have gotten together with insurance executives to come up with a variable annuity, one that earns high money market rates and/or allows you to take capital appreciation. The potential of this new way of participating in the money market is so great that I've written an extra chapter on the subject, just as this book goes to press.

### Money Funds—A Cash Management Tool for Business

*Small businesses are another category of money managers ready for the profitable use of money funds.* Somehow the idea has circulated among investors that money funds are for personal use only, that they aren't to be used by businesses. Nothing could be further from the truth. As I have pointed out, the original money funds were developed precisely with small businesses in mind—small in this instance referring to companies that didn't have a $100,000+ float around to invest.

The market changed radically with the advent of the money funds. Now a business doesn't need even $20,000 or $30,000 in cash in order to take advantage of the profitable money market. Just about any amount will do. So the local businessman, be he the owner of a pet store, a dry-cleaning establishment, or a small manufacturing concern, can and should integrate a money fund into his overall financial plan. Nearly two hundred thousand companies of all sizes currently have accounts at money funds.

My company, for instance, is the leader in its particular area of publishing. But it's far from being a McGraw-Hill or a Doubleday. Even though we publish three newsletters and present seminars and conferences all over the country, we're still a small business.

Our bills, on the other hand, usually don't seem so small. They come in from all over the place, from printers, speakers, hotels, and of course, American Express—bless 'em—for my travel expenses. Since most of these bills are for amounts over $500, we pay them with money fund checks. In one active six-month period, we earned over $2,000 in dividends simply by managing our cash using the money funds. I mean to tell you, it was a lot easier earning $2,000 that way than by traveling and lecturing.

*Look for the hidden cash in your business.* Then deposit it to your money fund. The amount of underutilized cash in business, even with today's sophisticated cash management, is staggering. One fast-food franchise out in Long Island, as a money fund manager tells the story, left $36,000 sitting in its checking account year after year. It could have been earning an additional $5,000 a year in interest at the current money fund rates.

But, you say, as a small business you have to leave a compensating balance at the bank to keep your rating up. It will mean an easier time for you in case of a future credit crunch. Wrong. Chances are that if you're not credit worthy when the next crunch or recession comes, no amount of compensating balances or good turns over the years past is going to help you.

Now, no one is saying it doesn't help to have a friendly banker on your side, particularly when the going gets rough. But your banker doesn't expect you to play the fool, either. He is, after all, getting a lot of your business. So consider paying for some of the bank services that are provided "free" for those who maintain a compensatory balance in their accounts, rather than maintaining the balance. Don't forget, too, that service charges are a deductible expense for tax purposes. The loss of interest you accept in getting these services "free" doesn't show up anywhere except on the bank's profit statement. So balance out all factors, and I think you'll find you can reasonably reduce your account to a minimum.

Level with your banker. Tell him exactly what you're going to do and why. Then when he sees a dramatic leveling off in your company's cash flow through his bank, he won't be worried about your going under. He'll understand that you're simply trying to put idle cash to work, trying to strengthen your company financially. As you grow, he stands to grow too. So he may look much more favorably than you might have thought on your taking some money out of his bank. He knows that whether it's personal money or company money that's involved, good cash management is the key to survival these days.

# 16

## Money Market Annuities—Adding Flexibility to Your Retirement Financing

*The latest wrinkle in the money market game is called a money market fund based variable annuity.* Now, that's a real mouthful, so let's just call it a money market annuity. Whatever you dub it, not only is this new approach to money management profitable, but it lets you defer taxes on the profits you make as well. Money market annuities don't allow you to eliminate taxes completely—no such luck. However, by deferring your taxes until such time as your tax rate is lower than it is during your peak earning years, you can at least reduce your tax load substantially.

Just as important in your long-range planning is the fact that since you are deferring taxes, the entirety of your high money market profits remains untouched for years. Your profits thus can be earning more profits until that inevitable date with the taxman. And they'll be earning profits for you rather than for the taxman.

But, you point out, this sounds just like a Keogh or an IRA retirement plan. Well, in some ways money market annuities do resemble these retirement plans. However, there are some big differences between the Keogh and IRA plans and variable rate annuities.

- *The crucial advantage of a money market annuity is that you withdraw the principal any time you want to, without paying penalties or taxes.* If you have a Keogh or an IRA plan, on the other hand, and you need to withdraw cash for some emergency, you are in big trouble. Expensive trouble, time-consuming trouble. Not only do you have to pay a penalty and extra taxes, but you have to refigure your income tax for all the years the plan has been in effect. You have to "undeduct" all those deductions you took for your Keogh or IRA contributions.
- *Another crucial difference is that you never have to liquidate a variable rate annuity as you do a Keogh or IRA plan.* You can use it as part of

your estate planning by, for instance, withdrawing all your capital, without paying taxes, upon retirement, and then using the accumulated earnings remaining in the account to purchase an annuity for your chidlren or grandchildren. When they finally cashed in the annuity, they would have to pay taxes on it. But by then the accumulated amount in the annuity would be so staggering they really wouldn't mind.

• *A third difference—a factor on the negative side for some savers—is that your contributions to money market annuities, unlike those to the IRA or Keogh plans, are not tax deductible.* But this is also the feature that enables you to withdraw the contributions to a variable rate money fund without any further ado and tax penalties.

### Switching with Annuities

Most annuity funds allow switching. You can push your savings around among money funds, bond funds, and stock funds to take advantage of fluctuating interest rates. Keeping the cash in a money fund when overall interest rates are high and then transferring it to a stock or a bond fund when interest rates fall generates much more profit than does simply leaving the money sitting, drawing whatever the prevailing rate of interest might be. And all the while your money is sheltered from the taxman.

*The only "leak in the shelter" is sprung by switching to a stock fund.* All annuities, even those from a brokerage house or mutual fund group, are actually issued by insurance companies. The sellers team up with the insurance companies as issuers because, under an insurance plan, the earnings from interest and dividends can be sheltered. Capital gains, however, are always treated differently from dividend and interest income. And in this instance the difference works against you, for in the case of capital gains distributions from a mutual fund, the insurance company is required to withhold 28 percent for capital gains tax. This essentially means that except in an explosive stock market rally, where the after-tax yield of a stock fund exceeds the money market yield, you should not switch into a stock fund.

The exception I've just referred to is a once-in-a-decade occurrence. However, when it happens, be prepared to latch on to the profits.

### Flash from the Money Market Front

I interrupted this book just as it was going to press because of a conversation with an executive of the Putnam Fund. Putnam is the distributor of the Galaxy variable annuity.

Galaxy allows you to switch your annuity into the Putnam Investors Fund, a concentrated portfolio of long-term growth stocks, without any withholding tax for capital gains. How do they do it? It's simple. The portfolio managers are instructed to trade all the stocks in the fund so that the holdings will always be less than 364 days. Since the fund has no holdings over a year, there are no capital gains.

Where there's a dollar to be saved, there's a way. Now back to the original book on press.

### Choosing an Annuity Fund

Besides the tax deferment distinction, there are other factors differentiating annuity funds from money funds. Here are the ones to take into consideration when choosing an annuity fund.

- First, there's the little matter of *sales and redemption charges*. Some annuity funds have them. Look out for your money.
- Second, there are the *annual fees*. These currently range from $25 plus 0.95 percent of the assets per year to $30 plus 1.4 percent of the assets per year. As yet there's no annuity fund that does not have annual fees. But you can expect this to be an area where competition heats up.
- The *minimum initial investment* ranges from $1,000 to $3,000. This and the minimum subsequent investment are both important considerations in tailoring an annuity plan to your pocketbook.
- Finally, check on the fund's *flexibility of payout*. You need a plan that gives you the option of either a lump sum payout or monthly checks.

The one thing you can be sure of in picking an annuity is that there *will* be one that's right for you. So let's look at the possibilities for the future using a money market annuity.

### How to Spend the Money and Still Have Three Times as Much Left Over

Let's say you're forty-five years old, the children have moved out, and you suddenly find that a house half the size of the one you've got would be a lot more convenient. You simply don't need that big old four-bedroom heat-it-till-you're-broke barn anymore. So you sell it. And, having had it for years, you make a big profit, even after buying a new comfortable-for-two house that gives you the low-upkeep freedom you want. With the savings in the bank, the extra money from the house sale, and the reduced expenses of a smaller family, chances are you can put together $100,000 in cash.

Let's look at what would happen if you put that money into a variable rate annuity. The annuity used as an example here is Old Republic Life of New York, an extremely conservative annuity, since it is calculated with a guaranteed minimum yield of 7.25 percent. With a bit of fund switching, and staying on top of the money market, you should be able to get at least 10 percent. But let's stay conservative. If the return looks good at 7.25 percent, think how much better your investment will look at 10 percent.

*Ten years after you purchased your $100,000 annuity, it will have grown in value to $201,135.* Now, let's say that when you're fifty-five, you suddenly need money. Perhaps you decide to switch careers, and you need cash to start a business. Or perhaps devastating hospital bills hit. Or there's a real estate deal simply too good to pass up. Or you just want to have some fun. Never mind the actual reason. You begin to draw $10,000 a year from your annuity account. You do so for a full ten years, until the $100,000 of your original investment has been completely eliminated from the account. You pay no taxes on this $10,000 annual withdrawal. It doesn't affect your taxable gross.

Meanwhile, the interest keeps accumulating on what is left in the account—that is, the tax-deferred profit from your original investment. At the end of another ten years, when you are sixty-five and ready to retire, the annuity will have a value of $264,974. Note that *this does not include the original $100,000 investment, for you've spent that.*

At the age of sixty-five, you can cash in the annuity for one $264,974 lump sum. If you do so, you'll be socked with a large tax bill. How large it is, of course, will depend on your tax bracket that particular year.

*You can build up your cash even more,* however, by leaving half of the money in the annuity contract untouched and buying a straight life annuity providing $13,768 a year for fifteen years. The annual payments will be taxable, but considered as supplements to social security, they should certainly carry you along. The half of your money remaining in the variable annuity meanwhile keeps on growing.

At the age of eighty years, when the $13,768 annual payments from your straight life annuity cease, you will have $351,675 remaining in your annuity fund. Again you can either draw it out in a lump sum or buy another straight life annuity and leave the extra capital untouched.

With this incredible program, then, you draw out your original $100,000 investment, plus another $206,520 in annual payments during retirement, and you end up with $351,675 in spare cash. With that you could purchase an annuity for the third generation of your family, and it would net them several million dollars when they finally cashed in the chips.

Is it any wonder that when Howard Stein, chairman of the mutual fund company Dreyfus Corporation, spoke of variable rate annuities, he said, "The money market fund was the innovation of the 1970s. I think this product will be the innovation of the 1980s."

# 17

## Money Funds and the Taxman

If money funds are the guardian angels of your savings base, then the tax-man is most certainly Lucifer. Even if it's not the case, you're going to have the devil to pay, there being extremely few sources of capital gains in the money market.

### Paying the Devil His Dues

Actually, although you can't count on it, you may find the devil's pitchfork somewhat blunted in the future. For there is a genuine tax revolt brewing in this country, which can be expected to come to a head during the eighties. A special IRS study indicates that a rapidly growing number of Americans are not only fed up with exorbitant taxes, but are asserting constitutional, religious, or moral reasons for not paying their federal income taxes as well. (One may wonder how many millions of dollars such an enlightening study cost. No matter. It was, after all, paid for by tax money.)

According to the study, the taxpayers' mood is turning ugly. In some areas of the country, agents are beginning to fear for their lives. Already, in fact, "IRS employees have experienced a wide range of threats, assaults and harassments from members of the illegal tax protest movement. In certain parts of the country—rural areas more than urban—violent protest has occurred. In many of these situations a seizure of property for nonpayment of taxes has evoked threats and assaults."

None of this is news, really. Revenuers have been shot at by moonshiners and other rural folk since the initiation of taxation.

*What's startling is that the IRS has declared tax protests illegal.* Not filing an income tax form is a criminal offense. The actual nonpayment of taxes is not really a criminal offense, although it does subject you to all kinds of fines and penalties. Now, however, the IRS has gone on record as stating that even protesting taxes is illegal. That's some step. But it shows you how determined the agency is to nail you if you step out of line. So does the fact that in the first nine months of 1979 alone, 100 protesters were convicted, for a total of 533 months in jail terms and fines of $1.4 million.

With that kind of determination, frankly, fighting the payment of taxes simply isn't worth it unless you are truly dedicated to the cause. For the average investor and citizen, tax protests don't make sense in terms of either money or time. So pay what you must—but not a penny more.

This admonition is particularly relevant for the self-employed and those receiving a substantial portion of their income from nonsalary sources. Besides the previously mentioned tactic of always using a money fund check to pay the IRS, a crucial ploy is to never overcredit your quarterly tax payment.

### The 80 Percent Rule—A Guideline for the '80s

You must keep 80 percent of your owed federal income taxes paid up at all times. Otherwise you are subject to interest charges, penalties, and sleepless nights. But the law requires 80 percent, not 100 percent.

Yet, fearful, many people pay the full amount or even a little extra. Worse yet, self-employed individuals often don't realize that the 80 percent is an estimate based on the *previous* year's income. If your income is irregular, there is indeed no other valid measure. After all, a year may start out with a fortuitous financial bang and then peter out into several checkless months. If you earned, say, $20,000 last year, that's the only thing your estimate for this year can reasonably be based on, even if you end up earning $30,000. If, for another example, in 1980 you paid $5,000 in federal income tax and by some lucky chance you make a fortune in 1981 on which you can expect to pay $50,000 in taxes, the 80 percent rule applies to the $5,000, not to the $50,000. In other words, your estimated tax payment for 1981 would be $4,000, not $40,000. It's all perfectly legal to keep that extra $36,000 for the year. However, when the final 1981 tax is due, you will, of course, have to pay it. In the meantime, you can earn a great deal of extra interest income through intelligent money market investment. Remember, it's not until the final quarter's payment that you can really determine the year's full result and make an extra payment if one is necessary. Meanwhile, your cash keeps earning high money market returns.

Let's look at the hypothetical case of two lawyers. Oh, yes, even lawyers make mistakes, and one of ours is going to. Let's say both our lawyers owe an estimated $20,000 in taxes for the year. Supercautious, Esq., overpays by $1,000 each quarter, sending in $6,000—"just in case." It doesn't really matter, since he'll get a refund. Close to the Vest, Esq., on the other hand, makes quarterly payments of just $4,000, 80 percent of the $5,000 payments required.

He puts the other $2,000 in a money fund the first quarter and each subsequent quarter. When he files his final income tax report, he pays the necessary $4,000.

Supercautious, Esq., receives a $4,000 refund—eventually. But meanwhile the money fund has made a considerable difference in our two lawyers' finances. Close to the Vest, Esq., with his $4,000 still invested in the fund plus another $600 to $1,000 in interest (depending on the rate) earned over the year on those quarterly $2,000 deposits, is well ahead in the money game.

Keeping this advantageous maneuver in mind, let's look at some bad news. One investor inquiring into the status of money fund income from a tax standpoint was told by an IRS official to report it as interest, since the income was derived from a bank-type financial institution. The IRS official was wrong, of course, and later corrected himself. Money fund earnings are, in fact, considered dividends for tax purposes. But they are a special kind of dividend, not eligible for the current $100 (or $200 on joint returns) dividend exclusion. This exclusion is limited to income from stocks.

And yes, your money fund will send you a copy of the 1099 form, or rat sheet, as it's known in the trade—the same one they send to the IRS informing them of the good news that they can expect to get more money out of you. So don't expect your money fund earnings to be overlooked.

*On the state tax level, there is an interesting ploy called the pass-through.* Unfortunately, it doesn't seem to be working, New York State being the latest casualty. Still, you should check with your fund on the possibility of any pass-through tax savings.

Essentially, the pass-through factor is a product of those funds investing entirely or in part in T-bills. Treasury bills are exempt from state and local taxes. Hence, the argument goes, earnings from a fund investing in these instruments should be exempt as well. However, New York State recently came to the conclusion that it would like its money and that the argument didn't hold water. Obviously, if New York State can tax these nontaxable earnings, then other states will probably do so too. Nevertheless, examine your own specific situation carefully, just in case someone in your local government happens to have retained his sanity.

There are legal ways to keep the taxman away from your money fund. But make sure they're not more expensive than simply paying the taxes would be. We've all become so IRS conscious—and rightfully so—that the words "tax exempt" seem almost magic.

### Tax-Free Money Funds

Tax-free money funds do exist. And queries about them are among the most frequent we get. The truth is, however, that they are not a viable medium for the average investor. Why not? Simply because their yield is proportionately lower than that of the taxable funds. At a time when ordinary money funds are yielding over 12 percent, the tax-free hybrids are yielding a little less than 6 percent.

Let's look more closely at what these funds are and when it pays to buy into them. Currently the five leading tax-free funds are Chancellor Tax-Exempt Daily Income Fund, Federated Tax-Free Trust, Fidelity Tax-Exempt Money Market Trust, Scudder Tax-Free Money Fund, and Warwick Short-Term Municipal Fund. All of them work on the same underlying principle. They invest in high-grade, short-term, tax-exempt securities. A new wrinkle is the short-term aspect of their portfolios.

Tax-free funds have been around for a long time. But recently they've had their portfolios murdered. As interest rates skyrocketed, their bond holdings plummeted in value because they were long-term obligations with relatively low yields. The forty-six municipal funds tracked by Lipper Analytical Services lost at least 7 percent of their principal in 1979. Some lost as much as 10 percent. And that was before interest rates really hit the fan early in 1980.

To make matters even worse, an investor, even one in the 50 percent tax bracket, retains more money after taxes from a general money fund yielding 13 percent than from a tax-free fund paying around 5 percent. Thirteen percent minus the half due the taxman leaves 6.5 percent. That's still a full percent and a half more than a tax-free 5 percent.

And so the hybrid municipal bond fund was born. Fund managers reasoned that interest rates were going to remain volatile, and therefore the way to avoid capital losses was to stay with short-term investments as the money funds were generally doing. What they had in mind, however, was not the 40–50 days around which the standard money funds kept their average maturities, since municipal investments with such time limits would be hard to come by in quantity. But by keeping the average dates to maturity in the 150-to-300-day range rather than in the traditional 10-to-20-year range, the municipal bond funds would be pretty well insulated against capital losses.

The yield of the new hybrid bond funds is less than that of the older tax-exempt funds because short-term paper almost always pays less than long-term paper. As John C. Bogle, chairman of the Vanguard Group, which is Warwick's sponsor, put it: "The longer-term bonds offered higher yields but additional price risk." It's the old trade-off between liquidity and yield all over again.

And yield can be a real problem for these funds any time general interest rates decline below 10 percent. That's why the tax-exempt money funds are simply not workable alternatives for most investors. It's a nice dream, that, not paying taxes. But remember, the after-tax yield of a regular money fund must be below that of the tax-free fund before the tax-free one pays. This usually happens only when you're in the 60 percent tax bracket or better. Even being in the 50 percent tax bracket isn't what it used to be.

### A Loophole on Your Keogh or IRA

A more profitable way to avoid taxes, or at least to defer them to a later date when your rates will supposedly be lower, is, as I've mentioned, to channel your retirement savings through a Keogh or an IRA plan where possible. However, there is an additional little money-earning twist you can take advantage of to get two months' interest a year on the untouchable cash tucked away in your IRA plan. Unfortunately, it doesn't work for the Keogh plan as well.

In effect, you give yourself an interest-free two-month loan from your retirement plan. That is to say, you pay no interest. There's nothing that says you can't earn interest for those two months instead of your IRA plan getting it.

Basically, the law allows you to shift your IRA account from one custodian to another once a year, and it gives you sixty days in which to do so. You must deposit in the new custodial account the same amount that you withdraw from the old one. But you don't have to do it the same day. In fact, you can put the money into a money fund account for the intervening two months. Parking the money between its departure from one IRA plan and its deposit to the next gives you sixty days' interest on the principal, interest that would otherwise be untouchable until your retirement.

Obviously, this is not an operation to put into effect continuously. First of all, you're only allowed to do it once a year. More important, the reason you set up an IRA plan is to supplement your social security payments when you retire. Since we all know social security simply isn't going to cover our needs—if indeed it doesn't go under before we retire—we don't want to cut into the accumulation of capital in our retirement plans very often. But the ploy is handy to know about in case of an emergency.

There are two points to keep in mind, though. You must deposit to your IRA account the full amount withdrawn and that deposit must be made within sixty calendar days, not business days. Fail to abide by these restrictions, and you're in for a heap of complications, not to mention tax penalties.

### MMCs Have a Sometime Advantage

*When it comes to money market certificates and the taxman,* another game plan may be in order. A money market certificate, unlike a money fund, does not pay its accumulated interest until the certificate matures. Consider a year when your dividend and interest income is running exceptionally high, or when your earnings are inflated by stock profits or the sale of other assets. You want to keep your cash invested, of course, but knowing you'll probably be making less money the following year, you would like to defer taking your interest income until then. The way out of the dilemma is simple. You buy a money market certificate in July. Since it doesn't mature until the following year, the interest is not recorded for tax purposes until then. Your money earns interest this year, but you don't get it until the beginning of next year. And the taxman, well, he doesn't get his until the year after that, when you file. Be absolutely sure, however, that your bank does not credit you with the MMC's interest until it actually matures. If, by a generous fluke, your bank credits you with MMC interest quarterly, the ploy will not work, even if you do not withdraw that interest. The IRS rule is that as soon as money is credited to you it becomes taxable.

### Corporate Investments

Another option, open to self-employed professionals such as doctors, lawyers, and Indian chiefs, is incorporation. A step of this nature obviously requires the assistance of a knowledgeable attorney and CPA. However, a point of interest often overlooked in weighing the advantages of incorporation is that the dividends earned by a corporation from its holdings in common and preferred stock of other corporations are 85 percent tax free. You pay taxes on only 15 percent of your dividend earnings if you're a corporation.

This is a rule of almost ancient standing, being based on one of the earliest Supreme Court decisions, back in the 1800s. The logic behind it is that a corporation's earnings have already been taxed, and therefore the stock-possessing corporation should not have to pay taxes a second time. Double taxation and all that.

You as an individual, of course, pay taxes too. So for you it's also double taxation.

Never mind trying to apply logic. Unless you're incorporated, it doesn't work. You're taxed on the full 100 percent of your dividends. Sounds like a game, doesn't it?

Well, that's what it is. Personal money management is a high-stakes game. If you don't play it to the full, your savings will be in trouble. So take advantage of every little twist and turn you can. If it's legal and profitable, do it. If it's questionable, don't. Play the game hard, and play to win. But when you play with the taxman, play by the rules.

# 18

## Moving Money Profitably

Most people think of money as a physical object. It has a static aura about it. Yet that twenty-dollar bill in your wallet is only a symbol. You don't need the symbol to use the money's purchasing power. You can pay for something by check or by credit card. The moment you do so, the seller considers the item paid for even though no money has physically left your possession. In today's world, it is possible to cover a full month's worth of business and personal transactions without physically handling any money at all.

### Creating Money

So what? you ask. Everyone knows about the explosive growth in credit cards and personal checking accounts during the last couple of decades. Credit is no different from paying in cash, except that in the case of credit cards you end up being billed a few weeks after your purchases.

But therein lies a crucial point that is often overlooked. It's not the element of putting off paying for something a week or two by using a credit card. Most people have that worked into their spending pattern. No, it's the fact that, because of the time factor, you *can actually create money*—just as the Treasury does, though unfortunately not with the same ease.

If you have $500, and you buy a $500 freezer with a credit card, paying for it thirty days later, for that period of time you actually have $1,000. You have, after all, your $500 plus the $500 freezer. Pay the credit card company with a money fund check, and it will probably take ten days for the check to clear. You receive 10 to 12 percent worth of dividends for forty days. (For you with sharp pencils, that's $6.56 @ 12 percent.)

### Don't Lose Interest—Even for a Day

*How you move money, not only to pay bills, but between investments as well, can mean the difference between a good return and only mediocre results.* Earning money on delayed payments and uncashed checks is a critical part of big-business strategy today. It's part of the game called "controlled disbursement," and so respectable that some of the best-known corporations use checks from distant banks to pay their local bills. A California company, for instance, may pay its bills with checks drawn on a Providence, Rhode Island, bank so they have to pass through at least two separate Federal Reserve districts, taking an extra interest-earning day or two to clear. Back in the bad old days, such a practice would have been considered questionable. Nowadays, renamed "controlled disbursement," it's simply good cash management. I know—I've taught the technique to thousands of corporations.

### Stretching the Float

What I'm suggesting here is not that you should set out to emulate the big corporations by acquiring a series of remote checking accounts at the opposite end of the continent from where you pay your bills. But you, too, should learn to move money in the most profitable way possible, starting with your money fund. Other considerations being equal, your money fund account should be located as far away from you as is feasible. This is one case where controlled disbursement pays. Since, unlike the case with your local bank, you will always be dealing with your money fund either by telephone—calling collect or on the free 800 number, of course—or by mail, the money fund's location might as well be put to good use. Columbia Daily Income Fund in Portland, Oregon, and Midwest Income Investment Company in Cincinnati, Ohio, are logical choices. Have you ever flown to Cincinnati? If you have, you know the nearest airport is in Kentucky. Well, the Federal Reserve has the same problem.

### Stockbroker Parking Lots

*One of the mechanics of moving money to be considered when you choose a money fund involves the stock market.* Are you one of those investors who swore off the stock market after its debacle in the seventies? Fine. I don't blame you. But if there's a chance that you might return to the equity market, perhaps you should consider a money fund that allows you free switching to its stock or bond funds and back. Then, by either a simple telephone call or a letter, you can exchange, say, $1,000 worth of your money fund holdings for a like amount of the stock or bond funds—with no commissions involved.

Many money funds offer free exchange privileges with their equity funds. First Investors Cash Management Fund, Dreyfus Liquid Assets, Fidelity Cash Reserves, and SteinRoe Cash Reserves are a few examples. Building the exchange privilege consideration into your money fund equation involves choosing a fund whose stock operation has performed well relative to Wall Street as a whole. You also want to make sure the stock and bond funds are of the no-load variety. The Dreyfus group, for instance, offers both the commission-charging Dreyfus Fund and the no-load Special Income Fund in addition to its money fund. If you exchange for the Dreyfus Fund, you pay the commission. And in today's enlightened age there's no reason for anyone to have his or her pockets picked by mutual fund commissions or "loads."

### Check This Out

*At the opposite end of the money-moving spectrum from the instant transfer is check cashing*, particularly if the check is an out-of-town one. Many banks will place a "hold" on a check for ten days, supposedly to make sure it clears. That means the bank has the free use of your money for a week and a half while you're left eating baloney.

For that's exactly what it is. A check does not take ten days to clear, nor are banks required to wait for that period of time before giving you access to your money, as so many of them claim. The ten-day rule, and in some banks the period is as long as twenty-one days, is strictly an internal regulation—one to which, with good banking relations, there's no need for you to be subjected.

The actual clearing process for a check, in almost every case, involves its passing through the Federal Reserve. And back in the old days, when checks made their way leisurely across the country stuffed in the mail sacks of transcontinental trains, the ten-day rule had some basis in reality. Today, however, the clearance is done by computer, with checks flying back and forth overnight in their very own special jets. As Ellen Stockdale, at the office of the Comptroller of the Currency in Washington, points out:

"It's not hunks of money being physically transferred from one bank to another. It's all done on computers. The minute that the Fed gets a little electronic impulse for your particular check, your bank is credited."

### Avoiding Unnecessary "Holds" on Your Cash

So your bank actually can often have the funds the same day your check is deposited or *at the very most two days* later. What, then, can you do about the delay in access to your money? Complain, that's what.

Speak to the teller, who will tell you it's the rule. Then work your way up, right up to the manager if necessary, until you get the rule waived for your account. If you are a good customer, it can be done, believe me. I've done it, and now I can use the money behind any checks deposited the same day. And don't think it's just because I happen to be involved in the financial world. According to a Federal Reserve study, 97 percent of the banks surveyed said they could alter their check clearance policy to accommodate customers. If your bank is one of the other 3 percent, find a new bank.

Money does come in two varieties, instant and delayed. Now, by delayed money I don't mean credit, which, of course, is also a form of spendable money. No, delayed money is funds that are actually deposited to an account but for the moment cannot be used, the kinds of funds, for instance, that your bank has when you deposit a check drawn on a different bank. Your bank does have to clear that check through the Fed. Once it's cleared, however, it becomes Fed funds, or Federal Reserve funds. And that's *real* money, available to the bank and to you.

This answers the second argument the bank will give you when you try to persuade them to give you instant use of any checks deposited. The argument that your checks must clear the Fed is valid, but it is valid for, at the most, only two days. And, as I've said, if you're a good customer, the bank should be willing to waive even this waiting time. After all, even if it takes two days for your deposited check to become real, genuine money (Fed funds), any check you write against that deposit will take the same amount of time to get back to the bank plus the time "your check is in the mail." At no time will the bank be out of funds. All it will be out is the free interest it's been collecting for years on your account. Now you know what the bankers mean when they say they're "enjoying the relationship."

Maybe the bank won't let you spend the $12,500 check you receive for selling your boat because it's worried about that particular check's collectibility. In other words, you're not in the habit of making deposits of that size, and it might bounce. In this particular case, the two-day clearance for funds doesn't really apply. Oh, the bank does get $12,500 worth of Fed Funds within two days, but the check could still bounce when it is sent on to the bank of origin, in which case the Fed would take back its funds from your bank. There is a legitimate reason, then, for a bank to hold back funds represented by a large check of unknown collectibility.

So let's not be petty about it. It's not worth switching banks for one check. Besides, in the span of time it would take you to find a good alternative bank and switch accounts, your original bank would probably have collected on that once-in-a-blue-moon check. Does that mean you should just deposit it and accept an interestless ten days?

Certainly not. Deposit the check to your savings account instead, and you will draw interest from the day of deposit. The instant-and-delayed money distinction does not usually apply to the interest-paying facet of savings accounts. You merely will not be allowed to withdraw on the capital amount until the check has cleared.

Then again, you have another alternative. You can simply endorse the check over to your money fund account. In that case you've invested almost as quickly and at a considerably higher yield—assuming the stop-and-start post office is making deliveries that week and you don't use the postage-paid return envelope supplied by the money fund. But call the fund first and inquire about their policy on "third-party" checks.

### Licking the Stamp Delay

*Saving a postage stamp will cost you a day's worth of dividends, or even more, from a money fund.* The fact is that the post office doesn't accord first-class service to postage-paid return mail. It spends an extra day accumulating the envelopes, counting the postage due, and charging the money fund's account. Of course, postage-paid mail isn't supposed to take longer. But the facts speak for themselves, as people who have availed themselves of this service can attest.

If New York City is the United States financial center, it's also the snafu center of the post office. Postal service is so fouled up that some Wall Street-based funds have resorted to using Newark, New Jersey, post office boxes, just to accelerate delivery. If you make numerous small deposits to your money funds by mail, choosing one located in California makes sense even if you live in, say, Boston, solely on the consideration of speeding up your deposits.

Our Holliston—outside Boston—office receives next-day mail service from California, whereas it may take five days or more to receive first-class mail from New York. Even ten or twelve days is not unusual. Special delivery, of course, adds additional time to your money's transit period.

### When to Wire

*If you have more than $10,000 to transfer, it usually pays to move your money by wire.* Please don't confuse wiring with Western Union, which can be even slower than the U.S. postal system, particularly on international transactions. To move large sums of money efficiently, the Federal Reserve wire system is the only way to fly. This wire system ties together all the Federal Reserve member banks. It's a private communication system for transferring funds. And since it's the big boy's money that's involved, the system is swift and efficient. Money is deducted from one account and deposited to another simultaneously. Not a moment's worth of interest is lost.

A bank will charge $5 to $15 fee for use of the Federal Reserve wire service, which is reasonable enough when weighed against the alternative. For amounts of $10,000 and over, the service not only pays for itself, but garners a profit as well. Consider postal transit and collection time. The average conveyance of funds from you to "them" takes seven days. If $10,000 remains invested for those seven days at 12 percent, you've gained $23. Deduct an average $10 wire charge, and you're still $13 ahead on each transaction. You're ahead a lot more with larger amounts, of course.

Conversely, if you need money in a hurry, you can call your money fund in the morning and have the funds wired to your bank by the same afternoon. It's not a check you're getting. The bank won't hold the funds for clearing. The money is yours to use at once.

Money funds are accustomed to wiring money. Banks are not, at least not for individual customers. Be prepared for snafus the first time you try to wire money through a bank, particularly if you're dealing with a branch bank rather than the main office. Once you have established your use of this service, however, things should run smoothly.

### The Secret of Joe Jones

A while back, a money fund account officer phoned me and recounted the story of a client who attended one of our cash management seminars. In the course of the seminar, I had mentioned that a check sent to someone's attention would be delayed in its deposit by at least a day. The point was a little contrived, I granted, but it was just the sort of entertaining bit one enjoys passing on in a seminar. The client had followed the suggestion in sending a tax payment due February 15 to the attention of "Mr. Joe Jones" at the IRS. It was not April and the half-million-dollar check still had not cleared. The client had been credited by the IRS, even though the check was outstanding. In response to the account officer's inquiry, the client replied, "Oh, does it have to be a real person? I just made up the name." Two weeks later the check cleared, having earned the client $958 (at 10%) in daily dividends.

The real name of the game, then, is to speed up the moving of money in your favor and to slow it down as much as possible as it leaves your possession. Time-saving techniques like wiring amounts over $10,000 and using a money fund's toll-free number for telephone redemptions can win you extra dollars. Writing large money fund checks to pay bills on Wednesdays to be mailed on Thursdays so you get that extra week of dividends spends time quite gainfully for you. How far you carry the delay-and-profit program, of course, is a personal choice. But do remember to keep time on your side when you move money.

# Appendix A.
# Money Fund Directory

## WHAT IS A MONEY FUND?

Money funds are mutual funds that invest in money market instruments such as Treasury bills, U.S. Government agency obligations, repurchase agreements, commercial bank certificates of deposit (CDs), commercial paper (corporate IOUs), and Eurodollar certificates of deposit. Until 1972, the year Reserve Fund was registered as the first money market mutual fund, such money market instruments were only available to those with $100,000 or more to invest.

Money funds were initially intended to help meet the cash management requirements of larger corporations. The individual investor was made aware of the advantages of playing the money market in 1978 when money market certificates were first offered by banks, savings and loan associations, credit unions, and mutual savings banks. This growing involvement in the money market led to increasing interest in money market mutual funds and, subsequently, money fund assets grew from about $4 billion in September 1977 to over $60 billion in February 1980. Money funds are now viewed as an ideal vehicle for cash reserves and have been incorporated into the portfolios of individual investors, bank trust departments, and pension funds.

## THE ADVANTAGES OF INVESTING IN A MONEY FUND

Investors enjoy flexibility by investing in a money fund. Most money fund accounts can be opened for as little as $1,000 or less. Returns on investments in money funds are comparable to those earned on direct investments in money market instruments (such as purchasing a money market certificate) and are higher than returns on a passbook savings account. One reason for this higher yield is the professional management of a well-diversified portfolio of money market instruments. Skilled portfolio managers can invest confidently and aggressively even within the conservative guidelines defined in money fund prospectuses. Your risk is reduced by being fully invested in a diversified pool of high-quality securities.

Investors often voice concern about the liquidity of their investment. Within certain constraints, shares of a money fund may be redeemed at any time by writing a check on your account at the fund or by calling the fund and requesting a telephone redemption which will normally place the requested amount in your bank account within 24 hours.

## HOW TO SELECT THE MONEY FUND THAT'S RIGHT FOR YOU

There are three classes of money funds to consider:

**1. General purpose money funds** are available to any investor and may be contacted and invested in directly. (It is usually not necessary to go through a stockbroker to invest in any money fund, though you may if you wish.) Some stockbrokers use the general purpose funds for their client accounts.

**2. Stockbroker-affiliated general purpose money funds** are money funds affiliated with stockbrokers, but are still available to all investors. Like general purpose money funds, they can be dealt with directly or through a stockbroker. (Those which require that you contact a stockbroker are noted in the **Directory** by **\*\***.) These funds tend to be designed for a more active investor and may not offer all the services of a general purpose money fund.

**3. Institutions-only money funds** are not available to individual investors except through an institution such as a bank trust department or a stockbroker. Minimum initial investments are usually higher for this type of money fund than they are for general purpose or stockbroker-affiliated money funds, and very few offer the check redemption privilege.

## POINTS TO CONSIDER BEFORE SELECTING A MONEY FUND

The funds have been categorized according to the three classes. Once you have determined which class(es) of funds best suit your needs, look for the investment requirements, services and individual policies which will help you meet your investment goals.

**Minimum initial and subsequent investments.** The first chart that follows lists the funds in sequence by minimum investment requirements. You can easily determine which group of funds allows minimum investments of $1,000 though some are lower and still others have no restrictions at all. Subsequent investments are typically in the $100 to $1,000 range, but, again, some funds carry smaller or no restrictions.

**Services offered.** The **check redemption** privilege permits you to withdraw your money simply by writing a check in an amount equal to or exceeding the minimum amount indicated. These checks are, in effect, the same as any bank check. They are drawn against an account which the fund sets up for you. The checks may be drawn to a third party such as your landlord, bank, or any other vendor. Many small businesses use these checks to pay all their bills over the minimum requirement and enjoy having daily dividends credited to their accounts until the check clears.

**Checking policies** vary from fund to fund. Most funds will provide a certain amount of checks (**cks. prov.**) with more supplied on request (**more on req.**) at no charge. Some will provide an unlimited amount (**U**) of checks to the investor. If for some reason you may not wish to use the checks supplied by the funds (corporate investors may have continuous form computer checks, for example), many funds will allow you to print your own checks at your own expense (**P**) as long as the checks conform to the fund's required format. Another concern of corporate investors may be whether the fund will accept a facsimile signature (**F**) such as a rubber stamp. Most funds have strict policies against this practice unless the alternate signature appears on the signature card (**sig. card**) or is printed by machine.

Some confirmation of check transactions will usually be offered by the funds (**ck. ret.**). Cancelled checks are returned as indicated on a monthly (**M**), quarterly (**Q**), or as-they-clear (**as clear**) basis. Some funds may only return a confirmation (**confirm.**) or photocopies of checks (**copies**) and others will do this only on request (**on req.**).

The **telephone redemption privilege** allows you to request by telephone that the fund redeem all or part of your investment in at least the amount of the indicated minimum. This privilege is typically used to request that the fund wire the money to your bank account. The standard minimum requirement on a Fed wire is $1,000, though an individual fund may require a larger minimum on a wire transfer. You may also request a check redemption by phone, but it is usually nore efficient to simply write the check yourself. Funds generally will only be wired to the one account designated on your application.

**Exchange privileges** permit you to exchange your shares of the money fund with the shares of another fund, usually an equity fund. Investors who feel that they would rather be in a bond fund or growth fund or some other fund will often switch their investments using this privilege. Others who feel they can time the market swings will use this more aggressively. The procedure for using the exchange privilege may vary between funds. You should check each fund's prospectus for limitations or restrictions.

None of the funds in this **Directory** (except the load funds listed in the **Special Purpose** section) have a sales charge (load) though some may charge a fee for services. Charges for check printing **(CP)**, wire redemption **(W)**, monthly service fee **(MS)**, one time set-up **(SU)**, sub-accounting **(SA)**, and exchange privilege **(E)** are indicated. The **normal sales charge** applied to the exchange privilege refers to a charge for exchanging shares of a no-load fund for those of a load fund.

**Dividend policy.** Most money funds declare dividends daily **(D)** and pay, credit, or reinvest dividends on a daily **(D)**, monthly **(M)**, or quarterly **(Q)** basis. The dividend policy has no effect on the size of an investor's yield only **when** the dividends are credited to his account.

**Note:** Yields reported in the **Directory** have been annualized to be fully comparable with each other. Yields are only recorded for those funds which were in operation for full years ending 12/30/78 and/or 12/30/79.

**Deadline for same-day investment by wire** refers to the time federal funds must be received in order to earn dividends as of the next pricing time. Most funds will begin crediting your investment with dividends 24 hours after receipt of a wired investment. All deadlines have been converted to eastern standard time and those funds whose policies require one-day lag are indicated.

If you choose to invest by check rather than by wire, you will not begin to earn dividends until at least one or two days after the check arrives. Money funds will not permit withdrawals of money invested by check for at least 10 days, though the money is invested promptly.

The **valuation method** (the means by which the fund prices its shares) is a highly technical matter still in the process of being refined by both the industry and the Securities and Exchange Commission. Money funds typically value shares at a 1.00 price per share (net asset value) and remain constant. Some funds do permit the price to float and adjust their yield accordingly, but this practice is quickly being outmoded by the constant net asset funds. There are currently four major valuation methods in use: **(1)** constant net asset value, market-to-market, **(2)** variable net asset value, market-to-market, **(3)** constant net asset value, 120-day maximum average maturity (penny rounding), **(4)** and amortized cost, straight line accrual. Each has its supporters. Methods **3** and **4** are most likely to assure a constant price per share and a more stable day-to-day yield. (Several funds have applied for valuation method number **3** — penny rounding. These are indicated by an asterisk **\*** in the valuation method column.)

**Approved investments** are the instruments in which the fund is permitted to invest. They are explained in detail in the fund's prospectus along with restrictions on investments, such as maximum maturities permitted and minimum quality ratings on permitted investments.

Most money funds restrict their investments to the following six investment instruments: **(1)** U.S. Treasury bills and notes, **(2)** U.S. Government agency obligations, **(3)** negotiable commercial bank certificates of deposit, **(4)** bankers' acceptances, **(5)** commercial paper, and **(6)** repurchase agreements.

Other instruments in which funds are permitted to invest are: **(7)** savings accounts, **(8)** Canadian government securities, **(9)** Yankee CDs or domestic deposits in foreign banks' U.S. branches, **(10)** reverse repurchase agreements, **(11)** corporate obligations, usually bonds with less than one year to maturity, **(12)** thrift institution obligations, **(13)** International Bank for Reconstruction & Development obligations, **(14)** letters of credit, **(15)** Eurodollar certificates of deposit (deposits in U.S. banks' foreign branches), **(16)** variable rate U.S. government guaranteed obligations, **(17)** floating rate notes, **(18)** documented discount notes, and **(19)** Eurodollar time deposits. Many of the last thirteen items have seldom been included in most portfolios, where approved, and are provided primarily to enable a money fund to take advantage of an investment opportunity consistent with the fund's investment goals.

Instruments actually included in a fund's portfolio are selected from the approved list at the discretion of the fund's portfolio manager and may vary with the market conditions. A telephone call to your money fund is usually sufficient to request a list of the securities currently included in the fund's portfolio.

### HOW TO INVEST IN A MONEY FUND

**1. By mail.** Mail your investment check with your application to the address designated on the prospectus, and as soon as the check arrives and is converted to federal funds (up to two days after its arrival) you will be invested.

**2. By wire.** Call the money fund and obtain detailed instructions on how to wire money to the fund, obtain an account number, call your bank and request it to wire the money as instructed (be precise in your instructions), and mail in your completed application. Your money should be invested that day.

If you are mailing your investment, put your own stamp on the envelope. The prepaid mail permits require the postal service to count the envelopes before delivery, a process that may delay the arrival of your investment. If you are wiring your money into the fund, you would be wise to go the bank's main office the first time and arrange for the wire. Most branch offices rarely wire funds and are more prone to making mistakes, while the procedure is fairly common in the main office. If you are investing less than $10,000, you will probably be better off investing by check. Larger amounts can make it worth your while to pay the wire charges to insure that your money is invested and earning more quickly.

**Special Purpose Money Funds** are money funds which exist for limited purposes and/or cater to a certain type of investor. **Tax-Free Money Funds** are a relatively new breed of money funds which provide tax-free income to their investors. The inclusion of these types of funds in this **Directory** is indicative of the growing, wide-spread popularity of the money market mutual fund concept.

**GUIDE TO SELECTING A MONEY FUND**

The following chart has been prepared to help you identify the funds which best meet your investment needs. All of the funds are listed in sequence by minimum initial investment requirements.

After you have determined how much you would like to invest, select the group(s) of funds which allow initial investments in that amount. Of the group(s) you select, find the funds which offer the services you wish to use: checking, telephone redemption, exchange privileges. Finally, compare the yields for the past two years to give you an idea of each fund's performance. Be more concerned with how well the annual rate of an individual fund's past yield compares to the past yields of all other funds rather than with the actual size of the yield itself. For example, a yield of 7.40% in 1978 may

## MONEY FUNDS AVAILABLE TO ALL INVESTORS

| Minimum Investment Initial / Subsequent | Fund Type | FUND NAME | Average Yield Full Year 12/30/79 | 12/30/78 | Checking / Minimum Check | Telephone Redemption | Exchange Privilege |
|---|---|---|---|---|---|---|---|
| None / None | SB | Alliance Capital Reserves, Inc. | 10.12 | — | Yes / $500 | Yes | Yes |
| None / None | GP | American Liquid Trust | 10.34 | 7.12 | Yes / 500 | Yes | Yes |
| None / None | SB | CMA Money Trust (Merrill Lynch)* | 10.52 | 7.23 | Yes / 500 | No | No |
| $500 / $50 | GP | Midwest Income Investment Co. | 9.82 | 7.30 | Yes / 350 | Yes | No |
| 500 / 100 | GP | Franklin Money Fund | 10.41 | 6.85 | Yes / 500 | Yes | Yes |
| 1,000 / None | GP | Capital Preservation Fund | 9.63 | 6.41 | Yes / 500 | Yes | No |
| 1,000 / None | GP | Centennial Capital Cash Management Trust | 9.93 | 7.24 | Yes / 500 | Yes | No |
| 1,000 / None | GP | Eaton & Howard Cash Management Fund | 10.37 | 7.08 | Yes / 500 | Yes | Yes |
| 1,000 / None | GP | Lord Abbett Cash Reserve Fund, Inc. | — | — | Yes / 500 | Yes | Yes |
| 1,000 / None | GP | Mass. Cash Management Trust | 10.47 | 7.35 | Yes / 500 | Yes | Yes |
| 1,000 / None | GP | NEL Cash Management Account | 10.27 | — | Yes / 250 | Yes | Yes |
| 1,000 / None | GP | Scudder Cash Investment Trust | 10.18 | 6.85 | Yes / 500 | Yes | Yes |
| 1,000 / None | GP | Scudder Managed Reserves, Inc. | 10.02 | 6.76 | Yes / 500 | Yes | Yes |
| 1,000 / None | GP | Union Cash Management Fund, Inc. | 10.69 | 7.24 | Yes / 500 | Yes | Yes |
| 1,000 / 25 | GP | Delaware Cash Reserve, Inc. | 10.58 | — | Yes / 500 | Yes | Yes |
| 1,000 / 25 | GP | John Hancock Cash Management Trust | — | — | Yes / 250 | Yes | Yes |
| 1,000 / 25 | SB | Oppenheimer Monetary Bridge | 10.64 | 7.13 | Yes / 500 | Yes | Yes |
| 1,000 / 50 | SB | Gradison Cash Reserves | 10.18 | 6.88 | Yes / 500 | Yes | No |
| 1,000 / 100 ck. 1,000 wire | GP | American General Reserves Fund | 10.88 | 5.89 | Yes / 500 | Yes | Yes |
| 1,000 / 100 | SB | Cash Equivalent Fund, Inc. | — | — | Yes / 500 | Yes | Yes |
| 1,000 / 100 | SB | Current Interest, Inc. | 10.12 | 7.21 | Yes / 500 | Yes | Yes |
| 1,000 / 100 | SB | Daily Cash Accumulation Fund, Inc. | 10.51 | — | Yes / 500 | Yes | Yes |
| 1,000 / 100 | GP | Federated Money Market, Inc. | 9.83 | — | Yes / 250 | Yes | Yes |
| 1,000 / 100 | GP | Financial Daily Income Shares, Inc. | 10.37 | 7.08 | Yes / 500 | Yes | Yes |
| 1,000 / 100 | GP | First Investors Cash Management Fund | 10.49 | — | Yes / 500 | Yes | Yes |
| 1,000 / 100 | GP | Kemper Money Market Fund, Inc. | 10.84 | 7.37 | Yes / 500 | Yes | Yes |
| 1,000 / 100 | GP | Lexington Money Market Trust | — | — | Yes / 250 | Yes | Yes |
| 1,000 / 100 | GP | Money Shares, Inc. | 9.49 | — | Yes / 1,000 | Yes | Yes |
| 1,000 / 100 | GP | Selected Money Market Fund | 10.41 | 7.04 | Yes / 500 | Yes | Yes |
| 1,000 / 100 | GP | United Cash Management, Inc. | — | . — | Yes / 500 | Yes | Yes |
| 1,000 / 100 | GP | Value Line Cash Fund | — | — | Yes / 500 | Yes | Yes |
| 1,000 / 250 | GP | Fidelity Cash Reserves | — | — | Yes / 500 | Yes | Yes |

* $20,000 relationship required. Only available at Merrill Lynch offices offering the Cash Management account.

not seem high in and of itself, but compared to yields of all other funds dealing in the same money market it would have been well above the 1978 average of 7.00%. Be aware that certain funds have a more conservative investment policy and, therefore, may have lower yields. If you are an extremely conservative investor you should not exclude these funds based on lower yields alone.

After you've selected a group of funds, read a more detailed analysis of each in the next few pages. (The money funds are listed in alphabetical order within the categories noted below: GP — General Purpose Money Fund; SB — Stock-broker-Affiliated General Purpose Money Fund.) Always read the money fund's prospectus before investing.

## MONEY FUNDS AVAILABLE TO ALL INVESTORS

| Minimum Investment Initial / Subsequent | Fund Type | FUND NAME | Average Yield Full Year 12/30/79 | 12/30/78 | Checking / Minimum Check | Telephone Redemption | Exchange Privilege |
|---|---|---|---|---|---|---|---|
| $1,000 / $250 | GP | First Variable Rate Fund for Government Income, Inc. | 10.30 | 7.47 | Yes / $500 | Yes | No |
| 1,000 / 500 | SB | Liquid Capital Income, Inc. | 10.36 | 6.95 | Yes / 500 | Yes | No |
| 1,000 / 500 | SB | Moneymart Assets, Inc. | 10.44 | 7.03 | Yes / 500 | Yes | Yes |
| 1,000 / 500 | GP | Columbia Daily Income Co. | 10.23 | 6.45 | Yes / 500 | Yes | No |
| 1,000 / 1,000 | GP | The Reserve Fund, Inc. | 10.67 | 7.24 | Yes / 500 | Yes | Yes |
| 1,250 / 100 | GP | Short-Term Yield Securities, Inc. | 10.38 | — | Yes / 500 | Yes | Yes |
| 2,000 / None | GP | Government Investors Trust | — | — | Yes / 500 | Yes | No |
| 2,000 / 100 | GP | Rowe Price Prime Reserve Fund, Inc. | 10.64 | 7.28 | Yes / 500 | Yes | Yes |
| 2,000 / 500 | GP | Putnam Daily Dividend Trust | 10.19 | 6.61 | Yes / 500 | Yes | Yes |
| 2,500 / 100 | GP | Dreyfus Liquid Assets | 10.37 | 6.81 | Yes / 500 | Yes | Yes |
| 2,500 / 100 | GP | IDS Cash Management Fund, Inc. | 10.44 | 7.02 | Yes / 500 | No | Yes |
| 2,500 / 100 | GP | Johnston Cash Management Fund | — | — | Yes / 500 | Yes | Yes |
| 2,500 / 100 | GP | MIF / Nationwide Money Market Fund | — | — | Yes / 500 | Yes | Yes |
| 2,500 / 100 | SB | National Liquid Reserves, Inc. | 10.28 | 6.90 | Yes / 500 | Yes | Yes |
| 2,500 / 100 | GP | SteinRoe Cash Reserves, Inc. | 10.69 | 6.77 | Yes / 500 | Yes | Yes |
| 2,500 / 500 | GP | Fund for Government Investors, Inc. | 9.79 | 6.78 | Yes / 500 | Yes | No |
| 2,500 / 500 | SB | INA Cash Fund, Inc. | — | — | Yes / 250 | Yes | No |
| 2,500 / 100 | GP | Mutual of Omaha Money Market Accounts | — | — | Yes / 500 | Yes | Yes |
| 3,000 / 100 | GP | Vanguard Money Market Trust: Portfolio I | 10.51 | 6.84 | Yes / 500 | Yes | Yes |
| 3,000 / 500 | GP | St. Paul Money Fund, Inc. | — | — | Yes / 500 | Yes | Yes |
| 5,000 / 50 | GP | Cash Management Trust of America | 10.49 | 6.72 | Yes / 500 | Yes | Yes |
| 5,000 / 100 | SB | Daily Income Fund, Inc. | 9.97 | 6.93 | Yes / 500 | Yes | Yes |
| 5,000 / 500 | SB | Legg Mason Cash Reserve Trust | — | — | Yes / 500 | Yes | No |
| 5,000 / 500 | SB | Paine Webber Cashfund, Inc. | 10.21 | — | Yes / 500 | Yes | No |
| 5,000 / 1,000 | SB | InterCapital Liquid Asset Fund, Inc. | 10.53 | 7.25 | Yes / 500 | Yes | Yes |
| 5,000 / 1,000 | SB | Merrill Lynch Government Fund, Inc. | 9.39 | 6.73 | Yes / 500 | Yes | No |
| 5,000 / 1,000 | SB | Merrill Lynch Ready Assets Trust | 10.61 | 7.24 | Yes / 500 | Yes | Yes |
| 5,000 / 1,000 | SB | Shearson Daily Dividend, Inc. | — | — | No | Yes | No |
| 5,000 / 1,500 | SB | Webster Cash Reserve Fund, Inc. | — | — | No | Yes | No |
| 10,000 / 1,000 | SB | Cash Reserve Management | 10.41 | 7.22 | Yes / 500 | Yes | No |
| 10,000 / 500 | GP | Fidelity Daily Income Trust | 10.73 | 7.40 | Yes / 500 | Yes | Yes |
| 100,000 / None | GP | Money Market Management | 9.68 | 6.71 | Yes / 500 | Yes | Yes |

## MONEY FUNDS AVAILABLE TO INSTITUTIONS ONLY

| Minimum Investment Initial / Subsequent | FUND NAME | Average Yield Full Year 12/30/79 | 12/30/78 | Checking / Minimum Check | Telephone Redemption | Exchange Privilege |
|---|---|---|---|---|---|---|
| $1,000 / None | FedFund (Shearson, Loeb, Rhoades, Inc.) | 9.74 | 6.59 | Yes / $500 | Yes | No |
| 1,000 / None | TempFund (Shearson, Loeb, Rhoades, Inc.) | 10.41 | 7.36 | Yes / 500 | Yes | No |
| 25,000 / None | Merrill Lynch Institutional Fund, Inc. | 10.50 | 7.13 | Yes / 500 | Yes | No |
| 50,000 / None 50,000 / None | ILA (Institutional Liquid Assets) Government Portfolio Prime Obligations Portfolio | — 10.47 | — 7.46 | Yes / None Yes / None | Yes Yes | Yes Yes |
| 50,000 / None | Money Market Trust (Federated) | 10.21 | — | No | Yes | No |
| 50,000 / $100 | Dreyfus Government Securities Series | — | — | Yes / 500 | Yes | Yes |

## GENERAL PURPOSE MONEY FUNDS (Available To All Investors)

| Average Yields Full Year 12/30/79 | 12/30/78 | FUND NAME, ADDRESS & PHONE NUMBER (date started) | Investment Advisor and Administrator/Distributor | Approved Investments | ASSETS (millions) As Of: 12/30/79 | 12/30/78 | Valuation Method |
|---|---|---|---|---|---|---|---|
| 10.88 | 5.89 | American General Reserve Fund P. O. Box 1411 Houston, TX 77001 (3/74) (800) 231-3638 (713) 526-8561 | American General Capital Management, Inc. | 1  6 2 3 4 5 | 36.6 | 11.4 | 3 |
| 10.34 | 7.12 | American Liquid Trust 99 High Street Boston, MA 02110 (7/75) (800) 225-2618 (617) 338-3300 | ALT Management Corp. (Sub. of Keystone Custodian Funds, Inc.) | 1 2 3 4 6 | 150.6 | 36.5 | 1 |
| 9.63 | 6.41 | Capital Preservation Fund 755 Page Mill Road Palo Alto, CA 94306 (10/72) (800) 227-8380 (800) 982-5844 (in CA) | Benham Management Corp. | 1 6 | 496.0 | 115.1 | 1 |
| 10.49 | 6.72 | Cash Management Trust of America P. O. Box 60829 Terminal Annex Los Angeles, CA 90060 (11/76) (800) 421-8791 (213) 486-9562 | Capital Research & Management Co. | 1  9  17 2  10  18 3  11 4  13 5  15 6  16 | 176.4 | 59.6 | 1 |
| 9.93 | 7.24 | Centennial Capital Cash Management Trust One New York Plaza New York, NY 10004 (7/74) (800) 221-5833 (212) 825-4000 | Centennial Capital Corp. STCM Management Co., Inc. | 1  7  15 2  9  16 3  11  17 4  12  18 5  13  19 6  14 | 22.8 | 31.5 | 1* |
| 10.23 | 6.45 | Columbia Daily Income Co. 621 SW Morrison Street Portland, OR 97205 (7/74) (800) 547-1037 (503) 222-3600 | Columbia Management Co. | 1  5 2  6 3  11 4  14 | 168.9 | 27.2 | 1 |
| 10.58 | — | Delaware Cash Reserve, Inc. Seven Penn Center Plaza Philadelphia, PA 19103 (8/78) (800) 523-4640 (215) 988-1340 | Delaware Management Co., Inc. | 1  6 2  9 3  11 4  15 5 | 246.5 | 9.5 | 4 |

**Valuation Methods:**
1   Constant Net Asset Value, Mark-to-Market
2   Variable Net Asset Value, Mark-to-Market
3   Constant Net Asset Value, 120-day Maximum Average Maturity (penny rounding)

4   Amortized Cost, Straight Line Accrual
*   Applied for #3 (penny rounding) valuation method
**  Available through sponsoring stockbroker

## MONEY FUNDS AVAILABLE TO INSTITUTIONS ONLY

| Minimum Investment Initial / Subsequent | FUND NAME | Average Yield Full Year | | Checking / Minimum Check | Telephone Redemption | Exchange Privilege |
|---|---|---|---|---|---|---|
| | | 12/30/79 | 12/30/78 | | | |
| $50,000 / $100 | Dreyfus Money Market Series | 10.48 | 6.99 | Yes / $500 | Yes | Yes |
| | Federated Securities | | | | | |
| 100,000 / None | Federated Master Trust | 10.26 | 7.52 | No | Yes | No |
| 100,000 / None | Trust / U.S. Government Securities | 9.72 | 6.98 | No | Yes | No |
| 100,000 / None | Trust / U.S. Treasury Obligations | — | — | No | Yes | No |
| | Fidelity Money Market Trust | | | | | |
| 250,000 / None | Domestic Portfolio | — | — | No | Yes | Yes |
| 250,000 / None | International Portfolio | — | — | No | Yes | Yes |
| 250,000 / None | U.S. Government Portfolio | — | — | No | Yes | Yes |

| Minimum Investment Initial / Subsequent | SERVICES OFFERED | | | | | | | Deadline For Same-Day Investment By Wire (EST) | Dividend Policy | | No. Of States Fund Is Registered |
|---|---|---|---|---|---|---|---|---|---|---|---|
| | Checking / Minimum Check | Checking Policies | Telephone Redemption / Minimum | Exchange Privilege | Funds Available For Exchange Privilege | Service Fees | | | Declared | Paid | |
| $1,000 / $100 check $1,000 wire | Yes / $500 | cks. prov.: 20 more on req. P F cks. ret. M | Yes / $1,000 | Yes | All load funds distributed by Capital Management, Inc. | E: $5.00 | | 12:00 PM | D | M | All |
| None / None | Yes / 500 | cks. prov.: 20 P F cks. ret. as clear | Yes / None | Yes | All funds in Keystone Group of funds | | | 4:00 PM | D | M | All |
| 1,000 / None | Yes/ 500 | cks. prov.: U P ck. copies ret. on req. | Yes / 1,000 | No | | W: $2.00 for under $5,000 wire | | 4:00 PM | D | D | All |
| 5,000 / 50 | Yes / 500 | cks. prov.: U F (if on sig. card) cks. ret. M | Yes / 1,000 | Yes | All funds in American Funds Group | E: normal sales charge | | 4:00 PM | D | M | All |
| 1,000 / None | Yes / 500 | cks. prov.: U | Yes / None | No | | | | 5:00 PM | D | D | 11 |
| 1,000 / 500 | Yes / 500 | cks. prov.: U P cks. ret. M | Yes / None | No | | W: $2.50 | | 4:00 PM | D | D | 8 |
| 1,000 / 25 | Yes / 500 | cks. prov.: U P cks. ret. M | Yes / 500 | Yes | All funds in Delaware Group of funds | CP: $5.00 set up W: $3.00 E: $5.00 | | 12:00 PM | D | M | 36 |

The 800 numbers are toll-free. If you are in the same state as the fund, however, call Collect.

## GENERAL PURPOSE MONEY FUNDS (Available To All Investors)

| Average Yields Full Year 12/30/79 | 12/30/78 | FUND NAME, ADDRESS & PHONE NUMBER (date started) | Investment Advisor and Administrator/Distributor | Approved Investments | | | ASSETS (millions) As Of: 12/30/79 | 12/30/78 | Valuation Method |
|---|---|---|---|---|---|---|---|---|---|
| 10.37 | 6.81 | Dreyfus Liquid Assets<br>600 Madison Avenue<br>New York, NY 10022 (3/74)<br>(800) 223-5525<br>(212) 223-0303 | The Dreyfus Corp.<br><br>Dreyfus Service Corp. | 1<br>2<br>3<br>4 | 5<br>6<br>15 | | 2,167.9 | 881.1 | 3 |
| 10.37 | 7.08 | Eaton & Howard Cash Management Fund<br>Box 336<br>Boston, MA 02101 (1/75)<br>(800) 225-6265<br>(617) 482-8260 | Eaton & Howard, Vance,<br>Sanders, Inc. | 1<br>2<br>3<br>4 | 5<br>6<br>7<br>12 | | 58.0 | 11.7 | 4 |
| 9.83 | — | Federated Money Market, Inc.<br>421 Seventh Avenue<br>Pittsburgh, PA 15219 (2/78)<br>(800) 245-2423<br>(412) 288-1948 | Federated Research Corp. | 1<br>2<br>3<br>4<br>5 | 6<br>7<br>9<br>12<br>15 | | 151.0 | 76.1 | 4 |
| — | — | Fidelity Cash Reserves<br>82 Devonshire Street<br>Boston, MA 02109 (5/79)<br>(800) 225-6190<br>(617) 523-1919 | Fidelity Management &<br>Research Co. | 1<br>2<br>3<br>4<br>5 | 6<br>9<br>11<br>15<br>19 | | 337.2 | — | 4 |
| 10.73 | 7.40 | Fidelity Daily Income Trust<br>82 Devonshire Street<br>Boston, MA 02109 (5/74)<br>(800) 225-6190<br>(617) 523-1919 | Fidelity Management &<br>Research Co. | 1<br>2<br>3<br>4 | 5<br>6<br>11 | | 2,376.0 | 846.8 | 4 |
| 10.37 | 7.08 | Financial Daily Income Shares, Inc.<br>P. O. Box 2040<br>Denver, CO 80201 (10/75)<br>(800) 525-9831<br>(303) 779-1233 | Financial Programs, Inc. | 1<br>2<br>3<br>4 | 5<br>7<br>11<br>12 | 14<br>15<br>16 | 62.2 | 16.4 | 2 |
| 10.49 | — | First Investors Cash Management Fund<br>120 Wall Street<br>New York, NY 10005 (10/78)<br>(212) 425-4026 (collect) | First Investors<br>Management Co., Inc. | 1<br>2<br>3 | 4<br>5<br>6 | | 76.2 | — | 1 |
| 10.30 | 7.47 | First Variable Rate Fund For<br>Government Income, Inc.<br>1700 Pennsylvania Ave., NW<br>Washington, DC 20006 (2/76)<br>(800) 424-9861<br>(202) 393-5330 | Government Securities<br>Management Co. | 1<br>2 | 6<br>16 | | 192.5 | 46.7 | 1 |
| 10.41 | 6.85 | Franklin Money Fund<br>155 Bovet Road<br>San Mateo, CA 94402 (1/76)<br>(800) 227-6781<br>(415) 574-8800 (collect) | Franklin Research, Inc.<br><br>Franklin Distributors, Inc. | 1<br>2<br>3<br>4<br>5 | 6<br>11<br>12<br>14<br>15 | | 91.5 | 9.8 | 1 |
| 9.79 | 6.78 | Fund for Government Investors, Inc.<br>1735 K Street, NW<br>Washington, DC 20006 (3/75)<br>(202) 452-9200 (collect) | Money Management<br>Associates | 1<br>2<br>6 | | | 201.1 | 53.3 | 4 |
| — | — | Government Investors Trust<br>1800 North Kent Street<br>Arlington, VA 22200 (7/79)<br>(800) 336-3063<br>(703) 528-6500 | Bankers Finance<br>Investment Management<br>Corp. | 1<br>2<br>6 | 10<br>13<br>16 | | 16.4 | — | 1 |
| 10.44 | 7.02 | IDS Cash Management Fund, Inc.<br>1000 Roanoke Building<br>Minneapolis, MN 55402 (8/75)<br>(612) 372-3158 (collect) | Investors Diversified<br>Services, Inc. | 1<br>2<br>3<br>4<br>5 | 6<br>14<br>15<br>18<br>19 | | 177.6 | 10.9 | 3 |

**Valuation Methods:**
1   Constant Net Asset Value, Mark-to-Market
2   Variable Net Asset Value, Mark-to-Market
3   Constant Net Asset Value, 120 day Maximum Average Maturity (penny rounding)

4   Amortized Cost, Straight Line Accrual
\*   Applied for #3 (penny rounding) valuation method
\*\*   Available through sponsoring stockbroker

| Minimum Investment Initial / Subsequent | SERVICES OFFERED | | | | | | | | | No. Of States Fund Is Registered |
|---|---|---|---|---|---|---|---|---|---|---|
| | Checking / Minimum Check | Checking Policies | Telephone Redemption / Minimum | Exchange Privilege | Funds Available For Exchange Privilege | Service Fees | Deadline For Same-Day Investment By Wire (EST) | Dividend Declared | Policy Paid | |
| $2,500 / $100 | Yes / $500 | cks. prov.: U P cks. ret. as clear | Yes / $1,000 | Yes | All funds in Dreyfus Corporation Group of funds | E: normal sales charge | 12:00 PM next day credit | D | D | All |
| 1,000 / None | Yes / 500 | cks. prov.: U F cks. ret. as clear | Yes / 1,000 | Yes | All funds in Eaton & Howard, Vance, Sanders Inc. Group of funds | E: normal sales charge | 4:00 PM next day credit | D | M | 40 |
| 1,000 / 100 | Yes / 250 | cks. prov.: U F (corp. only) cks. ret. M | Yes / 1,000 | Yes | Fed Tax-Free Income Fund: U.S.G. Securities. Fed High Income: Fed Tax-Free Trust: Fed Option Income: American Leaders | W: charge for under $5,000 wire | 4:00 PM next day credit | D | M | All |
| 1,000 / 250 | Yes / 500 | F (by machine) cks. ret. M | Yes / 5,000 | Yes | All no-load funds in Fidelity Group of funds | CP: .25 per ck. first 12 free W: $3.00 | 4:00 PM | D | M | All |
| 10,000  500 | Yes / 500 | cks. prov.: U F (by machine) cks. ret. M | Yes / 5,000 | Yes | All no-load funds in Fidelity Group of funds | MS: $3.00 | 4:00 PM | D | M | All |
| 1,000  100 | Yes / 500 | cks. prov.: U | Yes / 1,000 | Yes | Financial Industrial Fund; Financial Ind. Income Fund: Financial Dynamics Fund: Financial Bond Fund | | 4:00 PM | D | M | 49 |
| 1,000 / 100 | Yes / 500 | cks. prov.: U P cks. ret. M | Yes / 500 | Yes | All funds in First Investors Group of funds | E: normal sales charge | 1:00 PM | D | M | 28 |
| 1,000 / 250 | Yes / 500 | cks. prov.: U P F cks. ret. Q | Yes / None | No | | | 1:00 PM | D | D | 24 |
| 500 / 100 | Yes / 500 | cks. prov.: U P ck. copies ret. M on req. | Yes / 1,000 | Yes | All funds in Franklin Group of funds | E: $5.00 | 5:00 PM | D | D | All |
| 2,500 / 500 | Yes / 500 | cks. prov.: U at invest. exp. P F cks. ret. M | Yes / 500 | No | | | 12:00 PM | D | M | 3 |
| 2,000 / None | Yes / 500 | cks. prov.: U P F cks. ret. on req. | Yes / None | No | | | 1:00 PM | D | M | 41 |
| 2,500 / 100 | Yes / 500 | cks. prov.: Inv. $0-5,000 7 cks. $5-10,000 10 cks. $10 + 20 cks. ck. copies ret. on req. | No | Yes | All Mutual Funds distributed by IDS | E: normal sales charge W: $5.00 | 1:30 PM | D | M | All |

The 800 numbers are toll-free. If you are in the same state as the fund, however, call Collect.

## GENERAL PURPOSE MONEY FUNDS (Available To All Investors)

| Average Yields Full Year 12/30/79 | 12/30/78 | FUND NAME, ADDRESS & PHONE NUMBER (date started) | Investment Advisor and Administrator/Distributor | Approved Investments | | | ASSETS (millions) As Of: 12/30/79 | 12/30/78 | Valuation Method |
|---|---|---|---|---|---|---|---|---|---|
| — | — | John Hancock Cash Management Trust<br>John Hancock Place<br>P. O. Box 111<br>Boston, MA 02117 (10/79)<br>(617) 421-4506 | John Hancock Advisers, Inc. | 1<br>2<br>3<br>4<br>5 | 6<br>9<br>11<br>12<br>13 | 14<br>15<br>16 | 30.2 | — | 4 |
| — | — | Johnston Cash Management Fund<br>One Boston Place<br>Boston, MA 02106 (8/79)<br>(800) 343-6324<br>(617) 722-7250 | Douglas T. Johnston & Co., Inc. | 1<br>2<br>3 | 5<br>6<br>11 | | 29.5 | — | 4 |
| 10.84 | 7.37 | Kemper Money Market Fund, Inc.<br>120 South LaSalle Street<br>Chicago, IL 60603 (11/74)<br>(800) 621-1048<br>(312) 346-3223 | Kemper Financial Service, Inc. | 1<br>2<br>3<br>4 | 5<br>6<br>11<br>15 | | 618.0 | 129.0 | 1* |
| — | — | Lexington Money Market Trust<br>Box 1515<br>476 Hudson Terrace<br>Englewood Cliffs, NJ 07632 (1/79)<br>(800) 526-4791 | Lexington Management Corp. | 1<br>2<br>3 | 4<br>5<br>6 | | 31.1 | — | 1 |
| — | — | Lord Abbett Cash Reserve Fund, Inc.<br>63 Wall Street<br>New York, NY 10005 (7/79)<br>(800) 522-7519<br>(212) 425-8720 | Lord, Abbett & Co. | 1<br>2<br>3<br>4<br>5 | 6<br>11<br>12<br>15<br>16 | 17 | 78.9 | — | 1 |
| 10.47 | 7.35 | Mass Cash Management Trust<br>200 Berkeley Street<br>Boston, MA 02116 (12/75)<br>(617) 956-1200<br>(617) 423-3500 (collect) | Mass. Financial Services | 1<br>2<br>3<br>4<br>5 | 6<br>7<br>11<br>15 | | 152.1 | 28.5 | 1 |
| 9.82 | 7.30 | Midwest Income Investment Co.<br>508 Dixie Terminal<br>Cincinnati, OH 45202 (12/74)<br>(800) 543-0407<br>(513) 579-0414 (collect) | Midwest Advisory Services, Inc. | 1<br>2<br>3<br>4 | 5<br>6<br>11<br>12 | | 98.4 | 41.0 | 1 |
| 9.68 | 6.71 | Money Market Management, Inc.<br>421 Seventh Avenue<br>Pittsburgh, PA 15219 (1/74)<br>(800) 245-2423<br>(412) 288-1948 (in PA) | Federated Cash Management Corp. | 1<br>2<br>3<br>4 | 5<br>6<br>7<br>12 | | 75.7 | 83.6 | 4 |
| 9.49 | — | Money Shares, Inc.<br>1 Wall Street<br>New York, NY 10005 (2/78)<br>(212) 269-8800 | Calvin Bullock, Ltd. | 1<br>2<br>3<br>4 | 5<br>6<br>7<br>11 | 12 | 4.3 | — | 3 |
| — | — | Mutual of Omaha Money Market Accounts<br>3102 Farnum Street<br>Omaha, NB 68131 (7/79)<br>(800) 228-9011<br>(402) 342-3328 | Mutual of Omaha Fund Management Co. | 1<br>2<br>3<br>4<br>5 | 6<br>7<br>9<br>11<br>15 | 16<br>17<br>18<br>19 | 38.9 | — | 4 |
| 10.27 | — | NEL Cash Management Account<br>501 Boylston Street<br>Boston, MA 02117 (7/78)<br>(800) 225-7670<br>(617) 267-6600 | New England Mutual Life Investment Co.<br><br>NEL Equity Service Corp. | 1<br>2<br>3<br>4 | 5<br>6<br>9<br>10 | 11<br>12<br>15 | 133.8 | 32.9 | 4 |
| 10.19 | 6.61 | Putnam Daily Dividend Trust<br>265 Franklin Street<br>Boston, MA 02110 (9/76)<br>(800) 225-1789<br>(617) 423-4960 | Putnam Management Co. | 1<br>2<br>3<br>4<br>5 | 6<br>7<br>11<br>14<br>15 | | 75.4 | 21.6 | 1* |

**Valuation Methods:**
1   Constant Net Asset Value, Mark-to-Market
2   Variable Net Asset Value, Mark-to-Market
3   Constant Net Asset Value, 120-day Maximum Average Maturity (penny rounding)

4   Amortized Cost, Straight Line Accrual
*   Applied for #3 (penny rounding) valuation method
**  Available through sponsoring stockbroker

| Minimum Investment Initial / Subsequent | SERVICES OFFERED | | | Exchange Privilege | Funds Available For Exchange Privilege | Service Fees | Deadline For Same-Day Investment By Wire (EST) | Dividend Declared | Policy Paid | No. Of States Fund Is Registered |
|---|---|---|---|---|---|---|---|---|---|---|
| | Checking / Minimum Check | Checking Policies | Telephone Redemption / Minimum | | | | | | | |
| $1,000 / $25 | Yes / $250 | cks. prov.: 20 F (sig. card) cks. ret. M | Yes / $250 | Yes | All funds in John Hancock Group funds | MS: $1.00 W: $2.50 | 3:00 PM | D | M | All |
| 2,500 / 100 | Yes / 500 | cks. prov.: U cks. ret. as clear | Yes / None | Yes | The Johnston Income Fund; The Johnston Capital Appreciation Fund | MS: $1.25 | 12:00 PM | D | M or Q (option) | All |
| 1,000 / 100 | Yes / 500 | cks. prov.: U F cks. ret. M | Yes / None | Yes | All nine funds in Kemper Group of funds | E: normal sales charge | 1:00 PM | D | M | All |
| 1,000 / 100 | Yes / 250 | cks. prov.: U cks. ret. M | Yes / 1,000 | Yes | All four funds in Lexington Group of funds | W: $2.50 | 4:00 PM | D | D | All |
| 1,000 / None | Yes / 500 | cks. prov.: U P F cks. ret. M | Yes / None | Yes | All funds in Lord, Abbett Group of funds | | 12:00 PM | D | M | All |
| 1,000 / None | Yes / 500 | cks. prov.: 20 more on req. P cks. ret. M | Yes / None | Yes | All funds in Mass Financial Service's Group of funds | E: $5.00 | 4:00 PM | D | M | All |
| 500 / 50 | Yes / 350 | cks. prov.: U P F cks. ret. M | Yes / 1,000 | No | | W: $1.00 | 3:00 PM | D | D | 16 |
| 100,000/ None | Yes / 500 | cks. prov.: U F (corp. only) cks. ret. M | Yes / 1,000 | Yes | Fed Money Market; Fed Tax-Free Income; Fund for U.S.G. Sec.; Fed Option Funds; Fed High Income Fund; Fed Tax-Free Trust; American Leaders | E: normal sales charge | 12:00 PM | D | M | All |
| 1,000 / 100 | Yes / 1,000 | cks. prov.: U cks. ret. M | Yes / 5,000 | Yes | All funds in Calvin Bullock Ltd. Group except Tax-Free Shares, Inc. and New York Venture Fund, Inc. | E: normal sales charge plus $5.00 | 1:00 PM | D | M | 19 |
| 2,500 / 100 | Yes / 500 | cks. prov.: U P F | Yes / 1,000 | Yes | All funds in Mutual of Omaha Group of funds | MS: $1.50 W: $2.50 E: $5.00 | 4:00 PM | D | M | All |
| 1,000 / None | Yes / 250 | cks. prov.: U P F cks. ret. M | Yes / 1,000 | Yes | All other NEL Funds | MS: $.75 CP: $5.00 set up W: $2.50 | 4:00 PM | D | M | All |
| 2,000 / 500 | Yes / 500 | cks. prov.: U P F cks. ret. as clear | Yes / 1,000 | Yes | All open-end funds in Putnam & Eberstadt Group of funds | E: normal sales charge | 3:00 PM | D | M | All |

The 800 numbers are toll-free. If you are in the same state as the fund, however, call Collect.

## GENERAL PURPOSE MONEY FUNDS (Available To All Investors)

| Average Yield Full Year 12/30/79 | 12/30/78 | FUND NAME, ADDRESS & PHONE NUMBER (date started) | Investment Advisor and Administrator/Distributor | Approved Investments | ASSETS (millions) As Of: 12/30/79 | 12/30/78 | Valuation Method |
|---|---|---|---|---|---|---|---|
| 10.67 | 7.24 | The Reserve Fund, Inc. 810 Seventh Avenue New York, NY 10010 (2/70) (800) 223-5547 (212) 977-9880 | Reserve Management Co. | 1 12 / 2 14 / 3 15 / 4 19 / 6 | 1,760.6 | 630.5 | 1 |
| 10.64 | 7.28 | Rowe Price Prime Reserve Fund, Inc. 100 East Pratt Street Baltimore, MD 21202 (3/76) (800) 638-1527 (301) 547-2000 | T. Rowe Price Associates, Inc. | 1 6 15 / 2 8 16 / 3 9 17 / 4 11 / 5 12 | 716.5 | 150.7 | 2 |
| 10.18 | 6.85 | Scudder Cash Investment Trust 175 Federal Street Boston, MA 02110 (12/75) (800) 343-2890 (617) 482-3990 | Scudder, Stevens & Clark  Scudder Fund Distributors, Inc. | 1 6 16 / 2 8 17 / 3 11 18 / 4 13 / 5 15 | 104.9 | 29.8 | 3 |
| 10.02 | 6.76 | Scudder Managed Reserves, Inc. 175 Federal Street Boston, MA 02110 (5/74) (800) 343-2890 (617) 482-3990 | Scudder, Stevens & Clark  Scudder Fund Distributors, Inc. | 1 6 16 / 2 8 17 / 3 11 18 / 4 13 / 5 15 | 439.7 | 255.9 | 2 |
| 10.41 | 7.04 | Selected Money Market Fund 111 West Washington Street Chicago, IL 60602 (11/77) (800) 621-7321 (312) 630-2762 | Lincoln National Investment Management Co. | 1 6 / 2 9 / 3 11 / 4 12 / 5 15 | 13.9 | 2.8 | 4 |
| 10.38 | — | Short-Term Yield Securities, Inc. 1080 Dresser Tower 601 Jefferson Street Houston, TX 77002 (5/78) (713) 654-0640 | First City National Bank of Houston  AIM Advisors, Inc. AIM Distributors, Inc. | 1 6 / 2 15 / 3 / 4 / 5 | 13.2 | — | 1 |
| 10.69 | 6.77 | SteinRoe Cash Reserves, Inc. 150 South Wacker Drive Chicago, IL 60606 (4/76) (800) 621-0320 (312) 368-7826 | SteinRoe; Farnham | 1 6 / 2 11 / 3 15 / 4 16 / 5 17 | 211.4 | 55.9 | 3 |
| — | — | St. Paul Money Fund, Inc. Box 43284 St. Paul, MN 55164 (11 79) (800) 328-1062 (612) 738-4142 (in MN) | St. Paul Advisers, Inc. | 1 6 / 2 11 / 3 12 / 4 14 / 5 | 12.9 | — | 3 |
| 10.69 | 7.24 | Union Cash Management Fund, Inc. One Bankers Trust Plaza New York, NY 10006 (1/77) (800) 221-2450 (212) 432-4000 | Discount Corp. of NY  Money Market Advisors | 1 6 / 2 9 / 3 10 / 4 11 / 5 | 187.3 | 42.8 | 2 |
| — | — | United Cash Management, Inc. 1 Crown Center P. O. Box 1343 Kansas City, MO 64141 (8 79) (800) 821-5664 (800) 892-5811 (in MO) | Waddell & Reed | 1 5 / 2 6 / 3 9 / 4 15 | 40.9 | — | 1 |
| — | — | Value Line Cash Fund 711 Third Avenue New York, NY 10017 (4 79) (800) 223-0818 | Arnold Bernhard & Co., Inc.  Value Line Securities, Inc. | 1 5 / 2 6 / 3 11 / 4 12 | 17.9 | — | 1 |
| 10.51 | 6.84 | Vanguard Money Market Trust: Portfolio I P. O. Box 1100 Valley Forge, PA 19482 (6/75) (800) 523-7910 (800) 362-7688 (in PA) | Wellington Management Co.  The Vanguard Group, Inc. | 1 5 / 2 6 / 3 11 / 4 | 187.4 | 53.1 | 3 |

**Valuation Methods:**
1 Constant Net Asset Value, Mark-to-Market
2 Variable Net Asset Value, Mark-to-Market
3 Constant Net Asset Value, 120-day Maximum Average Maturity (penny rounding)

4 Amortized Cost, Straight Line Accrual
* Applied for #3 (penny rounding) valuation method
** Available through sponsoring stockbroker

| Minimum Investment Initial / Subsequent | SERVICES OFFERED | | | Exchange Privilege | Funds Available For Exchange Privilege | Service Fees | Deadline For Same-Day Investment By Wire (EST) | Dividend Policy | | No. Of States Fund Is Registered |
| | Checking / Minimum Check | Checking Policies | Telephone Redemption / Minimum | | | | | Declared | Paid | |
|---|---|---|---|---|---|---|---|---|---|---|
| $1,000 / $1,000 | Yes / $500 | cks. prov.: 15 sets more on req. P F cks. ret. Q | Yes / $1,000 | Yes | International Investors; 44 Wall Street; Templeton World; Templeton Growth | | 4:00 PM | D | D | All |
| 2,000 / 100 | Yes / 500 | cks. prov.: U P cks. ret. as clear | Yes / 500 | Yes | All funds in T.Rowe Price Group of funds. exchange by mail | W: $2.50 | 4:00 PM | D | M | All |
| 1,000 / None | Yes / 500 | cks. prov.: U P F cks. ret. M (corp. only) | Yes / None | Yes | All funds in Scudder Group of funds except Development Fund | | 12:00 PM | D | M | All |
| 1,000 / None | Yes / 500 | cks. prov.: varies w/vol. P F cks. ret. M (corp. only) | Yes / None | Yes | All funds in Scudder Group of funds except Development Fund | | 4:00 PM | D | M | All |
| 1,000 / 100 | Yes / 500 | cks. prov.: 5 reorder ck. copies ret. M | Yes / 1,000 | Yes | Selected American Shares; Selected Special Shares; Selected Tax-Exempt Bond Fund | | 4:00 PM | D | M | All |
| 1,250 / 100 | Yes / 500 | cks. prov.: U P F cks. ret. as clear | Yes / None | Yes | High Yield Securities. Inc.; Convertible Yield Securities. Inc. | | 12:00 PM | D | M | 47 |
| 2,500 / 100 | Yes / 500 | cks. prov.: U P F cks. ret. M | Yes / 1,000 | Yes | SteinRoe & Farnham Balanced Fund. SteinRoe & Farnham Bond Fund. Inc.; SteinRoe & Farnham Capital Opportunities Fund. Inc.; SteinRoe Tax-Exempt Bond Fund. Inc.: SteinRoe Special Fund. Inc. | W: $2.50 | 5:00 PM | D | M | All (plus Puerto Rico) |
| 3,000 / 500 | Yes / 500 | cks. prov.: U cks. ret. as clear | Yes / 1,000 | Yes | St. Paul Capital Fund. Inc.; St. Paul Growth Fund, Inc.; St. Paul Income Fund. Inc. | | 1:00 PM | D | M | All |
| 1,000 / None | Yes / 500 | cks. prov.: 50 more on req. P cks. ret. as clear | Yes / None | Yes | All funds in Union Service Group of funds | E: normal sales charge plus $5.00 | 4:00 PM | D | M | All |
| 1,000 / 100 | Yes / 500 | cks. prov.: U cks. confirm. ret. | Yes / 1,000 | Yes | All funds in United Group of funds | | 5:00 PM | D | M | 47 |
| 1,000 / 100 | Yes / 500 | cks. ret. as clear | Yes / 1,000 | Yes | All funds in Value Line Group of Mutual Funds | E: normal sales charge | 4:00 PM next day credit | D | M | All |
| 3,000 / 100 | Yes / 500 | cks. prov.: U on req. | Yes / 1,000 | Yes | All open-end funds in Vanguard Group of funds | W: $5.00 for wires under $5,000 | 4:00 PM | D | M | All |

The 800 numbers are toll-free. If you are in the same state as the fund, however, call Collect.

# STOCKBROKER-AFFILIATED GENERAL PURPOSE MONEY FUNDS

| Average Yields Full Year 12/30/79 | 12/30/78 | FUND NAME, ADDRESS & PHONE NUMBER (date started) | Investment Advisor and Administrator/Distributor | Approved Investments | | | ASSETS (millions) As Of: 12/30/79 | 12/30/78 | Valuation Method |
|---|---|---|---|---|---|---|---|---|---|
| 10.12 | — | Alliance Capital Reserves, Inc. 140 Broadway New York, NY 10005 (7/78) (800) 221-5672 (212) 425-4210 | Alliance Capital Management Corp. | 1<br>2<br>3<br>4<br>5 | 6<br>7<br>10<br>11<br>15 | | 330.5 | 60.4 | 3 |
| — | — | Cash Equivalent Fund, Inc. 120 South LaSalle Street Chicago, IL 60603 (3/79) (312) 346-3223 | Kemper Financial Services, Inc. | 1<br>2<br>3<br>4 | 5<br>6<br>7<br>9 | 11<br>15<br>18<br>19 | 546.5 | — | 1* |
| 10.41 | 7.22 | Cash Reserve Management** One Boston Place Boston, MA 02108 (10/76) (617) 523-7631 | Morgan Guaranty Trust Co. of New York<br><br>EF Hutton & Co., Inc. | 1<br>2<br>3<br>4 | 5<br>6<br>10<br>11 | 12<br>13 | 1,999.3 | 385.8 | 1 |
| 10.12 | 7.21 | Current Interest, Inc. 711 Polk Street Houston, TX 77002 (4/74) (713) 751-2400 (collect) | The Advisory Group, Inc. | 1<br>2<br>3<br>4 | 5<br>6<br>7<br>11 | 12<br>15 | 300.2 | 7.3 | 3 |
| 10.51 | — | Daily Cash Accumulation Fund, Inc. 3600 South Yosemite Street Denver, CO 80237 (7/78) (800) 525-9310 (303) 773-6483 | THE Management Group, Inc. | 1<br>2<br>3<br>4<br>5 | 6<br>11 | | 1,284.2 | 123.5 | 3 |
| 9.97 | 6.93 | Daily Income Fund, Inc. 230 Park Avenue New York, NY 10017 (7/74) (212) 697-8088 (collect) | Reich & Tang, Inc. | 1<br>2<br>3 | 4<br>5<br>6 | | 392.0 | 113.6 | 3 |
| 10.18 | 6.88 | Gradison Cash Reserves 580 Building Cincinnati, OH 45202 (12/75) (800) 543-1818 (800) 582-7062 (in OH) (513) 579-5700 | Gradison & Co., Inc. | 1<br>2<br>3<br>4 | 5<br>6<br>12<br>17 | | 239.4 | 60.0 | 1 |
| — | — | INA Cash Fund, Inc. Bedford Building 3531 Silverside Road Wilmington, DE 19810 (11/79) (800) 441-7786 (302) 478-9119 (in DE & AL collect) | Parkway Management Corp. | 1<br>2<br>3<br>4<br>5 | 6<br>7<br>10<br>11<br>12 | 13<br>15<br>16<br>18 | 72.4 | — | 4 |
| 10.53 | 7.25 | InterCapital Liquid Asset Fund, Inc. 1 Battery Park Plaza New York, NY 10004 (9/75) (800) 221-2685 (212) 422-6700 | Dean Witter Reynolds<br><br>InterCapital, Inc. | 1<br>2<br>3<br>4 | 5<br>6<br>11<br>12 | | 2,647.5 | 442.4 | 4 |
| — | — | Legg Mason Cash Reserve Trust** 421 Seventh Avenue Pittsburgh, PA 15219 (11/79) (800) 245-4270 (412) 288-1979 (in PA) | Fiduciary Research Corp. | 1<br>2<br>3<br>4<br>5 | 6<br>12<br>15 | | 40.1 | — | 4 |
| 10.36 | 6.95 | Liquid Capital Income, Inc. National City Bank Building Cleveland, OH 44114 (11/74) (800) 321-2321 (216) 781-4440 | Carnegie Capital Management Co. | 1<br>2<br>3<br>4 | 5<br>6<br>9<br>11 | 12<br>15<br>18 | 685.9 | 146.9 | 1 |
| 10.52 | 7.23 | Merrill Lynch CMA Money Trust** 165 Broadway New York, NY 10080 (9/77) (800) 221-4146 (212) 766-6310 | Fund Asset Management, Inc.<br><br>Merrill Lynch, Pierce, Fenner, & Smith | 1<br>2<br>3<br>4<br>5 | 6<br>10<br>11<br>12 | | 997.9 | 49.7 | 1 |

**Valuation Methods:**

1    Constant Net Asset Value, Mark-to-Market
2    Variable Net Asset Value, Mark-to-Market
3    Constant Net Asset Value, 120-day Maximum Average Maturity (penny rounding)

**4**    Amortized Cost, Straight Line Accrual
**\***    Applied for #3 (penny rounding) valuation method
**\*\***    Available through sponsoring stockbroker

## (Available To All Investors)

| Minimum Investment Initial / Subsequent | SERVICES OFFERED | | | Exchange Privilege | Funds Available For Exchange Privilege | Service Fees | Deadline For Same-Day Investment By Wire (EST) | Dividend Declared | Policy Paid | No. Of States Fund Is Registered |
|---|---|---|---|---|---|---|---|---|---|---|
| | Checking / Minimum Check | Checking Policies | Telephone Redemption / Minimum | | | | | | | |
| None / None | Yes / $500 | cks. prov.: 20 more on req. cks. ret. M | Yes / $1,000 | Yes | All funds in Alliance Capital Group of funds | | 4:00 PM | D | M | All |
| $1,000 / $100 | Yes / 500 | cks. prov.: U F cks. ret. M | Yes / None | Yes | All nine funds in Kemper Group of funds | | 1:00 PM | D | M | 36 |
| 10,000 / 1,000 | Yes / 500 | cks. prov.: U cks. ret. M | Yes / None | No | | | 12:00 PM | D | M or Q (option) | All |
| 1,000 / 100 | Yes / 500 | cks. prov.: U F (sig. card) cks. ret. M | Yes / 1,000 | Yes | Commerce Income Shares, Inc.; Industries Trend Fund, Inc.; Pilot Fund, Inc. | | 4:00 PM | D | M | 40 |
| 1,000 / 100 | Yes / 500 | cks. prov.: U F statements ret. as ck. clears | Yes / None | Yes | Hamilton Funds, Inc.; Hamilton Growth Fund, Inc.; Hamilton Income Fund, Inc.; Oppenheimer High Yield Fund, Inc. | E: $5.00 | 4:00 PM | D | M | 49 |
| 5,000 / 100 | Yes / 500 | cks. prov.: U cks. copies ret. on req. | Yes / None | Yes | Between Stock Funds | | 4:00 PM next day investment | D | D | All |
| 1,000 / 50 | Yes / 500 | cks. prov.: 30 mo. $100,000 P F cks. ret. option as clear M | Yes / 1,000 | No | | | 12:00 PM | D | D or M (option) | 10 |
| 2,500 / 500 | Yes / 250 | cks. prov.: U cks. ret. M | Yes / 1,000 | No | | | 12:00 PM | D | M | All |
| 5,000 / 1,000 | Yes / 500 | P | Yes / 1,000 | Yes | InterCapital High Yield Sec.; InterCapital Tax-Exempt Sec.; Inter-Capital Industry Valued Securities | | 12:00 PM | D | D | All |
| 5,000 / 500 | Yes / 500 | cks. prov.: U F (corp. only) cks. ret. M | Yes / 1,000 | No | | | 4:00 PM next day investment | D | M | All |
| 1,000 / 500 | Yes / 500 | cks. prov.: U cks. ret. as clear | Yes / None | No | | | 1:30 PM | D | M | 49 |
| None / None | Yes / None | cks. prov.: through VISA cks. ret. as clear | Yes 1,000 | No | | | 4:00 PM | D | M | All |

The 800 numbers are toll-free. If you are in the same state as the fund, however, call Collect.

# STOCKBROKER-AFFILIATED GENERAL PURPOSE MONEY FUNDS

| Average Yields Full Year 12/30/79 12/30/78 | | FUND NAME, ADDRESS & PHONE NUMBER (date started) | Investment Advisor and Administrator/Distributor | Approved Investments | | ASSETS (millions) As Of: 12/30/79 12/30/78 | | Valuation Method |
|---|---|---|---|---|---|---|---|---|
| 9.39 | 6.73 | Merrill Lynch Government Fund, Inc. 125 High Street Boston, MA 02110 (9/77) (800) 225-1576 (617) 357-1460 | Fund Asset Management, Inc. Merrill Lynch Funds Distributors, Inc. | 1 6 | | 69.8 | 14.4 | 3 |
| 10.61 | 7.24 | Merrill Lynch Ready Assets Trust 165 Broadway New York, NY 10080 (2/75) (800) 221-7210 (212) 766-6310 | Merrill Lynch Asset Management, Inc. Merrill Lynch Funds Distributors, Inc. | 1 6 2 10 3 11 4 12 5 15 | | 8,145.1 | 1,635.3 | 1 |
| 10.44 | 7.03 | Moneymart Assets, Inc. 100 Gold Street New York, NY 10038 (6/76) (800) 221-5168 (212) 791-7123 | Continental Illinois NB&T of Chicago Bache, Halsey, Stuart, Shields, Inc. | 1 6 2 10 3 11 4 15 5 | | 1,114.6 | 190.7 | 1 |
| 10.28 | 6.90 | National Liquid Reserves, Inc. 605 Third Avenue New York, NY 10016 (8/74) (800) 223-7757 (212) 661-3014 | Mutual Management Corp. | 1 6 2 11 3 14 4 15 5 | | 1,067.2 | 14.4 | 3 |
| 10.64 | 7.13 | Oppenheimer Monetary Bridge One New York Plaza New York, NY 10004 (4/74) (800) 221-5348 (212) 825-4000 | Oppenheimer Management Corp. | 1 5 14 2 6 16 3 11 17 4 12 | | 306.4 | 114.3 | 3 |
| 10.21 | — | Paine Webber Cashfund, Inc.** 815 Connecticut Avenue NW Washington, DC 20006 (5/78) (Call your local Paine Webber office) | Provident Institutional Management Corp. Paine, Webber, Jackson & Curtis, Inc. | 1 6 2 7 3 10 4 17 5 | | 1,541.4 | 270.6 | 1 |
| — | — | Shearson Daily Dividend, Inc.** 767 Fifth Avenue New York, NY 10022 (6/79) (800) 223-5525 (212) 935-6623 | Bernstein-McCaulay, Inc. Dreyfus Corp. | 1 6 2 7 4 9 5 15 | | 1,274.2 | — | 3 |
| — | — | Webster Cash Reserve Fund, Inc.** 10 Hanover Street New York, NY 10022 (8/79) (212) 747-3091 | Webster Management Corp. Dreyfus Corp. | 1 5 12 2 6 15 3 7 4 9 | | 324.6 | — | 3 |

# MONEY FUNDS AVAILABLE TO INSTITUTIONS ONLY

| Average Yield Full Year 12/30/79 12/30/78 | | FUND NAME, ADDRESS & PHONE NUMBER (date started) | Investment Advisor and Administrator/Distributor | Approved Investments | | ASSETS (millions) As Of: 12/30/79 12/30/78 | | Valuation Method |
|---|---|---|---|---|---|---|---|---|
| | | Dreyfus Money Market Instruments, Inc. 600 Madison Avenue New York, NY 10022 (800) 223-5682 (212) 935-6621 | The Dreyfus Corp. Dreyfus Service Corp. | | | | | |
| — | — | Government Securities Series (5/79) | | 1 5 2 6 3 15 4 | | 55.5 | — | 3 |
| 10.48 | 6.99 | Money Market Series (4/75) | | 1 5 2 6 3 15 4 | | 783.3 | 130.1 | 3 |

**Valuation Methods:**
1 Constant Net Asset Value, Mark-to-Market
2 Variable Net Asset Value, Mark-to-Market
3 Constant Net Asset Value, 120-day Maximum Average Maturity (penny rounding)

4 Amortized Cost, Straight Line Accrual
* Applied for #3 (penny rounding) valuation method
** Available through sponsoring stockbroker

## (Available To All Investors)

| Minimum Investment Initial / Subsequent | SERVICES OFFERED | | | | | | | | | No. Of States Fund Is Registered |
|---|---|---|---|---|---|---|---|---|---|---|
| | Checking / Minimum Check | Checking Policies | Telephone Redemption / Minimum | Exchange Privilege | Funds Available For Exchange Policies | Service Fees | Deadline For Same-Day Investment By Wire (EST) | Dividend Policy Declared | Paid | |
| $5,000 / $1,000 | Yes / $500 | cks. prov.: U P cks. ret. as clear | Yes / $1,000 | No | | | 12:00 PM | D | M | All |
| 5,000 / 1,000 | Yes / 500 | cks. prov.: on req. cks. ret. as clear | Yes / 1,000 | Yes | Merrill Lynch Capital Fund; Merrill Lynch Basic Value Fund; Merrill Lynch Municipal Bond Fund; Merrill Lynch High Income Fund; Merrill Lynch Special Value Fund | E: normal sales charge | 4:00 PM | D | M | All |
| 1,000 / 500 | Yes / 500 | cks. prov.: U P cks. ret. as clear | Yes / 200 | Yes | Chancellor High Yield Fund; Chancellor Tax-Exempt Daily Income Fund | CP: $5.00 | 12:00 PM | D | M | All |
| 2,500 / 100 | Yes / 500 | cks. prov.: U P F w/resolution cks. ret. as clear | Yes / 1,000 | Yes | National Securities Funds; Nat. Sec. Tax-Exempt Bonds, Inc.; Fairfield Fund, Inc. | E: normal sales charge | 12:00 PM | D | M | All |
| 1,000 /25 | Yes / 500 | cks. prov.: 20 P F cks. ret. on req. | Yes / 1,000 | Yes | Tax-Free Bond Fund; Oppenheimer Fund; AIM Fund; TimeFund; Special Funds; Option Fund; Income Fund of Boston; Opp. High Yield Fund | E: $5.00 | next day investment | D | M | All |
| 5,000 / 500 | Yes / 500 | cks. prov.: 20 P cks. ret. on req. | Yes / 1,000 | No | | | 1:00 PM | D | M | All |
| 5,000 / 1,000 | No | No | Yes / None | No | | | 2:30 PM | D | M | All |
| 5,000 / 1,500 | No | No | Yes / None | No | | | 12:00 PM | D | M | All |

| Minimum Investment Initial / Subsequent | SERVICES OFFERED | | | | | | | | | No. Of States Fund Is Registered |
|---|---|---|---|---|---|---|---|---|---|---|
| | Checking / Minimum Check | Checking Policies | Telephone Redemption / Minimum | Exchange Privilege | Funds Available For Exchange Privilege | Service Fees | Deadline For Same-Day Investment By Wire (EST) | Dividend Policy Declared | Paid | |
| $50,000 / $100 | Yes / $500 | cks. prov.: U P cks. ret. as clear | Yes / $1,000 | Yes | All funds in Dreyfus Group of Mutual funds | E: normal sales charge | 12:00 PM | D | M | All |
| 50,000 / 100 | Yes / 500 | cks. prov.: U P cks. ret. as clear | Yes / 1,000 | Yes | All funds in Dreyfus Group of Mutual funds | E: normal sales charge | 12:00 PM | D | M | All |

The 800 numbers are toll-free. If you are in the same state as the fund, however, call Collect.

## MONEY FUNDS AVAILABLE TO INSTITUTIONS ONLY

| Average Yields Full Year 12/30/79 | 12/30/78 | FUND NAME, ADDRESS & PHONE NUMBER (date started) | Investment Advisor and Administrator/Distributor | Approved Investments | | | ASSETS (millions) As Of: 12/30/79 | 12/30/78 | Valuation Method |
|---|---|---|---|---|---|---|---|---|---|
| | | Federated Securities 421 Seventh Avenue Pittsburgh, PA 15219 | Federated Cash Management Corp. | | | | | | |
| 10.26 | 7.52 | Federated Master Trust (12/77) (800) 245-2423 (412) 288-1948 (in PA) | | 1 2 3 | 4 5 6 | 12 | 1,090.1 | 424.3 | 4 |
| 10.21 | — | Money Market Trust (10/78) (800) 245-4270 (412) 288-1979 (in PA) | | 1 2 3 | 4 5 6 | 12 | 794.8 | 260.2 | 4 |
| 9.72 | 6.98 | Trust/U.S. Government Securities (12/75) (800) 245-4270 (412) 288-1979 (in PA) | | 1 2 6 | | | 2,120.0 | 870.3 | 4 |
| — | — | Trust/U.S. Treasury Obligations (11/79) (800) 245-4270 (412) 288-1979 (in PA) | Cash Management Research Corp. | 1 2 6 | | | 47.3 | — | 4 |
| | | Fidelity Money Market Trust 82 Devonshire Street Boston, MA 02109 (1/79) (800) 225-6190 (617) 523-1919 | Fidelity Management & Research Co.  Fidelity Distributors Corp. | | | | | | |
| — | — | Domestic Portfolio | | 1 2 3 | 4 5 6 | | 109.5 | — | 4 |
| — | — | International Portfolio | | 1 2 3 | 4 5 6 | 9 15 19 | 18.7 | — | 4 |
| — | — | U.S. Government Portfolio | | 1 2 6 | | | 77.5 | — | 4 |
| | | Institutional Liquid Assets 8700 Sears Tower Chicago, IL 60606 (800) 621-2550 (800) 621-2308 (312) 876-8888 | First National Bank of Chicago  Salomon Brothers | | | | | | |
| — | — | Government Portfolio (1/79) | | 1 2 6 | | | 495.4 | — | 4 |
| 10.47 | 7.46 | Prime Obligations Portfolio (1/76) | | 1 2 3 | 4 5 6 | | 1,371.5 | 367.4 | 4 |
| 10.50 | 7.13 | Merrill Lynch Institutional Fund, Inc. 125 High Street Boston, MA 02110 (10/74) (800) 225-1576 (617) 357-1460 | Fund Asset Management, Inc. | 1 2 3 4 | 5 6 11 | | 481.4 | 141.9 | 3 |
| | | Shearson, Loeb, Rhoades, Inc. Suite 203, Webster Building 3411 Silverside Road Wilmington, DL 19810 (800) 441-7690 | Provident Institutional Management Corp.  Shearson, Loeb, Rhoades, Inc. | | | | | | |
| 9.74 | 6.59 | FedFund (10/75) | | 1 2 | 6 | | 418.1 | 128.0 | 3 |
| 10.41 | 7.36 | TempFund (10/73) | | 1 2 3 | 4 5 6 | 7 12 | 1,828.8 | 901.8 | 3 |

**Valuation Methods:**
1  Constant Net Asset Value, Mark-to-Market
2  Variable Net Asset Value, Mark-to-Market
3  Constant Net Asset Value, 120-day Maximum Average Maturity (penny rounding)

4  Amortized Cost, Straight Line Accrual
\*  Applied for #3 (penny rounding) valuation method
\*\*  Available through sponsoring stockbroker

| Minimum Investment Initial / Subsequent | SERVICES OFFERED | | | Exchange Privilege | Funds Available For Exchange Privilege | Service Fees | Deadline For Same-Day Investment By Wire (EST) | Dividend Policy | | No. Of States Fund Is Regis- tered |
|---|---|---|---|---|---|---|---|---|---|---|
| | Checking / Minimum Check | Checking Policies | Telephone Redemp- tion / Minimum | | | | | Declared | Paid | |
| $100,000 / None | No | | Yes / None | No | | | 3:00 PM | D | M | All |
| 50,000 / None | No | | Yes / None | No | | | 3:00 PM | D | M | All |
| 100,000 / None | No | | Yes / None | No | | | 3:00 PM | D | M | All |
| 100,000 / None | No | | Yes / None | No | | | 3:00 PM | D | M | All |
| 250,000 / None | No | | Yes / None | Yes | Fidelity Money Market Trust's Int. Portfolio & U.S. Gov. Portfolio | SA: negotiable | 12:00 PM | D | M | All |
| 250,000 / None | No | | Yes / None | Yes | Fidelity Money Market Trust's U.S. Gov. Port- folio & Domestic Port. | SA: negotiable | 12:00 PM | D | M | All |
| 250,000 / None | No | | Yes / None | Yes | Fidelity Money Market Trust's Domestic Port. & Int. Portfolio | SA: negotiable | 12:00 PM | D | M | All |
| 50,000 / None | Yes / None | cks. prov.: U F cks. ret. M | Yes / None | Yes | Institutional Liquid Assets Prime Obligations Portfolio | | 4:00 PM (call by 12:00 PM) | D | M | All |
| 50,000 / None | Yes / None | cks. prov.: U F cks. ret. M | Yes / None | Yes | Institutional Liquid Assets Government Portfolio | | 4:00 PM (call by 12:00 PM) | D | M | All |
| 25,000 / 1,000 | Yes / 500 | cks. prov.: U P cks. ret. as clear | Yes / $1,000 | No | | | 12:00 PM | D | M | All |
| 1,000 / None | Yes / 500 | cks. prov.: U cks. ret. M | Yes / None | No | | CP: $5.00 set up | 4:00 PM (call by 2:30 PM) | D | M | All |
| 1,000 / None | Yes / 500 | cks. prov.: U cks. ret. M | Yes / None | No | | CP: $5.00 set up | 4:00 PM (call by 2:30 PM) | D | M | All |

The 800 numbers are toll-free. If you are in the same state as the fund, however, call Collect.

## "SPECIAL PURPOSE" MONEY FUNDS

| FUND NAME, ADDRESS & PHONE NUMBER (date started) | Investment Advisor and Administrator/Distributor | Funds Purpose and/or Availability | Approved Investments | Valuation Method |
|---|---|---|---|---|
| **LOAD FUNDS:** CG Money Market, Lutheran Brotherhood Money Market Fund, Inc., and MIF are all load funds; that is, they carry a sales charge (load) to open an investment account. | | | | |
| CG Money Market Connecticut General Life Insurance Co. Hartford, CT 06152 (1/75) (203) 726-6000 | CG Investment Co. CG Equity Sales Co. | All investors One time sales charge : $100 | 1  6<br>2  8<br>3  12<br>4  17<br>5 | 2 |
| Lutheran Brotherhood Money Market Fund, Inc. 701 Second Avenue South Minneapolis, MN 55402 (2/79) (800) 328-4363 (612) 339-8091 (in MN collect) | Lutheran Brotherhood Research Corp. Federated Research Corp. Lutheran Brotherhood Securities Corp. | Only members of Lutheran Brotherhood or the Lutheran Church Organization's trusts, employee benefit plans. One time sales charge: $100 | 1  5<br>2  6<br>3  7<br>4  15 | 4 |
| Mutual Investing Foundation — MIF/ Nationwide Money Market Fund One Nationwide Plaza Columbus, OH 43216 (3/80) (800) 848-0920 (800) 282-1440 (in OH) | Heritage Securities, Inc. | One time sales charge: $100 | 1  4<br>2  5<br>3  6 | 3 |

**LIMITED PURPOSE MONEY FUNDS:** Aetna Variable Encore Fund, Inc. is used strictly for the purpose of funding variable annuity contracts issued by Aetna Variable Annuity Life Insurance Company.

The Common Fund for Short-Term Investments provides investment management for educational institutions.

Massachusetts Municipal Depository Trust was established by the State Treasurer's office in 1975 to serve as an investment pool for cities, towns, retirement systems, regional school districts, housing authorities, regional transit authorities, and other political subdivisions of the Commonwealth of Massachusetts.

| | | | | |
|---|---|---|---|---|
| Aetna Variable Encore Fund, Inc. 151 Farmington Avenue Hartford, CT 06156 (1974) (203) 273-4806 | Aetna Variable Annuity Life Ins. Co. Aetna Financial Services, Inc. | Exists to fund variable annuity contracts | 1  6<br>2  10<br>3  11<br>4  18<br>5 | 4 |
| Common Fund for Short-Term Investments 635 Madison Avenue New York, NY 10022 (9/74) (212) 832-0230 | Fischer, Frances, Trees, Watts, Inc. | Only services educational institutions | 1  5  15<br>2  6  17<br>3  8  19<br>4  11 | 1 |
| Massachusetts Municipal Depository Trust P.O. Box 193 Boston, MA 02101 (800) 392-6095 | Fidelity Management & Research Co. FMR Service Co. | Only services cities, towns, and political subdivisions of the Commonwealth of Massachusetts | 1  5<br>2  6<br>3  7<br>4 | 4 |

**CANADIAN MONEY FUNDS:** AGF Money Market Fund is a Canadian money fund which invests strictly in Canadian instruments. **A:** Debt obligations of Canadian government or its Provinces; **B:** Canadian bank CDs and bankers acceptances; **C:** Canadian loan or trust company obligations (including CDs and guaranteed investment certificates); **D:** Short-term corporate obligations.

| | | | | |
|---|---|---|---|---|
| AGF Money Market Fund P.O. Box 50 Toronto Dominion Bank Tower Toronto, Ontario M5K 1E9 (416) 367-1900 | AGF Management LTD | Invests only in Canadian instruments | A<br>B<br>C<br>D | |

**Valuation Methods:**

| | |
|---|---|
| 1 | Constant Net Asset Value, Mark-to-Market |
| 2 | Variable Net Asset Value, Mark-to-Market |
| 3 | Constant Net Asset Value, 120-day Maximum Average Maturity (penny rounding) |
| 4 | Amortized Cost, Straight Line Accrual |
| * | Applied for #3 (penny rounding) valuation method |
| ** | Available through sponsoring stockbroker |

| Minimum Investment Initial / Subsequent | SERVICES OFFERED | | | | | | | | | |
|---|---|---|---|---|---|---|---|---|---|---|
| | Checking / Minimum Check | Checking Policies | Telephone Redemption / Minimum | Exchange Privilege | Funds Available For Exchange Privilege | Service Fees | Deadline For Same-Day Investment By Wire (EST) | Dividend Policy Declared | Paid | No. Of States Fund Is Registered |
| $300 / $500 | No | | No | Yes | CG Fund Inc: CG Income Fund Inc.; CG Municipal Bond Fund, Inc. | E: $5.00 | | D | M | All |
| 2,500 / 100 | Yes / $500 | cks. prov.: U F (corp. only) cks. ret. M | Yes / $1,000 | Yes | Lutheran Brotherhood (LB) Income Fund, Inc.; LB Municipal Bond Fund, Inc.; LB U.S. Gov. Securities Fund, Inc.; LB Fund | | 4:00 PM | D | M | All |
| 2,500 / 100 | Yes / 500 | cks. prov.: U P F cks. ret. confirm M | Yes / 1,000 | Yes | Among three other Mutual Investing Foundation MIF / Funds | W: $4.00 E: $5.00 | 2:00 PM | D | D | 38 |
| 5,000 / 5,000 | Yes / 5,000 | cks. prov.: U P F cks. ret. as clear | Yes 5,000 | Yes | The Common Fund for Equity Investments; The Common Fund for Bond Investments | | 2:30 PM | Q | Q | |
| None / None | Yes / None | cks. ret. confirm. M | Yes / None | No | | | 12:00 PM | D | M | |
| 1,000 / 1,000 | Yes None | | Yes | No | | | 12:00 PM | D | M | 1 |
| 5,000 / 1,000 | | | Yes | | | SU: $5.00 MS: $1.50 W: $2.00 plus cost | 2:00 PM Toronto time next day credit | | | |

The 800 numbers are toll-free. If you are in the same state as the fund, however, call Collect.

## TAX-FREE MONEY FUNDS
## (Recommended ONLY For Investors In Very High Tax Brackets.
## Explanation Below.)

| FUND NAME, ADDRESS & PHONE NUMBER (date started) | Investment Advisor and Administrator/Distributor | Funds Purpose and/or Availability | Approved Investments* | Valuation Method |
|---|---|---|---|---|
| Chancellor Tax-Exempt Daily Income Fund, Inc. 100 Gold Street New York, NY 10038 (8/79) (800) 221-7984 (212) 791-4654 (in NY collect) | Bache Halsey Stuart Shields Inc. | All investors | 5 10 | 3 |
| Federated Tax-Free Trust Federated Investors Building 421 Seventh Avenue Pittsburgh, PA 15219 (3/79) (800) 245-2423 (412) 288-1948 (in PA collect) | Federated Asset Management Corp. Federated Securities Corp. | All investors | 2 7 4 8 5 9 6 | 4 |
| Fidelity Tax-Exempt Money Market Trust 82 Devonshire Street Boston, MA 02109 (1/80) (800) 225-6190 (617) 726-0650 | Fidelity Management & Research Co. Fidelity Distributors. Corp. | All investors | 1 5 2 3 4 | 4 |
| Muni Fund Suite 203, Webster Building 3411 Silverside Road Wilmington, DE 19810 (2/80) (800) 441-7690 | Provident Institutional Management Corp. (sub. of Provident National Bank) Shearson. Loeb Rhoades, Inc. | Only to banks | 5 6 | 3 |
| Scudder Tax-Free Money Fund P. O. Box 1912 Boston. MA 02105 (1/80) (617) 328-5000 (in MA collect) | Scudder Stevens & Clark | All investors | 2 4 5 | 3 |
| Warwick Municipal Bond Fund Short-Term Portfolio P. O. Box 1100 Drummer's Lane Valley Forge. PA 19482 (1977) (800) 362-2688 (in PA) | Citibank, PA The Vanguard Group of Insurance Companies | All investors | 6 | 4 |

**Valuation Methods:**
1 Constant Net Asset Value, Mark-to-Market
2 Variable Net Asset Value, Mark-to-Market
3 Constant Net Asset Value, 120-day Maximum Average Maturity (penny rounding)

4 Amortized Cost, Straight Line Accrual
* Applied for #3 (penny rounding) valuation method
** Available through sponsoring stockbroker

## TAX-FREE MONEY FUNDS

Tax-Free Money Funds (Short-Term Tax-Exempt Mutual Funds) are actually a combination of municipal bond funds and money market mutual funds. Municipal bond funds offer tax-free income which appeals mainly to investors in high tax brackets. Municipal bond fund investments tend to be long-term, however, and when interest rates began to rise, the value per share tended to decline, making them less attractive. Money market mutual funds, with their high yielding portfolios of short-term investments, became the more popular vehicle.

Tax-Free Money Funds are money funds which tend to invest primarily in short-term municipal notes, thus providing a tax-exempt, but lower return to investors which is comparable on an after-tax basis with the return of money market mutual funds. These funds are not recommended for individual investors not in high tax brackets who might consider tax-free funds simply as a way to avoid paying taxes. The difference between tax free money funds and after-tax yields of regular money funds should be carefully evaluated. (For example, if you are in a regular money fund earning 13.73% and you are in a 49% tax bracket, the after-tax earnings of your investment would be 7%. If you were in a tax-free money market yielding only 5%, you could end up earning less on an after-tax basis.)

**\* Allowable Investments for Tax-Free Money Funds**

1. Rans: Revenue Anticipation Notes
2. Tans: Tax Anticipation Notes

3. Bans: Bond Anticipation Notes
4. Construction Loan Notes
5. Municipal Bonds
6. Industrial Development Notes

7. Project Notes
8. Serial Bonds
9. PreRefunded Municipal Bonds
10. Municipal Notes

| Minimum Investment Initial / Subsequent | SERVICES OFFERED Checking / Minimum Check | Checking Policies | Telephone Redemp- tion / Minimum | Exchange Privilege | Funds Available For Exchange Privilege | Service Fees | Deadline For Same-Day Investment By Wire (EST) | Dividend Policy Declared | Paid | No. Of States Fund Is Regis- tered |
|---|---|---|---|---|---|---|---|---|---|---|
| $2.500 / $500 | Yes / $500 | | Yes | Yes | Chancellor High Yield Fund Inc.; Money Mart Assets | CP: $5.00 set up | 4:00 PM | D | M | |
| 25,000 / None | No | | Yes / 5,000 | No | | W: $5.00 for $5,000 wire | 4:00 PM | D | M | |
| 20,000 / 1,000 | Yes / 1,000 | | Yes / 5,000 | Yes | All funds in Fidelity Group of funds | | | D | M | |
| 1,000 / None | Yes 500 | | Yes | Yes | TempFund; FedFund | | 4:00 PM | D | M | |
| 1,000 None | Yes | | Yes 5,000 | Yes | All funds in Scudder Group of funds except Scudder Development Fund | | 4:00 PM | D | M | |
| 3,000 50 | Yes 500 | | Yes 500 | Yes | Among the four port- folios and all funds in Vanguard Group of funds | W: $3.00 MS: $.75 | 4:00 PM | D | M | |

The 800 numbers are toll-free. If you are in the same state as the fund, however, call Collect.

## TAX-FREE EQUIVALENT TABLE                    December 1979

| Taxable Income* Joint Return | Single Return | Tax Bracket | 5% | 5½% | 6% | Tax-Free Yield 6½% | 7% Equivalent Taxable Yield | 7½% | 8% | 8½% | 9% |
|---|---|---|---|---|---|---|---|---|---|---|---|
| $ 20-25 | | 28% | 6.94% | 7.64% | 8.33% | 9.03% | 9.72% | 10.42% | 11.11% | 11.81% | 12.50% |
| | $15-18 | 30 | 7.14 | 7.86 | 8.57 | 9.29 | 10.00 | 10.71 | 11.43 | 12.14 | 12.86 |
| 25-30 | | 32 | 7.35 | 8.09 | 8.82 | 9.56 | 10.29 | 11.03 | 11.76 | 12.50 | 13.24 |
| | 18-24 | 34 | 7.58 | 8.33 | 9.09 | 9.85 | 10.61 | 11.36 | 12.12 | 12.88 | 13.64 |
| 30-35 | | 37 | 7.94 | 8.73 | 9.52 | 10.32 | 11.11 | 11.90 | 12.70 | 13.49 | 14.29 |
| | 24-29 | 39 | 8.20 | 9.02 | 9.84 | 10.66 | 11.48 | 12.30 | 13.11 | 13.93 | 14.75 |
| 35-46 | | 43 | 8.77 | 9.65 | 10.53 | 11.40 | 12.28 | 13.16 | 14.04 | 14.91 | 15.79 |
| | 29-34 | 44 | 8.93 | 9.82 | 10.71 | 11.61 | 12.50 | 13.39 | 14.29 | 15.18 | 16.07 |
| 46-60 | 34-42 | 49 | 9.80 | 10.78 | 11.76 | 12.75 | 13.73 | 14.71 | 15.69 | 16.67 | 17.65 |
| 60-86 | | 54 | 10.87 | 11.96 | 13.04 | 14.13 | 15.22 | 16.30 | 17.39 | 18.48 | 19.57 |
| | 42-55 | 55 | 11.11 | 12.22 | 13.33 | 14.44 | 15.56 | 16.67 | 17.78 | 18.89 | 20.00 |
| 86-109 | | 59 | 12.20 | 13.41 | 14.63 | 15.85 | 17.07 | 18.29 | 19.51 | 20.73 | 21.95 |
| | 55-82 | 63 | 13.51 | 14.86 | 16.22 | 17.57 | 18.92 | 20.27 | 21.62 | 22.97 | 24.32 |
| 109-162 | | 64 | 13.89 | 15.28 | 16.67 | 18.06 | 19.44 | 20.83 | 22.22 | 23.61 | 25.00 |
| 162-215 | 81-108 | 68 | 15.63 | 17.19 | 18.75 | 20.31 | 21.88 | 23.44 | 25.00 | 26.56 | 28.13 |
| over $125 | over $108 | 70 | 16.67 | 18.33 | 20.00 | 21.67 | 23.33 | 25.00 | 26.67 | 28.33 | 30.00 |

\* In thousands rounded

# Appendix B.
# Money Fund Valuation Methods —
# Pricing and Yield Considerations

Money market mutual funds are unique in that they declare and pay dividends daily. Each day the earnings on the investment portfolio securities are calculated very carefully and precisely. Since the proportional holdings of the shareholders could change daily, it is very important that each shareholder receive his or her fair share each day. To this extent all money fund valuation methods are similar.

## Changes in Market Value

Remember, however, that the value of the underlying portfolio changes independently of the earnings each and every day. An investment bought to yield an annual rate of 10 percent will be worth *more* today if similar instruments are selling at a rate at which the investor will earn only 8 percent. If the entire portfolio were to be sold on that day, it would be sold at a profit. It is only fair, then, that the investors in the fund that day should share in that unrealized (or theoretical) capital gain. It is on how the money funds handle these unrealized capital gains (or losses) that money fund valuation methods differ. The impact of these differences has been magnified in recent months as the interest rate roller-coaster ride has encountered steeper and steeper slopes. Last April and May, some money funds posted a 20 percent + annualized yield as other funds with similar portfolio holdings were offering yields declining rapidly from 16 percent to 10 percent. This difference is explained solely by the differing valuation methods.

## Alternative Valuation Methods

In a recent survey, 33 percent of the funds available to individual investors were using the conservative penny-rounding valuation method, 38 percent were using the traditional mark-to-market method with a fixed net asset value (per share price), 6 percent were using that same method with a variable net asset value, and 23 percent had opted for the amortized cost method—the most conservative of the four. Each method has its supporters and reasonable people differ on which is best, but the investor should have the facts in order to make up his or her own mind.

    *Traditional mark-to-market valuation* is used by the most funds at present but is losing out to the more recently authorized penny-rounding and amortized cost methods.

The portfolio earnings plus any appreciation (increase) or minus any depreciation (decrease) in market value is totaled, the management fee and expenses are deducted, and the result is divided by the number of shares outstanding at the end of the day to determine the per share dividend. To modify some of the volatility in daily yields resulting from violent swings in interest rates from day to day (as can happen in today's money market), any security with less than sixty days to maturity can be valued at cost rather than market value. This makes the yield much more stable.

The traditional method does not require that the last option be exercised. Merrill Lynch Ready Assets, for example, did not choose to use that option until May 1, 1980. This means that during the spring of 1980, the Ready Assets fund reflected in full the appreciation caused by the falling rates and, as a result, were paying over 20 percent. The fund has since elected to discontinue this practice.

The traditional method also has none of the limitations placed on funds opting for the penny-rounding or amortized cost methods. Thus mark-to-market funds may have much longer average maturities than others. This can be important in a period of falling interest rates, because the maturity can be extended dramatically to lock in high yields for a longer period. It can also increase the volatility of yield swings if situations change rapidly.

*Mark-to-market with a variable net asset value* is a method currently used by only a few funds and one that is currently going out of favor. The most visible supporter of this method is Scudder Managed Reserves, whose weekly yield will often fluctuate wildly because it pays out the net portfolio earnings in dividends and reflects the short-term capital gains (or losses) in a changing net asset value.

Scudder's price per share will change from $9.94 to $10.06, for example, and will change a penny at a time. Because the appreciation or depreciation must "build up" until it causes the penny change, the week the net asset value changes can result in a very high or very low yield. When rates are rising, Scudder's managers are "bums." When rates are falling, they are "heroes."

Over the cycle, Scudder will average in line with its peers, but if you go in for a short time at the wrong time, you could lose money or get an unexpected profit. For my money, that's not what money funds are for—I prefer more stability and less surprise.

Keep in mind, however, that Scudder is a fund to be *in* when interest rates are falling.

*Penny-rounding* refers to a method favored by many money funds, which offers additional assurance of a constant net asset value and a more stable yield. In exchange for this, the fund must agree to (1) limit the fund's investments to securities with a year or less to maturity, (2) have an average maturity of 120 days or less, and (3) carefully manage the fund's portfolio so that the price per share is a constant $1.00. Like the first category of fund valuation—mark-to-market—these funds *do* opt for the valuation at cost of securities with sixty days or less to maturity. The difference here is that this is a requirement, not an option.

*Amortized cost,* the most conservative method of valuation, is preferred by most institutional investors. It is similar to the penny-rounding formula except that *all* securities are valued at cost, and not just those with less than sixty days to maturity. Also, the board of directors has more flexibility in exercising its responsibility to maintain the constant net asset value at exactly $1.00.

The Federated Cash Management group in Pittsburgh—the largest fund group serving the bank trust market—has spent hundreds of thousands of dollars in convincing the SEC to approve this valuation formula so essential to the bank trust departments. In the end, their arguments proved persuasive, and the method has received wide acceptance.

### What Do Valuation Methods Mean to the Investor?

For the most part, mark-to-market, penny-rounding, and amortized cost, with their fixed $1.00 net asset value (price per share), will often appear very similar to the investor. When interest rates fall, however, the penny-rounding and amortized cost methods will decline more rapidly as their older, higher yields are replaced by newer, lower yields. On the other hand, the mark-to-market valuation method funds will reflect the appreciation in portfolio value faster.

You may wish to be in a mark-to-market fund when interest rates are falling (especially in a fund that values *everything* at mark-to-market), and in an amortized cost or penny-rounding fund when rates are on the rise, all things being equal. The last comment tells the tale, since some portfolio managers will be more aggressive than others and average maturity and portfolio holding differences can make significant differences in yields reported.

### Summary

With the SEC's latest ruling, there are now four methods of valuation, or recognition of income, for money funds. The four methods are mark-to-market with constant net asset value (MTM-CNAV), mark-to-market with variable net asset value (MTM-VNAV), amortized cost (AC), and penny-rounding—the latest method. Each method records income on a straight line basis as it is earned. The difference between the methods depends upon how its current market value is determined. The SEC has also differentiated between the funds by placing certain restrictions on their ability to invest in longer maturity instruments.

| Valuation Method | MTM-CNAV | MTM-VNAV | AC | Penny-Rounding |
|---|---|---|---|---|
| Appreciation/ Depreciation Recognition | in dividend | in NAV | in NAV but managed | in dividend |
| Transaction Accuracy (# digits used) | $1.000 | $1.000 | $1.00 | $1.00 |
| Max Maturity | none | none | 365 days | 365 days |
| Max Ave Maturity | none | none | 120 days | 120 days |
| Trading of Portfolio | at will | at will | none | at will |

# Index